SALVAGING CIVILIZATION

◆

Uniting America with Christian Values

Edward J. Mike, PhD

SALVAGING CIVILIZATION

1405 SW 6th Avenue • Ocala, Florida 34471 • Phone 352-622-1825 • Fax 352-622-1875
Website: www.atlantic-pub.com • Email: sales@atlantic-pub.com
SAN Number: 268-1250

Library of Congress Control Number: 2020922639

Printed in the United States

PROJECT MANAGER: Kassandra White
INTERIOR LAYOUT AND JACKET DESIGN: Vincent Saldana

TABLE OF CONTENTS

INTRODUCTION. ix

What Is This About? ix

What Is Christian Civilization? xi

What Am I About?. xi

SECTION I   CLARIFICATIONS. 1

CHAPTER 1   How Can We All Unite? 3

Introduction 3

Rudolf Karl Bultmann 4

Comparing Other Theologians. 7

Using the Example of Slavery 8

CHAPTER 2   What About Primitive Africa? 9

Working in Africa 11

Characterizing Their Sitz im Leben 11

The Missionaries' Sacrifices. 12

Mortality in Africa 13

How Did These People Get Along? 14

What About Slavery in Africa? 14

Devaluation of life 15

Cannibalism / Predatory Behavior 16

What About Wild Animals? 16

CHAPTER 3   What About Slavery in America?. 18

   Introduction 18

   Transition from Africa 19

   Stories of Abuse 20

   Positive Attitudes About Slavery 21

   Education and Learning Skills 25

   Church Attendance 25

   Ex-slaves Critical of Blacks 27

   Conclusion. 28

CHAPTER 4   Who Was Thomas Jefferson? 29

   Was Jefferson a Racist? 29

   Jefferson's Education 30

   Jefferson Made Slavery a Problem 30

   Jefferson's Concern for Slaves 31

   Was Slavery Ever the Problem? .33

CHAPTER 5   What About Organized Religion? 36

   If It Ain't Broke, Don't Fix It 36

   What Are We Up Against? 37

   What's the Objection? 37

   Aberrant Leaders of Organized Religion 39

   Are Churches Communist? 40

   What About the Catholic Popes? .41

   What About the Vatican Today? .43

   What About Homosexuality? 44

   What About the Vatican Bank? 45

CHAPTER 6   What About Atheism? .47

   Introducing Christopher Hitchens 47

   What About Sitz im Leben? 48

   What About Organized Religion? 49

   A "Rational Alternative" to Religion 53

   Conclusion. 54

SECTION II   ERADICATING CHRISTIAN CIVILIZATION 57

CHAPTER 7   What Is Communism About? 59

   Introduction 59

   Who Was Karl Marx? 60

   What Is Communism About? 61

   How Is the Communist Characterized? 65

CHAPTER 8   What About Communism in America? 68

   Introduction 68

   What's Wrong with Central Banking? 70

   What About Government-Controlled Education? 74

   What About Government-Controlled Labor? 74

   What About Control of Transportation and Communication? 76

   What About the Other Planks of Marx's Platform? 78

   Roosevelt and the Communist United Nations 82

   What Is Sustainable Development? 86

   What About Our Income Tax? 90

   Are We Destined for Revolution? 92

   What Is the Report from Iron Mountain? 94

   What Is the Club of Rome? 97

   What About Islam in America? 98

Who Was Muhammad? 99

Are Islamic Teachings Abhorrent? 99

Do Other Nations Have Problems with Islam? 99

CHAPTER 9   What About Public Education? 101

The Significance of Public Education 101

The Transformation in Public Education 102

The Corrosion of Public Education 103

Public Education in Universities 105

Universal Disinformation in Public Education 105

Exposing This Travesty 108

A Last Word 110

SECTION III   RESTORING CHRISTIAN CIVILIZATION 111

CHAPTER 10   The Good News in Perspective 113

Introduction 113

What Do We Know About God? 114

The Natural God 116

Clarifying Concepts 117

Reconciling Troubling Assertions 122

CHAPTER 11   Basic Themes of the Good News 126

Introduction 126

Love of Fellow Man 126

Universal Acceptance 129

Appropriate Associations 130

Taking Responsibility 131

Persistence 133

Using Common Sense 134

Single-Mindedness. .134

Unpretentiousness 135

Dangers from Wealth 136

Civil Obedience 137

Jesus on the Offensive 137

The Pharisees and Sadducees 138

What About Men? 139

What About Women? 140

What About Children? 142

A Virtuous Paradigm. 144

Conclusion. 152

CHAPTER 12 What Will It Take? 153

Meeting the Challenge 153

Confronting Business as Usual 156

CHAPTER 13 What to Do About Public Education? 158

Introduction 158

Are There More Reasons to Homeschool? 160

How Is Homeschooling Possible? 162

Will I Encounter Criticism? 162

How Much Will This Cost? 163

Can Parents and Children Adapt? 163

So What About Nuts and Bolts? 164

What About Going to College? 165

What Resources Are There? 167

Are Charter Schools the Answer? 167

What About Socialist Millennials? 168

CHAPTER 14 Getting All This Together 171

    Where Do Things Stand? 171

    What's the Plan? 174

    The Security of a Free State 179

    Should We Affiliate? 183

    Learning the Political Game 185

    Psyching Out the Politician 186

    The Communist Virus, Danger and Opportunity 187

    Conclusion. 190

APPENDIX **193**

    The Nervous System and Our Brain 193

    Our Human Executive Function. 194

    The Role of the Unconscious. 195

    What is Behaviorism? 197

NOTES **199**

INTRODUCTION

WHAT IS THIS ABOUT?

Thank you for choosing to read this book. That tells me that we share something. We are concerned that our nation isn't what it once was and that we are headed in the wrong direction. Love your neighbor is turning into hate your neighbor. We've become an identity politics nation at war with one another. It's becoming a sin to teach children virtue. We have become politically correct. We've lost our republic if we no longer are free to speak our minds and witness to our beliefs. Even the freedom to practice religion—guaranteed in the First Amendment—is no longer guaranteed. We are told that ours is no longer a Christian nation, and that is happening.

A broad study by the Pew Research Center[1] published in October, 2019, found that Christians now represent 65 percent of the population, down 12 percent in a decade. While 85 percent of the oldest population, born before 1945, describe themselves as Christian, there are thirty million more Americans who are "nothing in particular"—i.e., "nones"—in the past decade. Forty percent of millennials say they seldom or never attend religious services. This category accounts for 17 percent of the population. Ten percent of millennials identify with non-Christian faiths. Fully a quarter of the population describe themselves as atheist, agnostic, or nones.

The entire history of mankind, from the time humans grouped together sufficiently that some form of government became necessary, has seen one of the elite few dominating the rest of us, as William J. Federer spelled out in *Change To Chains: The 6,000 Year Quest for Control.*[2] He devotes thirteen pages of his book cataloging the various "major monarchs" in world history—from Gilgamesh in 2,500 BC through Vladimir Lenin in 1917 and Hitler in 1933 to Kim Jong-Il in 1994. Republics have been few, and the foremost republic in history has been the United States.

Gradually, over a thousand years of truth-seeking, we took control from the elites and asserted our human nature, resulting in our constitutional republic. Founded on Christian values, our republic accomplished what W. Cleon Skousen called *The Five Thousand Year Leap*,[3] superseding in a short time more than what had been achieved in advancing the human condition in the previous five thousand years. But Benjamin Franklin famously said, "We have given you a republic. It remains to be seen if you will be able to retain it." And President Ronald Reagan warned us, "Freedom is never more than one generation away from extinction. We didn't pass it to our children in the bloodstream. It must be fought for, protected, and handed on for them to do the same, or one day we will spend our sunset years telling our children and our children's children what it was once like in the United States where men were free."

Our Declaration of Independence proclaims, "We hold these truths to be self-evident, that all men are created equal, that they are endowed by their Creator with certain inalienable Rights, that among these are Life, Liberty and the pursuit of Happiness. That to secure these Rights, Governments were instituted among Men, deriving their just powers from the consent of the governed." Our founders signed their names to this declaration because, among other abuses, they worked two weeks out of the year to pay taxes to England, for which they did not consent. Americans who pay taxes today work six months out of the year to pay them to the federal "king," which, nonetheless, is saddling our posterity with debt that can never be repaid.

Our "situation in life" today finds us teetering on the edge of falling from the hard fought affirmation of these self-evident rights back into mankind's default form of governance—the abyss of communalism, communism in our day—which is pagan barbarism. Communism denies that we have any natural rights and holds that we are not self-determining, nothing but the equivalent of the farmer's herd of cows and flock of chickens, and thus disposable at the will of the elite. Individualism affirms that we each are, by our nature, self-determining and independent, secure in our person, and have an un*alien*able right to our life, our liberty, and our property, that is the wherewithal to secure these rights, so that we can each pursue happiness.

Thus, the battle line is drawn. These two "isms" are essentially conflicted and incompatible. The communists are well organized and determined. They have been at it a long while. We can't let them win. We must salvage individualism, our Christian way of life—our civilization, which is the fruit of Christian virtue and values—by finding common ground among all truth seekers, understanding what we are up against, clarifying what we need to salvage, and then developing action plans that we can pursue together. This is, admittedly, a Herculean challenge. By the time we get to the action plans, I hope you will commit to the cause before us. "'Whom shall I send, and who will go for us?' 'Here am I; send me'" (Isa. 6:8).

WHAT IS CHRISTIAN CIVILIZATION?

It is an ideal social contract where individuals in a society respect one another as equals—with the same essential human nature. Affirming one another, individuals create this quality of life together, supporting one another to achieve their full potential and freely pursue fulfillment and happiness. It is practicing love for neighbor, so that everyone can thrive. It is a personal commitment to strive to live the virtuous way, the way that is true to our nature, with uncompromising truthfulness, trustworthiness, and integrity, with everyone treating others as themselves, with empathy and care for one another.

Thus, individuals freely commit to be responsible for themselves, fulfilling their own potential, and also to be assets to the community, contributing to others' fulfillment. This personal responsibility enhances society, which, in turn, benefits everyone.

The free enterprise environment thus established enhances the capability of inventors and entrepreneurs to advance the human condition. It views leadership as a service to the community. Persons take no social advantage from economic success. It is the opposite of a predatory mentality. While these values represent an ideal, they remain the Christian aspirations that have created Western civilization, deficiencies notwithstanding, over many centuries.

WHAT AM I ABOUT?

Growing Up

I want to introduce myself to show how this book developed. The oldest of three from a white-collar family with a stay-at-home bookkeeper mom, I was definitely Roman Catholic. My dad and I would sacrifice Sunday mornings, when we would go trout fishing, to find a church in Northern Michigan, so we wouldn't miss Mass.

My eighth-grade teacher, Sister Tekla, said I should become a priest. She drafted me. I shined in high school. An Eagle Scout, I was also a Scout leader. I was valedictorian all four years, studied Latin all four years, and was president of the senior class of 408 students. My picture appeared in the paper occasionally. I organized the senior dance, and my mom came as a chaperone. They said she was my "date" since I never would ask anyone out.

Adults who had taken a shine to me, neighbors and professional people but never my parents, did their utmost to dissuade me from entering the seminary—to no avail. Mixing adolescent idealism with adolescent wisdom is an intoxicating cocktail, served up prior to the drinking age.

Becoming a Priest

So to the seminary I went. It was sobering, all right, but I was addicted. Two years of languages—Latin, Greek, Hebrew, French, Spanish—and then on to a degree in philosophy. For that, I am grateful. It taught me to pick information apart and to scrutinize it. That made a difference in my life.

As for theology, a few seminarians across America are selected every year to study in Rome. They live four years at the North American College (technically part of the Vatican) and attend the renowned Pontifical Università Gregoriana. The best Jesuit theologians taught there; several wrote the popes' encyclicals. I counted students from twenty-three countries, but we spoke a common language: Latin. By reviewing my verbatim lecture notes, I would orally defend the entire year's education each July. I acquired six languages and made strong European friends. That was the blessing.

The curse was the North American College. I was traumatized. It oriented the rest of my life. Confident and idealistic, we, the "Little Bishops"—that is, many of us—, soon discovered that the seat of the Roman Catholic Church, the Vatican, was nothing but a corrupt enterprise, in many ways the antithesis of the Christianity to which we had dedicated our lives. Almost daily we heard that "the essence of the priesthood is to get yourself a good name. Therefore, never take a controversial stand since it would alienate people." Put another way, "avoid controversy at all cost. Burn that incense before the idols."

Many of us became a loosely knit, secretive, underground community for mutual support. A homosexual seminarian, angry about being rebuffed by one of us, got drunk and took our names to the archbishop. This triggered a purge, and the respective bishops were summoned to Rome. But he missed my name, and this confirmed, in my mind, that God had a mission for me.

A great deal of my time was spent trying to keep the remnants from committing suicide. Later on, wearing my "neuropsychology hat," I realized that the mechanism in the unconscious brain that causes posttraumatic stress disorder in combat veterans is the same mechanism that causes PTSD in emotional trauma.

I did graduate with honors, with the equivalent of a master's degree in sacred theology. I celebrated my First Mass as a newly minted priest in the catacombs, where legend has it that the early Christians retreated to escape persecution. That was my pledge, to restore the original *kerygma*, the proclamation of the Good News of Christianity.

By the time I got back to the States, even my best friends did not think I would be able to have a functional life. You may say, "Why didn't you just get out?" Well, in my naiveté, I was all the more committed to carry on the Christian message, and this merely hardened me to show authentic Christianity by my works and to be God's witness. Now, wearing my "psychology hat," I know how this mechanism operates. By investing everything about you in your conviction, you find a way to maintain it. Doing otherwise is identity suicide.

The Parish Priest

So I became a parish priest and soon was counseling the parishioners. I developed quite a reputation; the doctors and attorneys in the area were adding to my clients. Sleep-deprived, I was "saving the world, one person at a time." Within three years, I had become quite influential; for example, I broke up a ring of taxicab drivers that provided underage girls for prostitution. With all that, the alcoholic monsignor got so jealous of me that he got the bishop to move me. I was heartbroken.

During the summer, I moved to Northern Michigan and acted as a kind of ombudsman for the (legal) Mexican migrant workers dwelling in a hundred scattered camps who came to harvest the cherries, pickles, etc. I was the court translator. I had Sunday Mass in barns.

I picked up where I left off at the new parish. Besides counseling and ordinary parish work, I eventually had a popular "underground church" and was teaching a pre-marriage course at the high school when I got a call from the bishop. The third assistant priest in a row in a parish in Northern Michigan had attempted suicide, so would I please take his place? Of course. The baron monsignor so intimidated the parishioners that I once noticed a stalwart farmer actually shaking when criticized by him. The monsignor simply canceled my scripture class, which had grown from a few to a great many parishioners. The experience there was what it took to make me admit that, to save some integrity, I had to move on. All the priests that I had admired had moved on. Several had killed themselves.

Moving On

What to do? Not much call for teaching Greek or Hebrew. My counseling experience convinced me that I was good at empowering other people to figure out their lives and thrive, so getting a PhD in clinical psychology was the ticket, and beyond all odds, Dr. John Mueller at the University of Detroit thanked me for giving him the opportunity to help me out and accepted me into that program. We became great friends and were developing a clinic together when he suffered a fatal heart attack.

I went on to get my PhD degree eventually, after many complications. I went on treating patients. Hearing of me, some travelled more than a hundred miles for their weekly session. One even flew from New Jersey!

I got married. When taking my two daughters around the U of D, folks thought they were my *grand*kids. Better late than never. My wonderful, gifted wife is a tremendous blessing.

So I practiced psychotherapy for forty-five years and was recruited as a neuropsychologist for the last twelve years. My basic education in neurology was outdated, so I had to catch up. Again, my reputation as a neuropsychologist grew, and I was getting referrals from physicians within a seventy-five-mile radius for neuropsychological assessments. And I was, once again, working too many hours.

I retired to finish this book that's been in my head awhile. Maybe I'm still trying to save the world, but I think it is vital that we unite now to save our tattered civilization, which mankind advanced for so many centuries at the cost of so much blood and treasure. As we go along, whether we agree with each other or disagree—and I predict there will be some of each— let's trust that we all have the sincerity, integrity, and good intentions as valid as our own.

SECTION I

CLARIFICATIONS

CHAPTER 1

HOW CAN WE ALL UNITE?

INTRODUCTION

As you learned from my history, I was traumatized to discover that the official Church was corrupt and did not represent my Christian values. I remain a practicing Christian, and that trauma hardened my resolve to live a Christian way of life and promote Christianity. Jesus remains Lord of the true Christian community, the living body of all those who aspire to live the Christian message—"the laws of nature and of nature's God," in the words of our Declaration of Independence.

My experience in Rome, coupled with the theology I learned there, has provided me a perspective that reaches out to those Americans who, like myself, have been disillusioned by official religion. There are many sincere Americans, dismayed by our eroding civilization, who no longer identify as Christian but who equally aspire to live a life of Christian values although they may identify as atheists, agnostics, or simply "nones." As the number of traditional Christians continues to decline, it is essential for all of us of goodwill, who are concerned about the erosion of our civilized way of life, to join forces. I reach out to them in this section. The task is to unite all of us in this common mission.

If America were as traditionally Christian as that of our forefathers, this book would not be necessary. Our Christian civilization would be assured. *If you are secure in your traditional Christian orientation, this section is not intended for you.* You continue to bear witness to the truth and uphold civilization. Because this section, instead, reaches out to the rest of America, you would find it an unnerving distraction at best. In a worse case, it could disillusion you to the challenge we have and our goal to unite all of us in this struggle. To prevent this, I recommend that you simply bypass Section 1 for now. You are already where you need to be. In this case, simply begin with Section 2, "Eradicating Christian Civilization."

Many Americans, no longer identifying as Christians, have fallen into the opposite camp and consider themselves socialists, another word for communists. Section 2 exposes communism for what it is and shows how it has infiltrated America. Once you have studied what we are up against and what we must do about it, especially if you have non-Christian friends and acquaintances who are sincere, then read Section 1. You will find it enlightening in understanding them and reaching out to them. It aligns them with all sincere Christians to salvage our Christian civilization. At that point, you will be able to put these ideas in perspective as another point of view. "In my Father's house there are many rooms."

In this book, I compare the situation in life at different periods in history to emphasize the importance of keeping events in perspective. From the work of the German theologian Rudolf Bultmann, I have coined his phrase, "Sitz im Leben." When you come across Sitz im Leben, that is what I have in mind. You will find in Section 1, by showing the importance of considering Sitz im Leben, that I disprove the racist divisiveness in our society today, comparing the situation in life of primitive Africans with that of slavery in America. I support our constitutional republic by showing that Thomas Jefferson and our founders were the slaves' heroes in the context of their Sitz im Leben.

RUDOLF KARL BULTMANN

Imagine being back in the sixteenth century, when the earth was flat. Copernicus, with his newfangled telescope, claims the earth isn't flat at all but, instead, is like a big ball circling around the sun, an even bigger ball, and there are other big balls doing that as well. Can you imagine! Then along comes Galileo[1] and says the same thing. What fools! Good thing they put that heretic in prison where he belongs. Actually, Copernicus wasn't the first. Somebody named Aristarchus of Samos[2] said the same thing three centuries before Christ. Nobody took him seriously of course.

But that was then; this is now. There remain some flatlanders out there, but almost everyone figures that Galileo got it right after all. In the history of man, we keep rethinking what we had taken for granted as we improve in knowledge and insight. That's what makes us *Homo sapiens*, the smart ones. We don't think today the way we did in the sixteenth century.

When I studied theology at the Università Gregoriana in Rome, those proud Jesuits couldn't get enough of the Lutheran theologian Rudolf Karl Bultmann[3] (1884–1976) and his unconventional explanation of scripture. His vision clashes with conventional ideas as strongly, perhaps, as Galileo's idea of the solar system. He focused—you guessed it—on putting into perspective the Sitz im Leben, meaning the "situation in life" or the mindset when Jesus lived and scripture was written.

People then were as human as we are. Human nature never changes; the laws of nature never change. But those people had no notion of science or testing things out to see what is true, and no one cared. They thought differently and talked a different language, literally and figuratively. We find it hard to think the way folks did in the sixteenth century. It's much harder to go back another sixteen.

For Bultmann, it is the essential philosophical truths of Christianity—teaching the right way to live, which are relevant and must be liberated from the mentality of that archaic Sitz im Leben. In other words, he taught that we must preserve the Christian message in our day and not reject these eternal truths because we fail to recognize or to take into account the archaic Sitz im Leben in which they were conveyed. He stated, "We cannot use electric lights and radios and, in the event of illness, avail ourselves of modern medical and clinical means but at the same time believe in the spirit and wonder world of the New Testament."[4]

The goal of Rudolf Bultmann, therefore, was to situate the "mythological" elements in the New Testament in that culture. He taught that "only faith in the kerygma"—that is, the proclamation of the Good News conveyed in the New Testament—"is necessary for Christian faith, not any particular facts regarding the historical Jesus."[5]

To this end, Bultmann taught that we must rid ourselves of the "supernatural" biblical interpretations of that Sitz im Leben—at that period in history—and discard their "temporal and existential categorizations," in other words discard the way they thought and spoke so long ago. He rejected such doctrines as the preexistence of Christ. He believed that this interpretation would allow modern audiences to grasp the significance of Jesus's teachings.

For Bultmann, Christian faith should be centered on the "transcendent Christ and the church," into which Jesus may be said to be risen, and not faith in the historical Jesus. Church, the "*ekklesia tou theou*," means the gathering together or community of Christians, not a religious denomination. Christ lives on in the community of practicing Christians. The truth of the Christian message, the right way to live, is the acting Lord, affirmed as mankind's Guide and Director, living on in those who believe and obey these teachings.

In this way, Bultmann sought to take us beyond both *subjective* (e.g., the resurrection as an experience of the disciples) and *objective* (e.g., the resurrection as a verifiable historical event) interpretations of the resurrection.[6] By emphasizing the significance of taking that Sitz im Leben into account, he sought to develop a theology of resurrection, which does justice to the primitive Christian proclamation—that the man who was put to death still lives and continues to act as the Lord *within the living Christian community.*

Scriptural "myths" from that archaic Sitz im Leben do, indeed, show us how to live virtuous lives aligned with our nature but conveyed in terms of the ideas and ways of thinking of the people at that time. These "myths" are the framework that was available to them, in that Sitz im Leben, which conveyed these "ultimate truths." It was the way they expressed the kerygma, the eternal Christian instructions about the right way to live.

When we think of a "myth," we assume it not to be true. Theologian Conrad Hyers explains,

> Myth today has come to have negative connotations which are the complete opposite of its meaning in a religious context... In a religious context, however, myths are storied vehicles of supreme truth, the most basic and important truths of all. By them people regulate and interpret their lives and find worth and purpose in their existence. Myths put one in touch with sacred realities, the fundamental sources of being, power, and truth. They are seen not only as being the opposite of error but also as being clearly distinguishable from stories told for entertainment and from the workaday, domestic, practical language of a people. They provide answers to the mysteries of being and becoming, mysteries which, as mysteries, are hidden, yet mysteries which are revealed through story and ritual. Myths deal not only with truth but with ultimate truth.[7]

One influence was Wilhelm Dilthey (1833–1911), according to whom we must project ourselves into the author's experience in order to relive it. Dilthey held that historical consciousness—*i.e.,* the consciousness of the historical relativity of all ideas, attitudes, and institutions—is the most characteristic and challenging fact in the intellectual life of the modern world. It shakes all belief in absolute principles, but it thereby sets people free to understand and appreciate all the diverse possibilities of human experience.[8]

Another influence was the existentialist philosopher Martin Heidegger (1889–1976), who provided the preunderstanding for Bultmann's existential theology.[9] Heidegger was initially a theology student but is known as a philosopher. He focused on being authentic to our culture.

So the task for Bultmann was to extract the kerygma in the New Testament from the "mythological" elements of that Sitz im Leben. He taught that only the essence of the Christian message is relevant and must be taken out of the particular "package" in which it was delivered then. We might say that we must "open the package" to see what is inside. If we let this sink in, he makes as much sense to me as Galileo.

COMPARING OTHER THEOLOGIANS

Bultmann was not the first theologian to grapple with the "spirit and wonder world" of scripture. A century before, in 1835, David Friedrich Strauss wrote *Das Leben Jesu, Kritisch Bearbeitet* (i.e., *The Life of Jesus Critically Examined*.[10]). In his two volumes, he denied the historical accuracy of the gospels, describing them as "historical myth," but he explained that his interpretation did not destroy Christianity because all religions are based on ideas, not facts.

He failed to adequately salvage the unchanging kerygma, which Bultmann preserved by transcending that Sitz im Leben. And he didn't understand "myth" as explained by Conrad Hyers. We might say that he "threw out the baby with the bathwater." Later influenced by the anti-Christian philosopher Georg Hegel (as was Karl Marx), he concluded that Christianity should be replaced by scientific materialism.

Other crusaders have fought to salvage Christianity, but I believe they fell short because, one way or another, they failed to grasp the illumination of Sitz im Leben, which is as clear to me as the solar system. They unconsciously presume that the authors of scripture somehow piggybacked to the twenty-first century.

For example, John Horvat II[11] uses my words—Christian civilization, individualism (which he misconstrues as intemperate selfishness)—and speaks of personal autonomy. He pays lip service to our constitutional republic and adherence to the natural law, but he is locked—in his unconscious Roman Catholic perspective—into stating that the people have "quasi-sovereign rights," while the state and, by implication, the Catholic hierarchy command "the supreme power." We have been climbing that mountain since before the Magna Carta, culminating in "governments instituted among Men, deriving their just powers from the consent of the governed." He demands that we return to the medieval feudal system. While he offers no autobiographical data to back it up, he trusts that, for the most part, the lords were benevolent and the vassals dependent and appreciative. He characterizes this system, it appears, to be equivalent to the American slave master–slave relationship that I portray below. So while I cheer his willingness to join the cause, he doesn't propose what it will take to win.

USING THE EXAMPLE OF SLAVERY

Interpreting the Sitz im Leben—the situation in life—is always the key to size up what history is really about. Bultmann contrasted the Sitz im Leben of scriptural times with ours today from a theoretical or philosophical point of view. This sets the theme for this book. I will now follow that with examples. I'm going to contrast the Sitz im Leben of slaves in Africa with their Sitz im Leben in America.

Christopher Caldwell has astutely observed that "today slavery is at the center of Americans' official history, with race the central concept in the country's official self-understanding." In his recent book, *The Age of Entitlement*,[12] he devotes twenty-five cogent pages to race.

Here are five reasons why I picked these examples. (1) This history of slavery allows us to examine firsthand facts and avoid conjecture. (2) In examining slavery, we have starkly contrasting Sitz im Lebens: Africa and America. (3) This comparison in Sitz im Leben 150 years ago underscores how necessary it is to interpret scripture with that perspective. (4) The Sitz im Leben in both primitive Africa—with the introduction of Christianity by devoted Christian missionaries—as well as in the Christian Southern states, drives home the essential value of Christian civilization and its contrast with barbarism. As a cogent example, the incessant identity politics, particularly labeling everyone and everything "racist" based on slavery, is herein exposed and repudiated. (5) Analogies can be noted regarding the Sitz im Leben in primitive Africa with the trends in today's pagan Sitz im Leben.

CHAPTER 2

WHAT ABOUT PRIMITIVE AFRICA?

So our first trek is to primitive Africa. To let that Sitz im Leben sink in, we discover how the slaves lived before coming to America. Our guides are two sterling Christian missionaries who followed the expansion of the British Empire into Africa. They forsook their civilized Sitz im Leben to bring it to a very primitive people. It would be hard to find a more cogent example of Christian love for our fellow man and the value of the Christian kerygma.

Given the importance of accurate firsthand examples of Sitz im Leben, I am going to quote extensively from the book *Tales of the African Frontier*,[13] particularly the firsthand account by Rev. Arthur Fisher among the first missionaries, capitalizing on the extension of the British Empire at the turn of the last century. He is a valuable resource providing an account of the lives of these primitive people at that time. He was among the first educated persons with a written language to live there. By inserting themselves into the Sitz im Leben of these people, he and his wife endured this culture shock and risked their lives virtually on a daily basis to introduce civilization to the people of this precivilized continent.

The coauthor, Daniel Maddix, was told, "You want to know about the early days in East Africa, the man for you to see is the Reverend Arthur Fisher. He's the last man alive who saw the hoisting of the British flag on the shores of Lake Victoria."[14]

True, our country was founded 150 years before, and there has always been slavery, but these primitive people in this dark continent still had no interest in recording history when the missionaries arrived. Their preoccupation was survival. It is a "given" that the African people weren't less primitive when the first slaves were brought to America.

Daniel Maddix actually is addressing the African Sitz im Leben with this key observation. He is not being "racist" by what he says. He calls these primitive people his "brother."

> The most difficult task that a writer can undertake is to give an intelligent description of a personality whose emotions and mental processes are completely alien to him. The writer is apt to reason, "If I were in this character's position, how would I think and behave?" This is particularly true of men who write about wild animals and attribute to the animals thoughts and emotions that an animal simply does not possess. It is equally true of authors who write about wild people. A savage does not think along the same lines as a civilized man. In some instances he may seem extremely shrewd and in other situations he may give the impression of incredible stupidity. But in few cases does he go through the same mental processes as his civilized brother.[15]

He visited the Fishers in their home.

> They took me into their living room, ornamented with African spears. "Everything here has a history to us," said Mrs. Fisher... She took down a cow's horn, ornamented with cowrie shells. "This was a witch doctor's medicine horn. The black, pitch-like substance around the tip is dried human blood. If a witch doctor thought a man was possessed of evil spirits, he would make a hole through his ear and drain off the blood into one of these horns." "Sometimes the patient didn't survive the treatment," added her husband... "We saw a man killed with one of these. The witch doctor cut too deeply. I remember the man scratched the ground for some time and then went into convulsions. Ruth and I worked over him that evening, but we couldn't save him."[16]

What led Arthur Fisher to Africa? He was inspired by evangelists, and he was determined to become a minister. While studying at the University of Dublin, he learned that a Bishop Tucker had sent missionaries to Baganda, now Uganda, but the king viewed this as a threat to his power, and so he tortured and killed over two hundred of the converts. Bishop Tucker intended to lead a new group there, and Arthur Fisher volunteered to be one of the seven missionaries.

WORKING IN AFRICA

Fisher said of getting there, "On their way across Kenya, the missionaries passed slave gangs being driven to the coast, the Arab slavers riding ahead on their magnificently caparisoned mules and behind them a long line of natives, yoked together."[17]

Surviving dangerous encounters, particularly with the Maasai, they finally reached Lake Victoria by December and arrived at Mengo (now Kampala, the largest city in Uganda) on Christmas Day. "Uganda was broken up into a number of small kingdoms and semi-independent villages all more or less at perpetual war with each other and each of these kingdoms had its own royal family."

Luckily, when he arrived, the king, Mwanga, hoping for British help in fighting his rival, Kabarega, decided not to kill Fisher. King Kabarega of Bunyoro was threatening King Mwanga's country. King Mwanga, described as nervous and weak, "might cringe before someone in the morning and have him put to death with the most horrible tortures in the afternoon. Mwanga's father had once had the inhabitants of an entire village thrown into Lake Victoria because a witch doctor said it would cure the queen's toothache."

What was Fisher's "job description"? In his own words, Fisher said:

I soon found that a missionary has more to do than stand under a fig tree and read the scriptures to a group of natives. In Uganda, he had to be a combination explorer, doctor, carpenter, linguist, big game hunter and with a bit of the politician thrown in too. The witch doctors had always acted as medicine men so the natives couldn't believe that we weren't doctors too. We did have some slight medical knowledge and with so much suffering about, one couldn't refuse to help." Soon, many of the missionaries found that virtually all their time was taken up treating the sick.[18]

CHARACTERIZING THEIR SITZ IM LEBEN

Fisher explained the context for preaching the gospel:

You see, they didn't really have a proper religion of their own. It was mainly what might be called devil worship. A man would pay the priests to give him a fetish to keep off evil spirits or, if he or his family were sick, he'd pay the priest to drive off the evil spirit that was troubling them. The priest usually did that through mutilation… You never saw a child who didn't carry the marks of the branding iron or the knife… In fact, natives would stop and stare at the children of our native converts because they weren't mutilated.[19]

Fisher found that, in Toro, he was unable to reach the women, who were suspicious of a strange man, so he sought women missionaries. "Several young ladies answered the call," Mr. Fisher told me proudly. "Among them was a Miss Ruth Hurditch. I liked her so well that I married her." "I'm afraid the poor man didn't have much choice," said Mrs. Fisher… "I was the only white woman in Toro. Now that I think of it, I didn't have much choice myself. It was either Arthur or a cannibal."[20]

Life in this primitive culture was precarious—for the missionaries as well—and life expectancy was short. Besides severe famine, one risked being eaten by a leopard, a lion, a crocodile, or by another human being. I detail this below. Tribes enslaved each other, and slavery was still universal, forty years after it was legally abolished in the United States. As noted, these accounts came 150 years after our nation's founding, but the situation in the Dark Continent then was not less primitive than we found it at the time Fisher recorded his observations.

THE MISSIONARIES' SACRIFICES

These Christian missionaries risked everything to carry out their mission. This heart-rending account by Mrs. Fisher is a striking example of the rigors they faced and their Christian sacrifice. For example, in that Sitz im Leben, they had to birth their children without benefit even of a midwife.

They were on a mission trip and expected to reach a village in plenty of time but were delayed by floods and other complications. Arthur was delirious with fever and not expected to live. Ruth said, "I felt that I was indeed 'in the land of darkness and the shadow of death' when the baby came. I had to do everything myself." But she was malnourished and so, to make the situation worse, had no milk for the baby. "One of the native porters heard my crying. He came to the door and asked, 'Mistress, what's the matter?' 'I haven't any milk for my baby.'"

The porter left without a word, but he returned, the next morning, with a gourd full of milk from a native village miles away in the jungle. He did this every evening, vanishing after carrying a heavy load all day and finding another gourd full of milk. "My child lived and she's now married and has a family of her own."[21]

MORTALITY IN AFRICA

Danger was everywhere, and the population was depleted, in part by the continuous intertribal warfare and predation. The main danger was simply starvation. Having food to eat was a never-ending crisis:

> With their fields destroyed, the cattle killed, the people [of Bunyoro] alternated between sullen indifference and a tendency to murder each other on the chance that the victim might have a few mouthfuls of food concealed on his person... Starving natives crawled out of their huts to beg a stranger for a mouthful of food and died while crawling. Young girls were wandering about, offering to sell themselves for a handful of grain.[22]

At one point, Fisher's native helpers came to him, saying, "Master, we've been talking things over, and we feel it is best that you go... We will stay. True, most of these people will be dead in the next few months, but there will be survivors. If we stay and work with them, those survivors will be Christians."[23]

Of course, he stayed as well. He sent an appeal to the Christian natives in Toro for help. But the Toro people were close to starvation themselves, reduced to such a state because of the constant Bunyoro raids on their country. The long native wars and an epidemic of rinderpest had wiped out most of their cattle.

In spite of this misery, King Kasagama of Toro rallied his people, and a few weeks later, caravans of Toro porters began to pour into the country carrying loads of food. King Kasagama sent word, "We are now Christians and must forgive our enemies."

But this was hardly the end of the story. The hut where the food was stored was alive with rats that were eating all the food. All the while distributing the food, Fisher and his helpers worked in relays for days to fight off the starving rats.

The poor little children had absolutely no clothing, and at night, they used to coat themselves with mud in an effort to stay warm. "I believe that the infant mortality rate must have been nearly ninety percent," said Mrs. Fisher. The women themselves weren't much better off:

> One afternoon, when I was sitting in the semidarkness of a hut talking to a local chief, I saw some creatures crawling about in the shadows searching for stray bits of food... I saw that they were the

chief's wives. The women seemed incapable of any thoughts except food and competition for their husband's favors.

HOW DID THESE PEOPLE GET ALONG?

Recall the words of Daniel Maddix: "In few cases does he go through the same mental processes as his civilized brother." Rev. Arthur Fisher states,

> Good works aren't enough. What good does it do to sew up a spear wound in a man's chest if the next week he's going out to raid another village and get a fresh one? The natives had no idea of sin. They couldn't understand why we thought it was wrong for a man to beat his wife to death or for a strong community to conquer their neighbors and sell them to the Arab slavers. Suppose a man's cattle and even his family are menaced by a lion. You say, I am a civilized, educated man so I will give this savage a gun to shoot the lion and protect himself. This is not enough. If the man is still a savage, he will promptly use the gun to shoot his neighbors and seize their property.[24]

> [T]he kings of Toro had been taking themselves so seriously that a few years before they would kill anyone who didn't prostrate himself on the ground as they passed. I remember [the king] had one servant run after him holding the imperial umbrella over his head all the time and another servant follow him with a stool in case he wanted to sit down.[25]

> It had been the habit of the Bunyoro king to mutilate any man who opposed him or violated any of the innumerable native laws. I don't believe there was a man in the entire country who was not mutilated in some way or other.[26]

WHAT ABOUT SLAVERY IN AFRICA?

Slavery continued throughout Africa. Tribes enslaved other tribes for their own use or to sell to Arab slavers. For example, "the Bunyoro had carried off many of the village of Toro's wives and children to be sold to the Arab slavers." Fisher further explained, "A village would say to me, 'our neighbors have raided us and stolen many young girls. As Christians we are forbidden to fight, but we must now invade their country and rescue our families.'"

There was also the problem with fugitive slaves: "Slaves would run away from their masters and take refuge with our converts. Their masters would demand their return and our converts would refuse to give them up. As slavery was the law of the land, I could only reluctantly say it must be done."[27]

DEVALUATION OF LIFE

We say that all men are created equal and have the right to life, liberty, and the pursuit of happiness. Recognizing these truths about human nature—Christian values—is the mark of civilization. Of this, the natives in Africa had no understanding. Beating one's wife to death, stealing the women and children from neighbors, and selling the women and children to the Arab slavers were standard procedure, as was mutilating children and adults at the witch doctor's or king's pleasure. In fact, in some instances, innocent women were buried alive:

> Some ten years later, [King] Kamurasi died. In accordance with native custom, the body was smoked to preserve it. Then a pit was dug and the king's wives forced to sit in the bottom in two lines facing each other. The royal corpse was laid across the women's knees. This was done during the night. When morning dawned, the royal guards seized as many people as possible as they came out of their huts, broke their arms and legs, and threw them into the pit to serve the king in the next world. Then cowhides were stretched across the pit and pegged down. The cowhides were covered with earth, which was stamped hard, and a grass hut erected over the spot. Some of the old palace servants were put in the hut to guard it. They were never permitted to go outside.[28]

The story goes on. The king's son, Kabarega, came to power by conquering his brothers. Shortly after he came to power, Kabarega's mother, Kamurasi's widow, appeared before the young king's palace to congratulate her son. Kabarega was shocked and infuriated that she was still alive. "If you were a decent woman, you'd have been buried alive like my father's other wives," he told her. However, there wasn't much he could do about it then, especially as the old queen had a substantial army.

Fisher said, "As long as the men felt there is nothing morally wrong in treating women like dogs, teaching crop rotation and healing the sick wouldn't do a mite of good." Mrs. Fisher also observed, "The natives believed that the birth of twins was unlucky. So if a woman had twins, the babies were left out in the forest to die. Then the witch doctor would say to the mother, 'Two dogs were born to you,' and that was the end of the affair."

CANNIBALISM / PREDATORY BEHAVIOR

Tribes were constantly warring and killing each other for food or selling others into slavery, so the natives needed to constantly be on guard and the missionaries as well. The following account is by Sir Gerald Porter:

> We plunged into the darkness of a dense belt of forest inhabited by the treacherous, cunning and hostile Kikuyu. Warned by the state of affairs… we were careful to keep all our people together, every man within a couple of paces of his neighbor. The Kikuyu very seldom or never show themselves and run the risk of a fight in the open, but lie like snakes in the long grass within a few yards of the line of march, watching for some incautious porter to loiter a few yards behind. Even then not a sound is heard but the twang of a small bow and the almost inaudible whizz of a poisoned arrow. A slight puncture in the arm, throat or chest is followed almost inevitably by death. Another favorite trick of the Kikuyu is to plant poisoned skewers in the path, set at an angle so they will pierce the stomach of anyone advancing through the underbrush. For a man to lag behind the others, even for a few seconds, means certain death.[29]

WHAT ABOUT WILD ANIMALS?

The natives were at continuous risk of being eaten by wild animals if not by one another. As stated, one of Fisher's tasks was that of big game hunter. "I never saw such a country for leopards as Toro," said Fisher.

The natives kept great fires going around their villages all night long to keep them away, but the leopards would still come in. They'd tear their way through the roofs of the huts to get at the people inside. When the natives went out to hunt them… [they] hunted with spears and I'd go along with my gun… I got quite handy at shooting leopards.[30]

This is the account of R. O. Preston about the cunning of lions. Imagine yourself trying to get a good night's sleep in Africa in those days:

> At first, I could scarcely believe the evidence of my senses… That a lion could take man after man in this manner without having the victims give a single cry to warn their friends sleeping around them seemed absolutely incredible… I know from many experiences with the brutes that a man-eater is a creature of great determination and cunning. An unarmed human being has less chance against one of these animals than a mouse has against a cat. A lion often breaks the neck of a sleeping man with one blow of his paw, and the stroke is delivered almost soundlessly. Then he picks up his victim in his jaws and trots off with him.[31]

For example, Lt. Col. John H. Patterson killed lions to safeguard the construction of the railroad, claiming that lions had killed 135 people. John Hunter, the coauthor of this book, was told, "You are the man best qualified for the task. We want the trouble-causing lions killed in the next three months [among the Maasai] to bring the lion population within control."[32] The following is but one vignette as he was able to kill more than one hundred lions: "During the night, two more prides came to the bait. When dawn broke, I saw a sight I doubt if anyone has ever seen before or will ever see again. Eighteen lions lay dead before me."

While there are more, these accounts peg the Sitz im Leben of primitive Africa. How does that Sitz im Leben compare with the experience of slaves in America?

CHAPTER 3

WHAT ABOUT SLAVERY IN AMERICA?

INTRODUCTION

We're now back in America. We consider the experiences of the slaves themselves—again, in their own words. As a psychologist-scientist, I seek firsthand information. There are at least 3,500 Sitz im Leben autobiographies, usually in the slaves' vernacular, from their interviews after the Civil War. I have not read them all, but in reviewing many of them, I have developed an accurate appreciation of their overall experiences as slaves.

As our Christian civilization erodes, we find ourselves awash in a sea of disinformation. As you shall see, their stories conflict with the ideas of slavery we have been sold. Perhaps you heard it said: "Tell a lie a hundred times, and it becomes the truth." So currently, virtually everyone and everything is being condemned as "racist" in this politically correct culture posited on slavery. Rather than trust those whose purpose is to divide and conquer us, those who argue their agenda instead of the facts, you will learn the truth about slavery in their Sitz im Leben.

You will see that there were instances of abuse, some severe. However, what I must emphasize is that the majority of the slaves—almost without exception—loved their masters and were loved in turn, and actually preferred being slaves to being emancipated. Slavery for them was a positive experience. Were I to provide stories about these positive experiences proportionately, those stories would need many more pages. I have had to limit these stories in order to provide some in each category. As it is, I found it difficult to sufficiently reduce the quantity of the accounts provided; each has a story to tell.

In the great majority of cases, the slaves had comfortable living quarters, copious food, quality clothing, quality health care, church attendance, recreation, and permission to visit neighboring plantations (always with written permission). Habitually taken care of, they were not prepared for a free enterprise way of life.

Unanimously, they condemned the post-slavery generation as being indolent and lacking in virtue. Should anyone desire more such accounts than I am providing here, there are many books still in print. For example, Applewood Books (www.awb.com), has a volume for each of the states of Alabama, Arkansas, Florida, Georgia, Indiana, Kentucky, Maryland, Mississippi, Missouri, North Carolina, Ohio, Oklahoma, South Carolina, Tennessee, and Virginia. These books are not all written in the same style, and some are more informative than others. There are abundant additional data from the Library of Congress (www. loc.gov). This is what the former slaves had to say. I decided not to reference each individual account.

TRANSITION FROM AFRICA

John Brown. "My grandmother was one of [the slaves coming from Africa.] A savage in Africa—a slave in America. Mammy told it to me. Over there all the natives dressed naked and lived on fruits and nuts… One day a big ship stopped off the shore. The ship men sent a little boat to the shore and scattered bright things and trinkets on the beach… Grandmother said everybody made a rush for them things soon as the boat left. Next day the white folks scatter some more… and the next day some of them walked up the gangplank to get things off the plank and off the deck… Two-three hundred natives on the ship when they feel it move. They rush to the side but the plank is gone… Folks on the beach started to crying and shouting. The ones on the boat was wild with fear. Grandmother was one of them that got fooled."

Clara Walker. "My mother was a slave before me. She come over from de old country, she was a-runnin' along one day front of a—a—dat stripedly animal—a tiger? An a man come along on an elephant and scoop her up an' put her on a ship…There was another fellow on a joinin' plantation. He was a witch doctor. Brought him over from Africa. He didn't like his master, 'cause he was mean. So he make a little man out of mud. An' he stick thorns in his back. Sure 'nuff, his master got down with a misery in his back. An' the witch doctor let de thorn stay in de mud-man until he thought his master had got 'nuff punishment. When he tuck it out, his master got better."

STORIES OF ABUSE

Henry Cheatam. "After Massa was kilt, Old Miss had a nigger overseer and dat was de meanest devil dat ever lived on de Lord's green earth. I promise myself when I growed up dat I was a-goin' to kill dat nigger if it was the last thing I ever done. Lots of times I'se see him beat my mammy, and one day I seen him beat my auntie who was big with a child, and dat man dug a round hole in de ground and put her stomach in it, and beat and beat her for a half hour straight till de baby come right out dere in de hole. Mistis allow such treatment only 'cause a heap of times she didn't know nothin' about it, and de slaves better not tell her, 'cause dat overseer whip 'em if he finds out dat dey gone and told."

W. L. Bost. "I remember how they kill one nigger whippin' him with the bull-whip. Many the poor nigger nearly killed with the bullwhip. But this one die. He was a stubborn Negro and didn't do as much work as his massa thought he ought to. He been lashed a lot before. So they take him to the whippin' post, and then they strip his clothes off and then the man stand off and cut him with the whip. His back was cut all to pieces. The cuts about half inch apart. Then after they whip him they tie him down and put salt on him. Then after he lie in the sun awhile they whip him agin. But when they finish with he, he was dead."

David Blout. "One boy ask if he could warm by de brush heap. Da overseer said no, and after awhile de boy had a chill. De overseer don't care, but dat night de boy am a sick nigger. De next mornin' de marster gets de doctor, and de doctor say dat de boy has got pneumonia. He tells 'em to take off the boy's shirt and grease him with some tar, turpentine, and kerosene, and when dey starts to take de shirt off dey finds dat it am stuck. Dey had to grease de shirt to get it off 'cause de blood where de overseer beat him had stuck de shirt tight to de skin. De marster was in de room and he asked de boy how come it, and de boy told him. De marster sorta turns white and he says, to me, 'Will you go and ask de overseer to stop here a minute, please?' When de overseer comes up de steps he asks sorta sassy-like, 'What you want?' De marster says, 'Pack you things and get off'en my place as fast as you can, you pesky varmit.' De overseer sasses de marster some more, and den I sees de marster fairly lose his temper for de first time. He don't say a word, but he walks over, grabs de overseer by de shoulder, sets his boot right hard 'gainst de seat of his pants and sends him, all drawed up, out in de yard on his face."

Henry Williams. "My master was Jason and Betsy Williams. He had a small plantation; the smaller the plantation the better they was to their slaves. Jim Johnson's farm joined. He had nine hundred ninety-nine niggers... He was rough on his place. He had a jail on his place... Put them in there and lock them up with a big padlock. He kept a male hog in the jail to tramp and walk over them. They said they kept them tied down in that place. Five hundred lashes and shot 'em up in jail was light punishment... They was rough on 'em, killed some...I think it was better times in slavery than now but I'm not in favor of bringing it back on account of the cruelty and dividing up families. My master was good to us. He was proud of us. We fared fine."

Henry Waldon. "A fellow by the name of Jim Holbert was mean to his slaves as a man could be. He would whip them night and day. Work them till dark; then they would eat supper. Cook their own supper. Had nothing to cook but a little meat and bread and molasses. Then they would go back and bale up three or four bales of cotton... Their backs would be bleeding just like they cut it with knives... I think things is worse than they ever was. Everything we get we have to pay for, and then pay for paying for it. If it wasn't for my wife I could hardly live because I don't get much from the railroad company... [Master] had a five or six horse farm. His land wasn't strong but we worked and had plenty. Mother cooked for white and colored. We had what they et 'cepting when company come ... We had plain eating er plenty all the time. You see I'm a big man. I wasn't starved out till I was about grown, after the war was over..."

Frank Childress. "Marse Bob, drawed me from de estate. He was good to me hisself, but dey hired a overseer, he couldn' hear good, so dey 'zempted him from the War. He was mighty mean, I doan know how many times he did whup me. He would come out of a mornin' an' want to whup everyting he seen."

POSITIVE ATTITUDES ABOUT SLAVERY

Jack Walker. "Couldn't a had no better master. That's the reason I' livin' like I do. Always too good care of myself... I remember when the War was gwine on. I didn't know nothin' only they was fightin'. Most of my work was around the house. I never paid no 'tention to that war. I was livin' to fine them days. I was livin' a hundred days to the week. Yes, ma'am, I did get along fine... We didn't have a bit of expense on us... Our doctor bills was paid and had clothes give to us and plenty of something to eat… Oh yes, ma'am, I had good white folks. I never was sold. No, ma'am, I born right on the old home place…"

Alfred Wells. "I wuz a small boy, dey called me nigger cowboy, cause I drive de cows up at night, and took 'em to de paster in the mornings… Ef I had my choice, I'd rather be a slave. But we can't always have our ruthers. Them times I had good food, plenty to wear, and no more work than was good for me. Now I was kinder [hu]militated, when I think of what a high stepper I used to be. Having, to hang around with a sack on my back begging de government to keep me from starving."

Henry Walker. "The folks had a hard time making a living. Old mistress had four girls and her baby Ed was one day older than I was. The children of the hands played around in the woods and every place and stayed in the field if they was big enough to do any work… White folks raised me up to play with Ed till I thought I was white. They taught me to do right and I ain't forgot it… Colonel Williams and Ed are both dead. They did give me a lot of fine clothes when I went to see them as long as they lived. I oughter never left my good old home and white folks. They was show always mighty good to me…

No, the slaves didn't leave Colonel Williams. He left them. He brought me and Ed and we went back and moved to the old Williams farm on Arkansas River close to Little Rock. Then he sent for my folks. They come in wagons. They worked for him a long time and scattered about. I stayed at his house till he said, 'Henry, you are grown; you better look out for yourself now.' I never did like to 'sociate or stay 'bout colored folks and I didn't like to mind 'em."

Carolyn Watson. "I was born in Mississippi. I never will forget my white folks. Oh, I was raised good. I had good white folks. Wish I could see some of 'em now… My old master, I can see him now—old Joe Shird. Just as good as they could be… But they done better fore surrender than they did afterwards—that is them that had to go off to themselves."

Dock Wilborn. "Slaveowners, as a rule, arranged for their Negroes to have all needed pleasure and enjoyment, and in the late summer after cultivation of the crops was complete it was the custom for a number of them to give a large barbeque for their combined groups of slaves, at which huge quantities of beef and pork were served and the care-free hours given over to dancing and general merry-making."

Uncle Dock recalls that his master, Dan Wilborn, who was a good-natured man of large stature, derived much pleasure in playing his "fiddle" and that often in the early summer evenings he would walk down to the slave quarters with his violin remarking that he would supply the music and that he wished to see his "niggers" dance, and dance they would for hours and as much to the master's own delight and amusement as to theirs."

Tom Windham. "Before the war my white folks was good to us. I had a better time than I got now. My father and mother was sold away from me, but old mistress couldn't rest without 'em and went and got 'em back. They stayed right here till they died. Us folks was treated well. I think we should have our liberty cause we ain't hogs or horses—us is human flesh."

Clara Walker. "When de war was over, young miss she come in an she say, 'Clara, you's a free as I am.' 'No, I ain't,' says I. 'Yes, you is,' says she, 'you ain't cause I can't pay you.' 'Well,' says I, 'I'll go home to see my old mother.' 'Tell you what,' says she, 'I ain't got nuff money to send you, only part—so you go down to whar' dey is a'pannin'gold. You can git a Job at $2.00 per day.' … I worked hard, an' young miss took care of me. When I got ready to come home I bought my stage fare an' I carried $300 [$9,300 today] on me back to my ol' mother… When I got home to my mother I found dat ol' miss had give all of 'em somethin' along with settin' 'em free. My mother had 12 children so she git de mos'. She get a horse, a milk cow, 8 killin' hogs and 50 bushels of corn… An' I stayed on wid her and help her farm—I could plow as good as a man in dem days."

John Cameron. "My old Marster was the bes' man in de worl'. I jus' wish I could tell, an' make it plain, jus' how good him an' old Mistis was… Us was 'lowed to sing, play de fiddles, an' have a good time. Us had plenty t' eat and warm clo'es an' shoes… How us could swing, an' step-'bout by dat old fiddle music always a-goin' on… Ol' Marster knowed how to comfort you in trouble."

Clarlie Davenport. "I growed up in de quarters. De houses was clean an' snug. Us was better fed den dan I is now, an' warmer, too. Us had blankets an' quilts filled wid home raised wool an' I jus' loved layin' in de big fat feather bed a-hearin' de rain patter on de roof… On Sundays us always had meat pie or fish or fresh game an' roasted 'taters an' coffee. On Chris'mus de marster 'ud give us chicken an' barrels o' apples an' oranges."

Henri Necaise. "When we was slaves Marster tell us what to do. He say, Henri, do dis, do dat. An' we done it. Den us didn' have to think whar de nex' meal comin' from, or de nex' pair o' shoes or pants. De grub an' clo'es give us was better'n I ever gits now… Dey didn't give us money, but, you see, I was a slave. Day sho' give me ever'thing else I need, clo'es an' shoes. I always had a-plenty t'eat, better'n I can git now. I was better off when I was a slave dan I is now, 'cause I had ever'thing furnished me den."

Isaac Stier. "Da slaves was well treated when dey got sick. My Marster had a standin' doctor what he paid by the year. He sho' was a gent'man an' a powerful good doctor. Dey was a hospital building near de quarters an' a good old granny woman to nuss de sick… Right now, I loves my marster an' his wife in de grave. Day raised me an' showed me kindness all dey lives. I was proud of 'em. At de present time I's under treatment o' young Dr. Stowers, my marster's gran'chil'. I trusts him an' he is sho' good to me."

Mary Anderson. "When Marster or Missus walked in the grove the little Negroes would follow along with them like a gang of kiddies. Some of the slave children wanted to stay with them at the Great House all the time. They knew no better, of course, and seemed to love Marster and Missus as much as they did their own mother and father… and the way the children loved and trusted them was a beautiful sight to see."

Charles Davenport. "My granny told me about a slave uprisin' what took place when I was a little boy. None o' de marster's niggers would have nothin' to do with it. A nigger tried to get 'em to kill dey white people and take dey land. But what us want to kill Old Marster and take de land when dey was de best friends us had?"

Mittie Freeman. "After a long time—oh maybe five years—one day they ask Pappy, 'Are you got some white folks in Arkansas?' He told them the Williams white folks in Camden on the Quachita. They's white. After while theys send Pappy home. Nobody ever seen such a homecoming. Old Miss and the young white folks gathered round hugged my old black pappy when he come home; they cry on his shoulder, so glad to get him back. That's what them Williams folks thought of their slaves."

Robert Wilson. "I didn't care whether I was free or not. 'Bout slavery—well, I thinks like this. I think they fared better then. They didn't have to worry 'bout senses. We had plenty chicken and everything. Nowdays when we pay the rent you ain't got nothin' left to buy somethin' to eat."

EDUCATION AND LEARNING SKILLS

Clara Walker. "When I was 13 years old my ol' mistress put me wid a doctor who learned me how to be a midwife. Dat was cause so many women on the plantation was catchin' babies. I stayed wid dat doctor, Dr. McGill his name was, for 5 years. I got to be good. Got so he'd sit down an' I'd do all de work… Brought as many white as culled children… I made a lot of money for ol' miss. But she was good to me. She give me lots of good clothes… An' I didn't have to work in de fields. In between times I cooked an' I would jump in de loom. Yes, ma'am, I could weave good."

Mary Williams. "Most generally the white folks was good to their darkies. My young master used to sneak out his Blue Back Speller and learned my father how to read, and after the war he taught school. He started me off and then a teacher from the North come down and taught us."

Jack Walker. "I never been to school but half a day. I went to work when I was eight years old, and been workin' ever since… The most work I done here in Arkansas is carpenter work. I'm the first colored man ever contracted in Pine Bluff."

Dock Wilborn. "During the period of slavery the more apt and intelligent among those of the younger Negroes were singled out and given special training for those places in which their talents indicated they would be most useful in the life of the plantation. Girls were trained in housework, cooking, and in the care of children while boys were taught blacksmithing, carpentrying, and some were trained for personal servants around the home. Some were even taught to read and to write when it was thought that their later positions would require this learning."

CHURCH ATTENDANCE

Martha Colquitt. "Us didn't have no separate church for colored folkses. De white folkses had a big Baptist chuch dey called Mill Stone Church down at Goosepond, a good ways down de road from Marse Billie's plantation. It sure was a pretty sight to see, dat church, all painted white and set in a big oak grove.

Colored folkses had dey place in de gallery. Dey weren't allowed to join the church on Sunday, but dey had regular Saturday afternoons for de slaves to come and confess dey faith, and join de church… All de baptizin' was done on Sunday by the white preacher."

Andrew Goodman. "[Marse Bob] built us a church, and a old man, Kenneth Lyons, who was a slave of the Lyons family nearby, used to get a pass every Sunday mornin' and come preach to us. He was a man of good learnin' and the best preacher I ever heard. He baptized in a little old mudhole down back of our place. Nearly all the boys and gals get converted when they's about twelve or fifteen year old. Then on Sunday afternoon, Marse Bob learned us to read and write. He told us we oughta get all the learnin' we could."

Marriah Hines. "When we would and see how the slaves on the joining farm was farming, 'twould almost make us shed tears. It made us feel like we was getting along most fine. Dat's why we loved and respected Master, 'cause he was so good to us. 'Cause Master was good and kind to us, some of the other white folks used to call him "nigger lover." He didn't pay dat no mind, though. He was as true Christian man, and I mean he sure lived up to it. He never did force any of us to go to church if we didn't want to. That was left to us to decide. If you wanted to you could; if you didn't you didn't have to. But he'd always tell us, you ought to go."

Nathan Best. "I b'long to de Methodis' church, I jined in 1866. We went to our marster's church in slavery time. He was a Methodis' an all his cullud folkses was Methodis', all dem dat b'longed to church. I takes de bus an' goes to church in Biloxi mos' ebery Sunday, I don' go ebery Sunday."

Mary Anderson. "We were allowed to have prayer meetings in our homes and we also went to the white folks' church. But they would not teach any of us to read or write."

Gabe Emanuel. "De mistis used to teach us de Bible on Sund'ys an' us always had Sund'y school. Us what lived in de Big House an' even some o' de fiel' han's was taught to read an' write by de white folks… One day I was out in de quarters when he brung back Oldman Joe from runnin' away… Dis time I's speakin' 'bout Marster Duncan [the overseer] put his han' on old Joe's shoulder an' look him in de eye sorrowful-lak. 'Joe,' hesay, 'I's sho' pow'ful tired o' huntin' you. I 'spect I's gwina have to git de marster to sell you some'r's else.' … After dat old Joe stayed close in an' dey warnt no more trouble out o' him."

EX-SLAVES CRITICAL OF BLACKS

Mary Williams. "The biggest part of these niggers puts their mistakes on the white folks. It's easier to do right than wrong cause right whips wrong every time into a frazzle."

James Lucas. "Slaves didn't know what to 'spec from freedom, but a lot of 'em hoped dey would be fed an' kep' by de gov'ment. Dey all had diffe'nt ways o' thinkin' 'bout it. Mos'ly though dey was jus' lak me; dey didn't know jus' zckly what it meant… Folks dat ain' never been free don' rightly know de fel of bein' free. Dey don' know da meanin' of it. Slaves like us, what was owned by quali-ty-folks, was sati'fied an' didn' sing none of dem freedom songs."

Charlie Cameron. "De young Niggers is heeded straight for hell. All dey think 'bout is drinkin' hard likker, goin' to dance halls, an' a-riden' in a old rattle trap car. It beats all how dey brags an' wastes things. Dey aint one whit happier den folks was in my day… Looks lak all mos' o' de young'n's is studyin' 'bout is how to git out o' hones' labor."

Dora Franks. "Lawd, Miss, dese here young folks today is gwine straight to de Devil. Al dey do all day an' all night is run 'round an' drink corn likker an' ride in automobiles. I'se got a grand-daughter here, an' she's dat wil'. I worries a right smart 'bout her, but it don't do no good, 'cause her mommy let her do jus' like she please anyhow."

Jack Walker. "Oh, don't talk about the younger generation. I just can't accom-plish 'em, I sure can't. They ain't got the 'regenious' and get-up about 'em they had in my time. They is more wiser, that's about all. The young race these days I don't know what's gwine come of 'em. If it wasn't for we old fogies, don't know what they'd do."

CONCLUSION

The "racist" narrative that has possessed our politically correct society today is exposed as a strategy to deflect attention from our real constitutional crisis and to divide and conquer us. Instead of being continuously on the brink of starvation, the slaves had good food in abundance. They had comfortable living quarters and were well cared for. Rather than being in danger of attacks and enslavement by neighboring tribes that continuously preyed on one another, their lives had stability. Christian morality was imposed.

Some were whipped by overseers—hardly ever by the slave owners themselves—but they didn't have spear wounds, were not mutilated, nor were they a cannibal's lunch. No women were beaten to death by their mates or buried alive. They had the best medical attention for the time, not witch doctors. I would prefer to be tracked by hounds than by a leopard or a lion. The vast majority loved their masters and were loved in return. Comparing their Sitz im Leben in Africa with that in the Southern United States, we might quip and say that they "went from hell to heaven" when brought to America. The black folks' troubles began *after* the Civil War.

CHAPTER 4

WHO WAS THOMAS JEFFERSON?

WAS JEFFERSON A RACIST?

Taking into account the Sitz im Leben in Thomas Jefferson's day provides another object lesson and has political implications. Everywhere, particularly on the campuses of many universities, "racist" seems to enter into every discussion. Thomas Jefferson, our preeminent founding father, is attacked as a "racist," so efforts are underway to tear down or deface statues of this key figure in the history of our constitutional republic.

One of the three accomplishments about which Jefferson most wished to be remembered was founding the University of Virginia, striving to reinvent higher education in America, where "professors and students alike could exercise their ingenuity, develop the tools of self-governance, and push the boundaries of knowledge in service of the common good." Today it is Virginia's premier university.[33] This is what it has come to:

> Earlier this week around 100 "students, faculty and community members" gathered at the University of Virginia and [covered] a statue of Thomas Jefferson in a black shroud…adorning it with signs that dubbed the former president a "racist" and "rapist." The protesters derided the statue as "an emblem of white supremacy," and demanded that it be "re-contextualized," lambasting the people who "fetishize the legacy of Jefferson," calling on the community to "recognize Jefferson as a rapist, racist, and slave owner."[34]

It is simply clueless to pluck Jefferson from the eighteenth and early nineteenth centuries—in his Sitz im Leben—and deposit him in the twenty-first century instead. That ignorance (and deceit by their Marxist professors) threatens our republic. Let's look at who he was in his day.

JEFFERSON'S EDUCATION

Thomas Jefferson[35] was arguably one of the most gifted, astute humans ever to walk the earth. His father, Peter Jefferson, himself well versed in Latin and Greek, placed him at the English school at five years of age and at the Latin school at nine, where he initially began learning French, as well as the rudiments of Latin and Greek. (Greek is especially challenging since it is complex and has its own alphabetic symbols: alpha, beta, gamma, delta, epsilon, zeta, eta, theta, … omega.)

Proficient, he then went to college for two years, where Dr. Small made him his daily companion. He went on to "read law" for five years and then practiced law and was also an architect. Fluent in five languages, he even mastered the Teutonic Anglo-Saxon language on the belief that English democracy and legal protections, dating from before the Magna Carta in 1215, had their origins in the Anglo-Saxons. He strove to reclaim the Anglo-Saxon birthright.[36]

JEFFERSON MADE SLAVERY A PROBLEM

Thomas Jefferson was more influential in abolishing slavery than was Abraham Lincoln, who stood on his shoulders. Jefferson, for the first time, actually made slavery a problem. As noted, he was chosen by the other founding fathers to be the draftsman of the Declaration of Independence: "We hold these truths to be self-evident, *that all men are created equal*, that they are endowed by their Creator with certain unalienable Rights, that among these are Life, Liberty, and the pursuit of Happiness" (emphasis mine).

President Lincoln said, in his Gettysburg Address, "Four score and seven years ago our fathers brought forth on this continent a new nation, conceived in Liberty, and dedicated to the proposition that all men are created equal."

I want to digress a bit. Even Lincoln's concern about slavery is challenged by G. Edward Griffin,[37] who asserts that it was only economic conflict pressured by northern monetary interests and not slavery that launched the Civil War. No doubt these elements were in play, but while Lincoln would have tolerated slavery in the south, neither he nor the Republican Party could allow extending slavery to the western territories. This is borne out in the 1860 Republican platform:

7. That the new dogma that the Constitution of its own force carries slavery into any or all of the territories of the United States, is a dangerous political heresy, at variance with the explicit provisions of that instrument itself, with cotemporaneous exposition, and with legislative and judicial precedent, is revolutionary in its tendency and subversive of the peace and harmony of the country.

8. That the normal condition of all the territory of the United States is that of freedom; that as our republican fathers, when they had abolished slavery in all our national territory, ordained that no 'person should be deprived of life, liberty or property, without due process of law,' it becomes our duty, by legislation, whenever such legislation is necessary, to maintain this provision of the constitution against all attempts to violate it; and we deny the authority of congress, of a territorial legislature, or of any individuals, to give legal existence to slavery in any territory of the United States.[38]

Even so, it was Thomas Jefferson and all the founding fathers that sealed the fate of slavery in America, not Abraham Lincoln. In fact, it was the Civil War that enflamed animosity between the races.

JEFFERSON'S CONCERN FOR SLAVES

Jefferson eventually owned over six hundred African-American slaves, and by 1776, he was one of the largest "planters" in Virginia. Nonetheless, he spoke out against the international slave trade and criminalized it as president, signing the bill in 1807. In fact, he had attacked the British for sponsoring human trafficking as a grievance justifying the revolution, and in 1778, slave importation was banned in Virginia under his leadership. While James Madison was primarily responsible for writing the constitution, it was Thomas Jefferson who convinced him to add the Bill of—un*alien*able, immutable, universal—Rights. Jefferson was in Europe when this occurred, but he reported in his autobiography:

I wrote strongly to mr Madison urging the want of provision for the freedom of religion, freedom of the press, trial by jury, habeas corpus, the substitution of militia for a standing army, and an express reservation to the states of all rights not specifically granted to the union. he accordingly moved in the first session of Congress for these Amendments.[39]

In his *Farm Book* journal, he meticulously noted the quantity and quality of the clothing purchased for his slaves and considered it his duty to provide "those poor creatures" desirable blankets. There is no record that he ever physically abused a slave, although his overseers, when he was away, disobeyed his orders not to whip them and were sometimes cruel.

He kept the slave families together, so there was often more than one generation living on the plantation. He would buy and sell slaves to keep families together. He also paid the slaves in money and clothing for work in important positions, and several were known to be able to read and write. He recorded the productivity of the children and selected the most productive to be trained as artisans, blacksmiths, carpenters, and coopers. Some of his slaves held leadership roles, managing the house slaves and maintaining the property as master carpenter, blacksmith, painter, and gardener.

In 1779, as a practical solution to end the legal enslavement of humans, Jefferson supported gradual emancipation, training, and colonization of African American slaves rather than unconditional release from slavery, believing that releasing unprepared people with no place to go and no means to support themselves would only bring them misfortune. He did free two men since they had been trained and could find employment. His wisdom is confirmed by the stories of the slaves themselves.

In 1784, Jefferson proposed federal legislation banning slavery in the New Territories of the North and South after 1800, but it failed to pass Congress by one vote. Had this passed, we would *not* have had a Civil War since the spread of slavery into the western territories was Lincoln's impetus for the war as noted. With the mechanization of farming and our evolving Sitz im Leben, slavery in America would gradually have died a natural death.

Thus, the history of Jefferson, when placed in his Sitz im Leben, reveals, to the shame of his ignorant critics, that he, together with the other founding fathers, was not only an American hero giving us our Declaration of Independence and our Bill of Rights, but he was also a champion of freedom for all mankind. As noted, he kept his slaves since they would flounder if freed at that time, never abused them, was concerned to keep families intact, made sure they had what they needed, and trained those who were suited, so that they could be independent. To attempt to displace a deeply entrenched societal platform on a dime would have resulted in catastrophic harm, which is what happened with the Civil War. As I noted, he had more to do with freeing the slaves than did Abraham Lincoln.

We, therefore, leave the founding fathers, and particularly Thomas Jefferson, where they belong: in the eighteenth and early nineteenth centuries. We cannot rationally pluck him out, put him in the twenty-first century, and demand that he fit here. In his time, he was an example of Christian values, the right way to act. In his Sitz im Leben, he was the slaves' hero, not a villain.

WAS SLAVERY EVER THE PROBLEM?

I digress here because slavery is a national obsession. Once we learn the Sitz im Leben of the slaves themselves, we find that slavery was not the problem; ironically, the Civil War and emancipation advanced the race problem. Not only did the Civil War kill six hundred thousand Americans, it mortally wounded the republic. Adding all the civil rights legislation that eventually followed, the republic is now on life support.

While slavery is obviously incompatible with Christian civilization, it was not incompatible with Christians being Christians and caring for their slaves and bringing Christianity to them. It should be noted that slavery is still legal in ninety-four countries around the world.[40] America was a leader in outlawing slavery.

There are always exceptions, but I have learned through the years that, on the whole, a group of people can "make a broad jump" but cannot "be long-distance runners." That is, the next generation can make another "broad jump." Had black people been able to transition, with education and job training for several generations, they would have had a chance.

Remember that the former slaves had the same words in criticizing the generations that followed them as were used by the white folks. They were considered irresponsible, immoral, shiftless, and lazy. But they were not to blame. Most of them floundered, having been dumped from a culture that provided all their needs into a free enterprise economy they didn't even want and in which they were not emotionally prepared for. And they lacked the necessary skills with which to succeed.

The scourge of that war had demolished the social and economic order of a stable, century-old social platform. The resulting chaos affected blacks as much as the former slave owners. There was "Reconstruction" for fourteen more years. How could this social disruption—with the deaths of so many men, as well as the destruction of their property and their society itself—not be expected to evoke fear and rage in the white population? These blacks didn't fit in and were made-to-order scapegoats.

They had been accustomed to go to church together, and the children all played together. In many cases, the former slaves preferred to and were permitted to remain with their former masters throughout their lives. Now a wall literally came up between the races. There was segregation.

Actually, there was an exception to the rule. The small community in Southwest Michigan, Covert, was always integrated. Children attended school together, adults socialized and intermarried, and blacks held supervisory positions in the community from the 1860s on.[41] Regrettably, their example did not convert the nation.

The Supreme Court, in *Brown v. Board of Education*, 1954, unanimously re-wrote the Fourteenth Amendment of the Constitution. It acknowledged that the schools were equivalent in quality, and their decision against segregated schools was not based on jurisprudence or stare decisis reasoning ("let stand what was already determined"). It was based on the argument that separating the children in schools "generates a feeling of inferiority," with such arguments as black children preferred white dolls over black dolls. (The white daughter of a prior patient actually prefers her black doll over her white dolls. Is that because she feels inferior?)

Then came the civil rights movement, which Christopher Caldwell covers in his book, *The Age of Entitlement*. "The changes of the 1960s, with civil rights at their core, were not just a major new element in the Constitution. They were a rival constitution, with which the original one was frequently incompatible."[42] Civil rights gradually turned into a license for government to do what the Constitution would not previously have permitted."[43] "The new system ... became the model for overthrowing every tradition in American life."[44]

The well-worn saying "Never let a crisis go to waste" gave leftist politicians, for whom acquiring more federal power is always their goal, the opportunity to use the havoc ongoing since the Civil War to eviscerate the freedoms founded in the Constitution and foster efforts already established to bring communism to America.

We are equal in that our immutable human nature is shared by each of us. But we are not all destined for the Basketball Hall of Fame. We are individuals in almost infinite ways, as I explain in the appendix. We now have black billionaires in America.[45] We also have bloodshed in the streets. Fueled basically by drug wars, blacks are killing blacks out of proportion. Perpetrators and victims virtually all have prior criminal records. We still have a long way to go, but black unemployment was finally at an all-time low before the Wuhan virus epidemic. We must celebrate progress (always encouraging) rather than set unrealistic benchmarks (always discouraging).

If any "reparations" might be due, the reason should not be slavery. Are they now due American citizens four or more generations removed from the slaves themselves? Is it not demeaning that people need compensation because they are black? Perhaps those of mixed blood could be awarded three-fifths. Sorry for being sarcastic.

Nonetheless, reparations are in the works in politically correct America. For example, Evanston, Illinois, announced, in December 2019, plans to provide taxpayer-sponsored financial reparations for slavery, taxing marijuana sales at 3 percent to create a reparations fund for all its black residents. Private donations (I suspect, from self-confessed "racists") are expected to add to the pot.[46]

Addressing racism and reparations defeats black people because it characterizes them as victims. Victims are, by definition, powerless. Psychology teaches us to take responsibility for our lives. Only by feeling responsible do we acquire the power to fix our lives and actively pursue our happiness. Dr. Phil wrote an excellent book on this subject: *Life Strategies*, with the slogan "Your attitude determines your altitude."[47]

Bob Woodson[48] is in total agreement and has done something about it. Founded in 1981, his Woodson Center works in the inner cities to empower blacks to take responsibility for their lives and uses their success stories to inspire others. He laments that "blacks kill more blacks in a year than were lynched in fifty years." He states that blacks led moral lives, and 85 percent of children were born in married homes until the civil rights movement split money from income and made blacks a financial commodity. He states that the people's "door is locked from the inside, not the outside." He is an exemplary activist.

CHAPTER 5

WHAT ABOUT ORGANIZED RELIGION?

IF IT AIN'T BROKE, DON'T FIX IT

Although it should make sense now that every segment in history must be set in its Sitz im Leben, the breakthrough of Rudolf Bultmann is an emotional challenge for many readers. Now we have another hurdle for many of us. After this, we're home free. From my history, you know that I was traumatized by my exposure to the business of organized religion. Here, I address organized religion in detail, but please don't misunderstand me. We surely want to celebrate the many Protestant ministers and Catholic priests and their solid Christian communities who love their neighbors, are sincere, and are admirable citizens. As a priest, I was among that group.

How do we tell? Simply "by their fruits will you know them." Christians are responsible for themselves as individuals, as many scriptural quotations attest. Any teaching that infers that we are essentially inadequate, powerless, and dependent is false—erroneous psychology and erroneous theology. Demanding "politically correct" behavior, whether the enforcer be organized religion or government intrusion, conflicts with "the freedom of the Children of God."

I am free to do whatever I choose if I don't infringe on or jeopardize that same right for others. For example, I'm not free to drive drunk because it puts others in jeopardy. Prohibition from eating meat on Friday is an example of enslavement—poisonous fruit. An example of the subversion of the Christian kerygma—the poisonous fruit—is seen in "Christian" Ireland, where the Catholic religion and the Protestant religion have been at a bloodletting war with each other for a century. "Hate your neighbor" is not scriptural. Christianity encourages everyone to aspire to the Christian values we noted: to live the right way, according to everyone's conscience.

So if you attend church in a congregation of an organized religion and are blessed to have a minister or priest who is attuned to the true kerygma of scripture and is a guide for you in discerning the right way to live, be thankful and stick with it. "There are many rooms in my father's house" (John 14:2).

As we shall see, those appear to be the exceptions. We know that our Christian civilization is in trouble. Our slippery slope bottoms into a pagan, barbarian society. The churches are empty. Statistics warns us that we are losing the fight to salvage this Christian message. Christians are becoming extinct.

WHAT ARE WE UP AGAINST?

If we study the history of animals that have become extinct, we realize that they were incapable of adapting in time to keep up with their evolving Sitz im Leben. Their ribbon of life frayed and eventually broke. This is what we see happening. As I noted in the introduction, 85 percent of the older generation identify as Christian, while 40 percent of millennials virtually never go to church and 10 percent identify with non-Christian religions. Polls show that more than half of the millennials consider themselves socialists. Again, the churches are emptied.

As we are marginalized more and more, our influence to sustain civilization within our society dissipates. We need to bring together every sincere person seeking the truth about the right way to live in our common society, including the significant number of atheists, in name or in practice. We are losing our grip on civilized society. Our status quo isn't maintaining it.

Which brings me to the issue of organized religion. We must learn to distinguish and affirm the immutable Christian truths by liberating them both from an archaic Sitz im Leben and also from the business of organized religion. Too often, organized religion becomes bait and switch. The parishioners end up controlled with doctrines that are not correlated with the Christian kerygma and which actually undercut authentic Christianity.

WHAT'S THE OBJECTION?

This is a story that was told to me a long time ago by a good friend who was a Protestant minister. I don't recall which denomination.

Some folks, living on the coastline in a dangerous spot where there were frequent shipwrecks, resolved to do what they could to rescue those whose lives were periodically in jeopardy. They pooled their money, rented an old warehouse, and purchased several appropriate boats. They were on notice to respond and actually did save lives. They got a lot of publicity for their service, as well as considerable contributions.

So they spent some money carpeting and decorating their warehouse and buying comfortable furniture. It became a pleasant meeting spot. But that presented a problem. The ship-wreaked souls, wet and dirty, were ruining the carpet and furniture. A decision had to be made. They could no longer accommodate the survivors there.

Some from the group were still concerned. They pooled their money, rented an adjacent warehouse, and purchased the boats of the original organization. They got back to rescuing the survivors of shipwrecks. Soon they also were recognized, and contributions poured in. So they spent some money carpeting and decorating their warehouse, buying comfortable furniture. They enjoyed gathering there. But that presented a problem. The ship-wreaked souls, wet and dirty, were ruining the carpet and furniture. So, a decision had to be made. They could no longer accommodate the survivors there.

This is the irony. The wealthy and powerful marketers of religion may well be our greatest stumbling block to any credibility in our struggle to salvage true Christian values. We know the saying "All power corrupts, and absolute power corrupts absolutely."

Living in Europe, I determined to visit the shrine of Our Lady of Fatima in Portugal. Even sixty years ago, this was big business that marketed everything imaginable. I can only guess how that has expanded. I may still have a tiny bottle or two of the miraculous water that cures any disease. I have not visited Bethlehem, but you can see from the news that they have outdone Fatima in spades.

In absolute contrast were the peasant pilgrims who, barefoot, walked for over a week or two to get to the shrine. I marveled that the soles of their feet were as thick as those of my shoes. They slept in a blanket around the shrine. These *anawim*,[49] the poor of Yahweh, given to loving devotion and surrender to God, were the true Christians, not the money changers. "The meek [i.e., *anawim*] shall inherit the earth" (Psalm 37:11). They "delighted in the Lord because they were rooted in him."[50]

ABERRANT LEADERS OF ORGANIZED RELIGION[51]

Tony Alamo. Headed a Santa Clarita commune. Convicted of tax evasion in 1994 and then resided in a halfway house in Texarkana. In 2009, he was convicted of ten federal counts of taking minors across state lines for sex and was sentenced to 150 years in federal prison.

Matthew F. Hale. Former leader of Creativity Movement sentenced to a forty-year prison term for soliciting an undercover FBI informant to kill a federal judge.

Warren Jeffs. Once president of Fundamentalist Church of Jesus Christ of Latter-Day Saints (a polygamist Mormon sect), convicted of rape as an accomplice (overturned in 2010). Jeffs was convicted in a Texas state court of child sex charges and sentenced to life plus twenty years. He is incarcerated at the Powledge state prison. He also awaits trial in other states and in the federal court system.

Jeffrey Lundgren. Headed splinter group from Reorganized Church of Jesus Christ of Latter-Day Saints. Executed October 24, 2006, for multiple murders.

Ervil LeBaron. Led a small sect of polygamous Mormon fundamentalists and was convicted of involvement in the murder of two people and plotting to kill another person in 1981.

Roch Theriault. Former head of the Ant Hill Kids commune. Served a life sentence in Canada for the murder of Solange Boislard.

Yahweh Ben Yahweh. Head of Nation of Yahweh, convicted for federal racketeering charges and conspiracy involving fourteen murders.

Joseph Smith Jr. The founder of the Latter-Day Saint movement. Was subjected to approximately thirty criminal actions during his life. Another source reports Smith was arrested at least forty-two times. Smith was killed by a mob while in jail awaiting trial on charges of treason against Illinois.

Jim Bakker. Created the PTL organization. Convicted of fraud and conspiracy charges after illegally soliciting millions of dollars from his followers.

Kent Hovind, aka Dr. Dino. Convicted of fraud in collecting, accounting for, and paying federal income taxes; knowingly structuring transactions in federally insured financial institutions to evade the reporting requirements; and obstructing and impeding the administration of the internal revenue laws.

L. Ron Hubbard. Founder of Scientology. He was convicted of illegal business practices, namely, making false claims about his ability to cure physical illnesses in France. He was sentenced to four years in prison, which was never served.

Henry Lyons. Former president of National Baptist Convention, USA, Inc. Convicted for racketeering and grand theft.

These self-serving ministers are merely the small-time players, not adept at getting away with it. The major organizations are "six feet tall and bulletproof," protected and too big to fail. Additionally, many have been captured by communist liberation theology.

ARE CHURCHES COMMUNIST?

Communists began infiltrating social institutions, all religious denominations, and the government in America virtually from Karl Marx's lifetime. In 1919, the official communist party in America, Communist Party USA(CPUSA), was established.

The Harvard-educated Methodist, Dr. Harry F. Ward, became an ethics professor at New York's Union Theological Seminary in 1918 and remained there until 1941.[52] He was a card-carrying Communist. In 1906, Ward had founded the Methodist Federation for Social Service in order to transform the Methodist Church and Christianity into an instrument for the achievement of socialism. He founded the Federal Council of Churches in 1908 (currently the National Council of Churches). He was selected to head the American League Against War and Fascism created by the Communist Party to resist law enforcement, conduct soviet espionage, and infiltrate churches, seminaries, and youth organizations.

A member of the federation, Jack McMichael, was head of the communist front organization, the American Youth Congress. By 1950, it included half of the church's sixteen bishops. One of Ward's students, Bishop Bromley Oxnam, became bishop of Washington, DC. They are now active in more than thirty-eight chapters. Dr. Paul Kengor uncovered a four-page letter, dated December 1920, which identified various religious college professors, in addition to Ward, who were targeted by the Soviet Comintern and American Communist Party, enabling the party to get its materials on the shelves of seminary and college libraries.[53]

The CPUSA instructed thousands of their members to operate as cells within the churches to take control for communist purposes. "Their efforts had enormous impact upon the 'mainline denominations' such as the Methodists, Presbyterians, Lutherans, and Episcopoalians."[54]

Additionally, the Protestant Justice Action organization adds to these the Baptists, United Church of Christ, and Disciples of Christ. Besides infiltrating the Democratic Party since the 1960s, The CPUSA has emphasized recruiting black pastors.[55]

Of course, the most conspicuous of all and the one I have been following for sixty years is the Roman Catholic Church. A truly terrifying book was written by Douglas Valentine, *The CIA as Organized Crime*[56] —guaranteed to turn your stomach and keep you up at night, and he exposes, as well, its collusion with the Vatican. Since the excesses of the Vatican have alienated so many people of good-will for so long and my goal is to unite us, I need to expose the Vatican.

WHAT ABOUT THE CATHOLIC POPES?

A Google search will expose the worst of the popes, and of course, not all popes were equally debauched. One list called Pius XII the worst pope in history. I was actually in Rome when he died, and therefore, I am privy to his history. Many accusations were afloat that he had supported Hitler, but others argued that he actually had protected the Jews. Actually, he was one of the more "Christian" popes. As the secretary of state under Pius XI, he condemned the National Socialist Party of Hitler and already prohibited Catholics from membership in the party. He incurred the wrath of Hitler for his pro-Jewish policies. He helped save some Jews.

My point is that some of these biographies may result from people having their own agenda, but even given what we know, the Catholic Church has a disgraced legacy. It is the institution itself that is corrupt. All power corrupts. As I said, I focus on the most extreme examples because they attest to a systemic fault. These are some of the most corrupt popes through the ages:

Damasus I (366–84). Bought and sold women and children as slaves for income. When he seized lands, he burned the people alive. Forty-four bishops condemned him for his adultery, so he ordered the murder of them all.

Stephanus VII (896–7). Exhumed his predecessor to try him for his crimes post-humously. He ordered his fingers cut off and threw the corpse in the Tiber. The people stripped him of his vestments, imprisoned, and then strangled him.

Sergius III (904–11). Killed Pope Leo V and Pope Christopher in order to become pope. He was the father of the illegitimate Pope John IX. His era was known as the pornocracy era.

Joannus XII (955–64). Installed at age eighteen, he developed a reputation for raping his two sisters and papal visitors, including the men, in the papal palace. He had massive orgies. He castrated and then murdered a cardinal. He blinded and murdered his confessor. His son became Pope John XIII. An outraged husband found him in bed with his wife and killed him; the same fate of his son.

Benedictus IX (1032–48). Elected through his father's bribery and was accused of many adulteries and murders. He was deposed but regained the papacy, only to be thrown out. He returned with an army to successfully regain the papacy but then sold it to his godfather for a fortune. With his army, he tried again, but this time, he failed.

Alexander VI (1492–1503). One of the Borgias, bought the papacy and celebrated by hosting the most elaborate orgies ever seen in the Vatican, with fifty prostitutes crammed into a hall for him and his clergy. He married and sired countless children within and outside of marriage. He ignored all the laws and traditions of the church. He used his daughter, Lucrezia, as bait for wealthy merchants. Finally, an assassin poisoned him.

Paul III (1534–49). Killed his own mother and niece to inherit the family fortune. Once he became pope, he executed anyone who annoyed him by strangulation. Following a theological dispute between two cardinals and a Polish bishop, he had them hacked to death with swords. He managed 45,000 prostitutes in Rome for a proportion of their revenues.

Pope Julius III (1550–5). Had picked up a teenage boy off the street and adopted him as his "nephew," thus making him a cardinal while still an adolescent. He had Michelangelo decorate his home with sculptures of young boys having sex with each other.

WHAT ABOUT THE VATICAN TODAY?

Those popes lived many years ago. Many popes were surely not so debauched, but these stories are but the worst of a sordid tradition.

To clarify the current state of the Vatican, under Pope Francis, we study his predecessor, Pope Benedict XVI, aka Joseph Ratzinger, a theologian from Bavaria. It is quite clear that Ratzinger was forced to resign in order to replace him with Pope Francis, the elected icon of the contemporary Catholic Church.

Ratzinger held a position about scripture that hints at the thesis of this book. Ratzinger held that the static Bible-based concept of divine revelation was nonexistent in the thirteenth century.[57] He held that God reveals and revealed himself in history *and throughout history* and not just once to the authors of the Bible.

> He taught that the Bible is not a natural science textbook, but rather it is the essential testimonial of God's revelation; one cannot get from it a scientific explanation of how the world arose. One can only glean religious experience from it. Thus, scripture would not wish to inform us about how the different species of plant life gradually appeared or how the sun and the moon and the stars were established. Its purpose ultimately would be to say one thing: God created the world. [58]

According to this conservative theologian, church doctrine must be preserved and not accede to modern pressures to change teachings on ordination of women to the priesthood, divorce, birth control, abortion, and homosexuality. While he viewed homosexual inclinations as "an objective disorder," he also denounced "violent malice in speech or in action" against homosexuals. He objected to homosexual couples adopting children. He attacked rock 'n' roll as "the expression of elemental passions." He was staunchly opposed to "moral relativism," even more conservative than his predecessor. Here is a quote:

> Precisely in those places where the Marxist liberating ideology had been applied consistently, a radical lack of freedom had been produced, the horror of which now appeared out in the open before the eyes of world public opinion. The fact is that when politics are used to bring redemption, they promise too much. When they presume to do God's work, they become not divine but diabolical.[59]

The point is that Pope Francis, who was selected to replace him and characterize the Catholic Church, is the antithesis of Pope Benedict. He embodies the current stance of the Roman Catholic Church, not Benedict. Among many other critics, George Neumayr wrote a book, *The Political Pope: How Francis Is Delighting the Liberal Left and Abandoning Conservative Catholics*.[60] He explores the pope's embrace of Marxism. Francis is quoted to have "met many Marxists in [his] life who are good people." Neumayr states, "He rolled out the red carpet for Raul Castro, which flabbergasted Cubans who have suffered under the heel of his communist thuggery." He quotes Fidel Castro: "I may convert again to Catholicism, even though I am a communist."

"Pope Francis has turned the Vatican into a bully pulpit for the left's favorite causes, including: open borders, gun control, climate-change activism, the abolition of the death penalty and lifetime imprisonment, universal distribution of wealth, and the socialism of central planners."

Pope Francis's mentor, Cardinal Oscar Rodriguez Maradiaga, has collaborated with George Soros to promote socialism in the church. Soros is a wealthy anarchist, notorious for funding Antifa and many other terrorist organizations that attack America. Pope Francis called Esther Ballestrino a "fervent communist," stating, "I owe so much to that great woman… She taught me so much about politics." She provided him with Marxist literature.

He restored communist liberation theology that had been called "diabolical" by Pope Benedict. There is a lot of confirmation of his promotion of communism in Neumayr's book, and Francis reveals it by what he says. Communism is the antithesis of Christianity: communalism versus individualism—individuals taking responsibility to live life the right way, in accord with our nature.

WHAT ABOUT HOMOSEXUALITY?

As early as 2018, there were calls for Pope Francis to "resign."[61] Archbishop Carlo Maria Vigano wrote a detailed 7,000-word letter to the pope, accusing him of covering up the rampant sexual abuse in the official church around the world. Vigano described "dismay and sadness over the enormity of what is happening." A columnist for *The National Catholic Reporter* said, "We are a step away from schism."[62]

For example, Cardinal Theodore McCarrick recently resigned and was laicized, having been found guilty of sexual abuse against both adult seminarians and minors since, at least, 1993.[63] He raised over $6,000,000 over seventeen years for the Vatican and others in the church hierarchy—donations meant to help the poor.[64] His crimes had been known by the Vatican for the past twenty years.

Bishop Robert Morlino said, "It is time to admit that there is a homosexual subculture within the hierarchy of the Catholic Church."[65] A Pennsylvania grand jury detailed decades of sexual misconduct by priests and the failure of their bishops to deal with the problem.[66]

For quite a few years, as a psychologist, I was the consultant to a bishop and got a broad look at the behavior of priests. I assume nothing has improved. While not a scientific research study by any means—simply by my estimate—80 percent of American priests are homosexuals. There are acknowledged associations of homosexuals within religious orders. Celibacy is a magnet for homosexual men since it provides them with ample opportunity for sexual connections and a cover for why they did not date women or want to marry.

WHAT ABOUT THE VATICAN BANK?

The Vatican Bank, aka IOR, *Institute per le Opere di Religione*, founded in 1942, is called "the most secret bank in the world." It is an entity unto itself but under the pope's jurisdiction. Records are systematically destroyed, and it cannot be forced to release the source of any deposit. Thus, untold millions can be deposited into the IOR on a continuous basis and channeled into Swiss bank accounts with no chance of detection. Thus it has become the world's money launderer, serving the narcotics trade of the American CIA and the Sicilian Mafia, among others.[67]

"In the months before the 1948 [Italian] national election, the CIA had already dumped $65 million of its black money into the Vatican Bank."[68] This black money was in cash, delivered in large suitcases by the Sicilian Mafia and affiliated clerics. The money came from the heroin trade, smuggled under various façades. Charles "Lucky" Luciano was caught with a half ton of heroin to be shipped to Havana, heroin supplied for African American ghettos.

One Vatican collusion was code-named Operation Gladio,[69] set up by the CIA and NATO to thwart communist influence in Europe. It set up various false flag operations. As an example, a bombing at the Bologna train station, on August 2, 1980,[70] killed eighty-five people and wounded two hundred. It was blamed on the Red Brigades but eventually exposed. Such false flags are a page from Hitler's playbook. The goal was to convince the populace to rely on the state for more security. Such cooperation with the CIA and the Mafia grew stronger in the next thirty years. The Vatican got in the act under Msgr. Don Giuseppe Bicchierai, agent of the pope, who assembled a terror gang to create these false flags to beat up Communist candidates and intimidate voters. Money, guns, and jeeps were supplied to him by the CIA.[71]

Rigging the elections, the Christian Democrats returned to power. It was estimated by William Colby, later head of the CIA—eventually murdered[72]—that the communists would have gotten 60 percent of the vote otherwise. Fearing a new communist takeover, the CIA supported the Christian Democrats by expanding the drug trade. Using Catholic priests, they funneled billions more into various Catholic banks, safe from scrutiny because the Vatican is a sovereign state.[73] There is no reason to question that the money-laundering service is still being provided by the Vatican.

CHAPTER 6

WHAT ABOUT ATHEISM?

INTRODUCING CHRISTOPHER HITCHENS

I reach out in this chapter to all well-meaning atheists and agnostics and to anyone else who has turned away from organized religion. I believe that you are likely to identify with Christopher Hitchens, a poster-child atheist, and discover that we actually are all truth seekers. If thinkers are at odds, we must find out what we're missing. Truth is always the same. Two plus two always equals four. The stumbling block must be misunderstanding. If we can resolve that, we can rally behind our common goal to salvage our civilization.

Christopher Hitchens (1949–2011)[74] authored and coauthored thirty books and many articles. He was a man of varied experiences and spoke the Romance languages, as well as English. He apparently even knew Latin, Greek, and Hebrew. In his book, titled *God is not Great: How Religion Poisons Everything,*[75] he provides a lot of information about the reasons sincere atheists think as they do, and I touch on that here. While I have not been able to speak to him directly—he is deceased—I have "attended" some of his debates and lectures via the internet. I am impressed with Hitchens's intelligence, his openness, his multilayered experience, and his ability to spell out clearly what he thinks.

Former prime minister Tony Blair, who had debated him in Toronto in 2010,[76] characterized him, following his death: "Christopher Hitchens was a complete one-off… He was fearless in the pursuit of truth and any cause in which he believed. And there was no belief he held that he did not advocate with passion, commitment, and brilliance." David Horowitz was a good friend of Hitchens and said, "If ever a man appreciated blunt candor, whether on the dishing out or the receiving end, it was my friend, Christopher."[77] He seems like the kind of person anyone would value as a friend.

I believe that Hitchens, in fact, was not an "antitheist"—his label—at all. He practiced Christian virtue while affirming his theoretical atheism. He championed various social causes. He noted that once, shivering in fear as a correspondent in a war zone, he took off his flak jacket and gave it to a woman who was even more terrified. What better example could we find of "love your neighbor"?

I review examples of his objections to the "religion that poisons everything." He was "anti" the phony hypocrisy of the organized religion business, and he didn't realize Bultmann's idea of liberating the Christian message from that scriptural Sitz im Leben. His criticisms, as they stand, are valid.

WHAT ABOUT SITZ IM LEBEN?

Hitchens confronts the "spirit and wonder world" of the New Testament, as Bultmann describes it, but didn't make the leap to simply mark that Sitz im Leben and preserve the unchanging kerygma, the Christian truths about the right way to live. He says,

> We distrust anything that contradicts science or outrages reason. We ought to be glad that none of the religious myths has any truth to it, or in it. The Bible may, indeed does, contain a warrant for trafficking in humans, for ethnic cleansing, for slavery, for pride-price, and for indiscriminate massacre, but we are not bound by any of it because it was put together by crude, uncultured human mammals."[78]

> These mighty scholars [Augustine, Aquinas, Maimonides, and Newman]... [have been] laughably ignorant of the germ theory of disease or the place of the terrestrial globe in the solar system, let alone the universe... Religion spoke its last intelligible or noble or inspiring words a long time ago.[79]

> God did not create man in his own image. Evidently, it was the other way about.

If we implant that ancient Sitz im Leben into modern times and imagine that we literally are created in God's image, we anthropomorphize—*anthropos* (man) and *morphe* (image)—God in the image of man. If man is literally the mirror image of

God, the old man in the white beard that shows in the mirror, guarding the pearly gates, is not a stretch. I don't buy that either, and I discuss this below, analyzing the Sitz im Leben of scripture and the idea of God.

However, this is not to claim that man created the natural laws. We have a nature and are born naturally. The laws of nature and of nature's God create man's essence and, therefore, define the right way for man to live, aligned with the laws of nature and exemplified in Christian civilization.

Here is an example of a belief that defies science and is clarified by orienting Sitz im Leben. He addresses the virgin birth of Jesus by reminding us that this was a way of speech in the Sitz im Leben when the scriptures were written. He provides examples: the Greeks had Danae; Buddha came unnaturally; the Aztec god Huitzilopochtli as well; Atis was another one; so were Krishna, Mercury, and Romulus; and even Genghis Khan.[80] Yes, virgin birth was a typical "myth"—in the meaning of that word discussed above—announcing, in that Sitz im Leben, the birth of an extraordinary human being. He pegged that Sitz im Leben.

Hitchens asks reasonable questions. "If Jesus could heal a blind person he happened to meet, then why not heal blindness?… Why did I have to keep saying, in public, that I was a miserable sinner? Why was the subject of sex considered so toxic?" Appreciating Sitz im Leben and then separating Christian civilization from the fabrications of organized religion would clarify all such misunderstanding.

WHAT ABOUT ORGANIZED RELIGION?

As is true of many atheists, Hitchens cannot simply set religion aside. Religion wouldn't go away, and he had to address it. The intellectual struggle with religion challenged him to write a very thoughtful book about religion. One might quip and say, "He doth protest *too much*." As I said, he was "religious"; that is, he practiced Christian virtue. Again, the catch is that he did not rescue the Christian "Good News" from *organized* religion.

Occasionally he specifies organized religion:

Violent, irrational, intolerant, allied to racism and tribalism and big-otry, invested in ignorance and hostile to free inquiry, contemptuous of women and coercive toward children: organized religion ought to have a great deal on its conscience.[81]

He has carefully analyzed this disconnect of organized religion from Christian civilization. He has "taken the words out of my mouth."

We are entitled to at least three provisional conclusions. The first is that religion and the churches are manufactured, and that this salient fact is too obvious to ignore. The second is that ethics and morality are quite independent of faith, and cannot be derived from it. The third is that religion is—because it claims a special divine exemption for its practices and beliefs—not just amoral but immoral... Those who claim a heavenly warrant for the cruelty have been tainted by evil, and also constitute far more of a danger.[82]

There are multiple issues here. Yes, *organized* religion is a manufactured and generally corrupt business. The scriptural word *church* (i.e., *ekklesia tou theou*) means the gatherings of the people of God, the Christian community—the antithesis of the Anglican Church or the Holy Roman Empire. And yes, there is no correlation between behaving in a Christian manner and avoiding sin by not eating meat on Friday or missing Sunday Mass, let alone many other enslaving religious taboos. I am thinking about the universal mutilations inflicted on the African natives for violating those innumerable laws.

Again, he confuses organized religion with Christian civilization when he states:

[Believers claim] not just to know, but to know everything. Not just to know that god exists, and that he created and supervised the whole enterprise, but also to know what 'he' demands of us—from our diet to our observances to our sexual morality... One faction...has the sheer arrogance to tell us that we already have all the essential information we need.[83]

As Catholics, we were told that Protestants could only get to heaven because of their invincible ignorance. To the contrary, true Christianity teaches that we are all, as individuals, under the judgment and are expected to love one another and to discern the right way to act responsibly. The arrogance he alleges actually characterizes both organized religion and communism, as we shall see, and not the message of scripture. Once again, we concur.

He continues, "This is the painless explanation for the profusion of gods and religions, and the fratricide both between and among faiths, that we see all about us and that has so retarded the development of civilization."[84]

Indeed, he has in mind organized religion, which, too often, has given Christianity a bad reputation. By crippling the faithful, teaching that we are inadequate and powerless to be responsible for ourselves, "the development of civilization" is impeded.

Instead, America thrived as an authentic Christian nation, at least until recently. As I have noted above, Cleon Skousen, in his book *The 5,000 Year Leap*, has aptly shown how Christian values and corresponding free enterprise have transformed American society in the past 250 years more than mankind had progressed in the prior 5,000 years, enriching the entire world. Civilization blossomed under Christianity. Indeed, America, as a Christian nation, has been more generous to support the needy than any other culture ever has been.[85]

Hitchens specifically criticizes organized religion by naming the Anglican Church, in which he was baptized.

> [The Anglican Church is] the descendant of a church that has always enjoyed a state subsidy and an intimate relationship with hereditary monarchy, it has a historic responsibility for the Crusades, for the persecution of Catholics, Jews, and Dissenters, and for combat against science and reason… It must see to interfere with the lives of nonbelievers, or heretics, or adherents of other faiths. It may speak about the bliss of the next world, but it wants power in this one.[86]

Hitchens also recognized problems that included, in addition to the Anglican archbishop of Canterbury, the Vatican, as well as Jews. That is, he noted that Salmon Rushdie wrote a novel, *The Satanic Verses*, and the Ayatollah Khomeini of Iran issued a fatwa and publicly offered money, in his own name, to murder him. One of his Italian or Japanese translators was "savagely mutilated as he lay dying." His Norwegian publisher was "shot in the back several times with a high-velocity rifle and left for dead in the snow." Hitchens was himself warned by the American State Department about "chatter" that he and his family would be murdered, as Rushdie had been a house guest. Why is this significant?

> In considered statements, the Vatican, the archbishop of Canterbury, and the chief Sephardic rabbi of Israel all took a stand in sympathy— *with the ayatollah*. So did the cardinal archbishop of New York and many other lesser religious figures.[87] (Emphasis mine)

But of course. These all are politically corrupt businesses marketing themselves as religion. Birds of a feather flock together. Here is an example of Pope Francis:

Most churches opposed the effort to remove Saddam Hussein, and the pope disgraced himself utterly by using a personal invitation to the wanted war criminal Tariq Asis, a man responsible for the state murder of children. Not only was Asis welcomed at the Vatican as the senior Catholic member of a ruling fascist party... he was taken to Assisi for a personal session of prayer at the shrine of Saint Francis.[88]

Hitchens could also find many examples of harmful doctrines in organized religion. I have some of my own. In doing so, we are soul mates.

We have no way to quantify the damage done by telling children that masturbation will make them blind, or that impure thoughts will lead to an eternity of torment, or that members of other faiths including members of their own families will burn.

There is much to this, and we must escape this brainwashing. I regret of what I was deprived in pursuit of my bogus virtue. As a Catholic priest, I encountered parishioners who had lived their lives for many years under a dark cloud, convinced that they would eventually go to hell because of some childish foible. In fact, one lady comes to mind who would not drink water on Fridays since the water might have been contaminated by some microscopic protein and she would go, unwittingly, to hell for eating meat on Friday. What a curse to bear!

But where do we find such nonsense in scripture? Where are these proscriptions found in the Creator's laws of nature? What do these rules and regulations have to do with living a Christian life? I submit; their purpose is domination by organized religion.

Once again, I wholeheartedly agree with him that organized religion is no keystone to virtue:

We believe with certainty that an ethical life can be lived without religion. And we know for a fact that the corollary holds true—that religion has caused innumerable people...to award themselves permission to behave in ways that would make a brothel-keeper or an ethnic cleanser raise an eyebrow.[89]

While I never had the chance to meet him, I did "attend" some of his lectures/debates on the internet, as I said. On these occasions, he clearly affirmed that the natural law directs us to the right way to live. He attacks the "enslavement" of *organized* religion. I'm still with him there. He simply fails to distinguish the Sitz im Leben of that period when scripture was written and thus "throws out the baby with the bathwater." He affirms the virtue but is blinded from seeing that the kerygma, the Christian message that proclaims it, is in scripture for the taking.

A "RATIONAL ALTERNATIVE" TO RELIGION

For many years, Hitchens described himself as a Democratic Socialist and Marxist, but he worked his way through that:

> For a good part of my life, I had a share in this idea [the yearning of the poor and oppressed to rise above the strictly material world and to achieve something transcendent] that I have not yet quite abandoned. But there came a time when I could not protect myself, and indeed did not wish to protect myself, from the onslaught of reality… [T]he very concept of a total solution had led to the most appalling human sacrifices… Those of us who had sought a rational alternative to religion had reached a terminus that was comparatively dogmatic.[90]

I believe that all truth seekers will conclude that they are not Marxists after all, once they understand communism objectively—the "religion of hate"—and recognize the cruelty and devastation communism pledges to inflict on mankind. We will get to that next. The millions of truth-seeking fellow antitheists won't identify with that.

In the *Monitor on Psychology*, July/August 2020, Kirsten Weir reported research comparing atheists and traditional Christians on many characteristics. The research found them to be equivalent. It found that both groups consider family and freedom as the most important values in their own lives. While religious people are more likely to volunteer or give to charitable causes related to their beliefs, atheists appear to be more generous to a wider range of causes and dissimilar groups. They are equivalent in finding meaning in life, loving their families, working hard, and simply being a good person. Indeed, it was found that "it's actually the most secular countries on Earth right now that are doing the best job taking care of their most vulnerable, not being violent and doing things that seem moral."

All of us have the same human nature, the same essence, expressed in the same essential characteristics. Although these values are articulated in the Christian kerygma, it should be no surprise that everyone is capable of practicing the essential values we have learned and are embodied in our common nature. To do so is to obey "the Laws of Nature and of Nature's God." There is no rational justification for the antagonism between atheists and traditional Christians. Realizing that we are all on the same page, we should respect and affirm one another as sincere human beings. We must come together to promote these universal values and salvage our civilization.

Is humanism the same as Christian civilization? Hitchens affirmed, "I can think of a handful of priests and bishops and rabbis and imams who have put humanity ahead of their own sect or creed… But this is a compliment to humanism, not to religion."[91]

I don't equate them. As the practice of Christian virtue erodes in society, replaced by secular humanism, society itself erodes as history shows over and over. Civilization is undone. Secular humanism seems mechanistic and doesn't orient to living the right way.

CONCLUSION

This brings us to the end of section 1. When I think of identity politics, what comes to mind are those primitive tribes constantly throwing spears at one another. Then I think of the story of the starving Bunyoro tribe. The Christians warned the missionaries to "get out while the gettin' is good." Instead, the Christian Toro tribe, themselves malnourished, carried foodstuffs to save them, explaining, "We are now Christians and must forgive our enemies." That would be heroic in cultures with a "civilized" Sitz im Leben.

I think of the plight of Mrs. Fisher, who had no milk for her infant. Learning of this, the Christian porter, after carrying a heavy load all day, slipped into the jungle every night and was able to return with a gourd of milk and saved the baby's life. These stories demonstrate the power of the Christian kerygma—even in primitive Africa—drawing out the best in human nature. The porter heroically saved Mrs. Fisher's infant. Contrast that with the primitive law that twin babies had to be murdered, the witch doctor saying simply, "Two dogs were born to you."

As I write, Governor Northam of Virginia recently stated that a woman has the right to murder her newborn, should she choose. What has become of that self-evident, un*alien*able right to life? You know, "thou shalt not kill." Which way are we headed?

To paraphrase Ronald Reagan, Christian civilization is never more than one generation away from extinction. America appears hell-bent on eradicating two thousand years of Christian civilization and returning mankind to the Dark Ages and barbarism, starkly depicted for us in primitive Africa.

Thomas Jefferson provided the platform for ending slavery in our Declaration of Independence: all men are created equal. In 1819, he founded the flagship university in Virginia, the University of Virginia. In our day, its students and their professors are covering his statue with a black shroud and plastering it with signs saying "racist," "rapist," and "slaveholder," lambasting those who "fetishize the legacy of Jefferson." This five-thousand-year leap of civilization is being covered with a black shroud.

To this challenge mankind cannot simply turn a blind eye. All of us who sincerely seek the truth must eschew identity politics and affirm common ground. The barbaric enemy—communism—is at the gate.

ERADICATING CHRISTIAN CIVILIZATION

CHAPTER 7

WHAT IS COMMUNISM ABOUT?

INTRODUCTION

Let's get past the pseudonym socialism and call it by its name, communism. Marx used the term *socialism* more commonly than *communism*, but both have identical underpinnings. The only distinction given between socialism and pure communism is the ruthlessness of the vicious and total annihilation of mankind that both embrace.

The modern American communists—the millennials and Generation Z and the majority of those in public office—most likely know less about the philosophy of communism than we will review here. They are but the marionettes of the invisible communist puppeteers who pull their strings. They are not so much theoretical communists as unthinking, selfish, dependent recruits in the movement. The goal of their puppeteers is to abolish our republic and enslave us. The ignorance of these unwitting disciples makes them more dangerous. They are "flying blind," if you will. There is no opening for dialogue.

In this chapter, I introduce the creator of communism, Karl Marx, and briefly examine the major tenants of his theories. Then we consider characteristics of the communists themselves. Finally, we consider how this movement has infiltrated America. First, then, a snapshot of the person who brought this dark devastation, communism, into existence.

WHO WAS KARL MARX?

Talking about Karl Marx could be considered an ad hominem attack on communism, yet "good trees bear good fruit while bad trees bear bad fruit," and that is the argument for even paying him attention.

Marx descended from a long line of distinguished Jewish scholars in Germany, and he did manage to get a PhD degree. He was a very intelligent man. He was also as loathsome a human being as you would ever have the misfortune to encounter. He never worked to earn a ha'pence in his entire life, being supported by Engels as best he could. Driven from Germany, France, and Belgium, he took refuge in the London slums.

Even there he, his wife, and his children were always on the verge of eviction, threatened to have all their belongings confiscated to compensate the landlord. In our day, Child Protective Services would have placed his children in foster homes. Two died of malnutrition, and two others committed suicide. In letters to Engels asking for money, he would complain about his wife's incessant crying but noted also that he was spending his days in the library, studying mathematics.[1] He surely behaved like the world owed him a living. Quoting Cleon Skousen, here is one example of his psychopathic character:

> During a particularly desperate period [his children were starving] Marx made a trip to Holland where a prosperous uncle generously handed him one hundred sixty pounds. This was enough to put Marx on his financial feet, pay off the debts and give him a new start. But with money in his pocket, Marx decided to take a tour of Germany. He visited his mother in Treves, proceeded to Berlin, undertook a number of drinking excursions with his old friends, had himself photographed and generally played the role of a gentleman of leisure. Two months later he returned home. Frau Marx welcomed her tourist husband thinking that now bills could be paid, clothing and furniture could be purchased, and better rooms rented. She was horrified to learn that practically nothing remained of the hundred and sixty pounds.[2]

Marx tried repeatedly to establish an International Socialist Movement throughout Europe, but he repeatedly failed. He was so egotistic and so insecure that whenever one of his disciples would show some quality of leadership, Marx would concoct a series of lies about him, destroy his reputation, and banish him. He died sitting in a chair, alone. Engels and a half-dozen others attended his funeral.

There are those who "talk the talk" and those who "walk the walk." Typically, the pretentious "talkers," without any corrective experience to test and balance their theories, are unquestioning about their wisdom and the least likely to get it right. Marx never had a clue about living the right way as a human being. So he knew it all.

As a neuropsychologist, I understand how the human brain creates "templates" from life experiences and programs us *unconsciously* to perceive the world through that mindset. These are, if you will, bad "brain habits," and persons are trapped, projecting these distortions on their experiences unconsciously and misconstruing them. Being unaware of it consciously, people can't correct themselves. I elaborate this in the appendix.

WHAT IS COMMUNISM ABOUT?

Marx's revolt against functional behavior in a free enterprise economy led, instead, to attacking the economy as the reason for his own dysfunction. He created a view of the world that led to an eventual utopia that would bestow on mankind a cornucopia of whatever was desired.

> His personal attitude toward religion, morals and competition in everyday existence led him to long for an age when men would have no religion, morals or competition in everyday existence. He wanted to live in a classless, stateless, noncompetitive society where there would be such lavish production of everything that men, by simply producing according to their apparent ability, would automatically receive a superabundance of all material goods.[3]

To bring this about, he brooked no opposition. Governments, economic systems, everything must be destroyed, so his new perfect world could take their place. Cleon Skousen quotes, "I shall stride through the wreckage a creator."[4]

Since he considered man to be nature's ultimate achievement, with the highest intelligence in existence, it behooves man to recreate the world. Thus, the creature of nature becomes the creator of his creator. Of course, not just any human being is up to it. The communist elite alone have the intellectual capacity to know what has to be done. The bulk of human beings have no intrinsic rights and no self-determination, so they are expendable without remorse. It will not be easy and surely not painless. Marx's dictum was, "everything that exists deserves to perish."

> Marx and Engels accepted the fact that the remaking of the world will have to be a cruel and ruthless task and that it will involve the destruction of all who stand in their way... In other words, whatever tends to bring about the Communist concept of material betterment is morally good, whatever does not is morally bad... It is not wrong to cheat, lie, violate oaths or even destroy human life if it is for a good cause.[5]

Proclaiming to be all knowing to cover up his social alienation and insecurity, he created a philosophical framework that, somewhat ambitiously, explained everything in existence. (The psychological term is to *reaction form*, balancing the scale by thinking the opposite: insecure→ all knowing.) In this way, he enticed the intelligentsia. I did not say the intelligent. Everything can be explained by matter, the total explanation for space, nature, man, psychic consciousness, human intelligence, and every other aspect of existence. Since he knows all there is to know about matter, he knows everything. So here are Marx and Engels's three important Laws of Metaphysics.[6] Don't fret if you don't understand these. Neither do I.

The *Law of Opposites*.[7] The existence of all objects is inclusive in each other. None exists separately. Like electricity has protons and electrons, unified but contradictory forces, everything (i.e., matter) in existence has dialectic (read: conflicting) forces and is in a state of motion. Cleon Skousen put it this way: "Two inert elements could no more produce a conflict and create motion than a thousand dead capitalists and a million dead communists could produce a class war."

The *Law of Negation of The Negation*.[8] Each entity negates itself to reproduce itself in greater quantity. A barley seed dies and germinates and produces a plant, which dies and produces many barley seeds. He thus comes to the conclusion that individual private property, based on individual labor, is negated by capitalist private property. (You miss the connection? So do I.) Well, elephants are not barley and repeatedly reproduce for more than a hundred years. It is a rare tragedy when a woman dies in childbirth, surely not in accord with the natural law. The young need care from the adults to maintain the ribbon of life, and human neonates will not reach "the age of maturity" for eighteen years.

The *Law of Transformation*.[9] Matter is not only auto-dynamic and inclined to increase itself numerically but also increases through quantitative accumulations. From time to time, a particular class in nature "leaps" and becomes an entirely new form. The model used by Marx was the incremental periodic table. An example would be H (hydrogen, a flammable gas) and O (oxygen, a gas, needed for fires); if they get together as H_2O, we have a liquid, water, which you might use to put out a fire. But his formula is grossly inadequate and inconsistent with the theory of evolution.

Marx is left to justify his affirmation that all work is of equal value. He comes up with a very complex transformative formula, calculating "living labor," "normal" labor parameters, and "dead labor" (i.e., the cost in terms of raw materials, etc.). He cannot factor into his formula higher-paid skilled labor with lower-paid unskilled labor since he requires homogeneity. He cannot explain how an unnatural misunderstanding of the laws of nature suddenly leaps to create the perfect society.[10] His "perfect society" glosses over the payoff of this communist philosophy, the most horrible crimes of the twentieth century. Adding up the murders of communists' innocent citizens compares to one-third of all the American citizens in the fifty states!

These are his ten essential tenets of communism.[11] I will examine them below, showing how they have infected the United States.

- Central banking system
- Government controlled education
- Government controlled labor
- Government ownership of transportation and communication vehicles
- Government ownership of agricultural means and factories
- Total abolition of private property
- Property rights confiscation
- Heavy income tax on everyone
- Elimination of rights of inheritance
- Regional planning

Communism—that is communalism—clashes head-on with individualism, believing that we, as individuals, have self-determination and unalienable rights. Our Christian civilization is founded on individualism and is showcased in the American Constitution. "We hold these truths to be self-evident: that all men are created equal; that they are endowed by their Creator with certain unalienable rights; that among these are life, liberty, and the pursuit of happiness"—each one of us.

The communist isn't disposed to take personal responsibility to live the right way and pursue happiness. Marx and his followers, as individuals, are misfits in society and long to blend themselves into a communal identity where they can be swallowed up and, at last, belong. They feel validated by being absorbed into the movement. Thus, communism requires mindless humans to be cogs on the communal wheel. Such people have no individuality or any rights. They cannot be self-determining. Some people would elevate animals to the same plane as human beings. Communism degrades human beings to the level of a farmer's herd of cows and flock of chickens to be managed by the elite, with their superior intelligence, who are creating a new world. We are, therefore, as dispensable as they may require.

Skousen points out,

> Perhaps, without quite realizing it, Marx was setting out to create a race of human beings conditioned to think like criminals… Today this breed of criminally conditioned man walks the earth in sufficient numbers to conquer countries or continents, to change laws and boundaries, to decree war or peace… He lives exclusively by the jungle law of selfish survival… The subordination of other men's minds to the obscuring of truth is not deceit but a necessary governmental tool.[12]

Marx would seize upon ideas with some validity but then misconstrue them to fit his mindset. For example, one theory is the *Activist Theory*. In this theory, after the brain receives impressions from the outside world, it automatically moves the individual to take action. Action inevitably must be taken. Once again, this reduces human nature to that of lower animals. From a neuropsychological understanding, this is equivalent to the brain of the beagle. Smelling a rabbit, it immediately takes action, not stopping to think that the rabbit ran across a busy highway with bumper-to-bumper traffic. Besides that "old brain," similar to that of the animals, the human brain has an "executive" function, like the executive in a corporation. I explain this in the appendix. This exclusively human executive function can be pictured having a dialogue with the impulsive "old brain." We weigh the value and risk of an action and which action, if any, would be best. A human being knows better than a beagle. Not so for Karl Marx, who dehumanizes man to the level of a herd of cows. Unless you are Karl Marx.

> The victims of adversarial ideologies do not fit into the believer's [i.e., Communist's] agenda, and so they do not matter and are not, ultimately, even human in his eyes. Because they are not human for

him, the believer sees them as enemies and, therefore, supports their extermination.[13]

Communism is equivalent to group psychopathy. Psychopaths are unable to experience empathy. To shoot a child or shoot a tin can off the fence are equivalent for them. Just as those who are not psychologists cannot adequately comprehend psychopaths and are, therefore, their prey, civilized societies cannot comprehend the communist mind. This places the rest of us at a disadvantage. Think of the notorious Ted Bundy, who murdered more than thirty women. He would play the cripple and elicit their sympathy until he could shove them into his car. We see this same strategy in play with communists, and we need not look beyond the United States. Our orientation to "do unto others as you would have them do unto you" doesn't work with psychopaths. They have no empathy.

Another analogy is cancer. Cancer cells and healthy cells are not on an even playing field. Cancer cells draw upon the body's resources to proliferate, invading normal tissues and organs and eventually spreading throughout the body. Cancer is like a suicide bomber, killed when it kills its host. Such it is with communism. It invades and metastasizes. You cannot "turn the other cheek" with cancer or communism; you must do all you can to eradicate it before it kills you—and itself.

HOW IS THE COMMUNIST CHARACTERIZED?

The evils of a free enterprise society that communism promises to eliminate are actually much worse in Communist countries, but that is irrelevant. Communists are not truth seekers. They are hate obsessed. As Dr. Jamie Glazov observed, the communist believers in America and elsewhere flocked to Stalinist Russia in great numbers when this genocide was at its worst.

> The less brutal an ideology is, the less interest the average believer has in it and the less praise he is inclined to give it. By contrast, when the death cult is in full gear, the believer supports it most strongly… The fellow travelers always flocked to communist regimes in largest numbers when the mass murder had reached a peak.[14]

You are not likely to succeed in converting communists; you cannot "convert" cancer either. Again, as Glazov points out,

[T]he political faith, therefore, is not at all a search for the truth. It is a movement. For the believer, consequently, changing his views becomes nearly inconceivable, since doing so means losing his entire community and, therefore, his personal identity: he is by necessity relegated to "non-person" status. Even so, many believers have gathered the courage to abandon the movement.[15]

People who are satisfied with their lives don't want to rock the boat. Those who are square pegs in a round hole and either haven't figured out how to fit in or don't care to get it right hate the hole. They blame their misalignment on the hole. They are committed to destroy it and find themselves a new one—a new society—in hopes they will finally fit in. Christian civilization—the right way to live—empowers us to take control of our lives and pursue happiness. Instead of taking individual responsibility for their lives, communists borrow a sense of control by uniting with the communist movement. They renounce individualism and replace it with communalism. They renounce their identity and replace it with a communal identification.

As I have said, I seek firsthand accounts rather than theories. We find such an account in Dr. Jamie Glazov's book, *United In Hate: The Left's Romance With Tyranny and Terror*. He was born in Russia and came with his family to America. The following is a capsule of what he said about the Communist mind.

This struggle for "self"-preservation is achieved by self-rejection in favor of melding into the powerful movement. But they can't leave it at that. Glazov points out that "the suffering of capitalism's supposed victims is somehow [their] personal business."[16]

Those who get it right in the first place don't join in, of course, casting doubt on the communist solution and leaving their movement incomplete, so communists are consumed with hate toward them. In fact, "human joy and cheer are tacit endorsements of the present order that [leftist] utopians want to destroy."[17]

The believer must tell himself that these individuals are content with their own society only because they have been brainwashed. In other words, they think they are happy but they are not… and they can only be liberated from this mental enslavement by the revolution that the believers have appointed themselves to lead.[18]

Similarly, while they denounce the perceived materialism, poverty, and all supposed injustices in their society, these are not actually their concerns since all these imperfections are far worse in Communist societies. They are not truth seekers. Only the movement, the party line, has credibility for them. Since they cling to it for dear life, getting them to see the light is virtually impossible.

Seeking truth is central to our nature. We are *Homo sapiens*, the wisdom-seeking, truth-seeking animals. This has gotten us out of caves and appears to have gotten us to the moon. Even the Roman Cicero acknowledged this natural "law of right reason" in us all. It is the engine driving our progress.

Having renounced their individuality, communists are at a loss to develop personal relationships. Glazov points out that this newfound "brotherhood" is but an illusion:

> [Communists'] friendships are seldom based on what they might actually like about each other as human beings; they are based only on how their political beliefs conform to one another's... [and so they are] completely undisturbed by the arrests and deaths of their friends in the Stalinist purges.[19]

Glazov notes that the communists in the "educated class" rationalize their alienation by convincing themselves they're smarter than ordinary folks, and therefore, their destiny is to manage them. After all, Marx reassured them that he knew everything.

Following the philosopher Rousseau, they also became enamored with the innocence of "the noble savage." The virtue of the noble savage clashes with the decadence of the "deplorables" in the Western world, a world in which they are a superior class. As Glazov also pointed out, in actuality, it was the very savagery of primitive man that was so enticing, endorsing their quest to destroy all liberty and all of society's achievements. From our discovery of life in primitive Africa, I doubt they would have enjoyed living there. Yet this dark path is where communism inexorably leads.

CHAPTER 8

WHAT ABOUT COMMUNISM IN AMERICA?

INTRODUCTION

A movie about Ayn Rand begins with the image of a magnificent oak tree, most likely growing there for two hundred fifty years. Then a powerful thunderstorm ensues, with lightning flashing all around. The narrator informs us that the oak tree crashed to the ground. And we found that it was all hollow inside.

The communist "termites" in America have been at work for more than a century, hidden, underground. Then, in 2016, something unpredicted occurred. Donald J. Trump painted the map of America red and was chosen to be America's leader and, in many ways, the leader of the free world. The communists' secretive game plan aborted, they panicked and came out of hiding. It is now all or nothing for them. They realized that their well-oiled efforts were imperiled. Their chance was to spy on him to uncover some flaw, hamstring his ability to function, or, if all else failed, to impeach him. And they have been at it ever since.

We set ourselves up for this. In a way, our success has been our undoing. There is a theoretical cycle called the Tytler cycle, named after Judge Alexander Fraser Tytler.[20] In fact, it was spoken by Henning Webb Prentis Jr. in 1943 and basically goes like this: nations transition from bondage to spiritual faith, from spiritual faith to courage, from courage to freedom, from freedom to abundance, from abundance to selfishness, from selfishness to complacency, from complacency to apathy, from apathy to fear, from fear to dependency, and from dependency to bondage.

A democracy cannot exist as a permanent form of government. It can only exist until the voters discover that they can vote themselves largesse from the public treasury. From that moment on, the majority always votes for the candidates promising the most benefits from the public treasury with the result that a democracy always collapses over loose fiscal policy, always followed by a dictatorship. The average age of the world's greatest civilizations has been 200 years.[21]

Our nation seems to be at the point of apathy and fear, stoked by the Wuhan virus and the continued rioting, leading to dependency. If communism prevails, we will surely be in bondage. By this gauge, we're running on empty.

Since the advent of mankind, humans have been self-reliant. Not too long ago, we had to raise our vegetables and care for livestock and a chicken coop to have food. Fish came from a nearby lake or stream, but they had to be caught, not prepackaged for us in the supermarket. Transportation came from maintaining a hayburner (i.e., a horse). Wood had to be cut in the summer to stay warm in the winter. Even the coal furnace, which needed tending, is long gone, now replaced with a thermostat. Ice had to be cut and stored in the winter to keep up the icebox in the summer. Today city dwellers would have no opportunity for any of that.

The homegrown auto mechanic has given way to computerized diagnostics. We need not be responsible for checking tire pressure; an icon on the dashboard warns us. We don't even crank down the car windows. Push a button. Deprivation is lacking a cell phone. As I type this, the computer tells me if I misspelled a word and even substitutes its idea of what word is better: *There* when I want *their* for example. You know what I mean.

Every time, something is done for us in this way, we need not be personally responsible for it. Our individualist identity is diminished, and we are being programmed—literally—to become the dependent slaves of mushrooming technology.

Self-reliance is married to freedom. As the American slaves preferred their slavery to emancipation, since all their needs were provided to them, so are many Americans today being trained to rely on the government to take care of us—enslave us—instead of asserting our freedom and shouldering the responsibility to take care of ourselves. So we are becoming prey to Karl Marx.

As I said, the infiltration of communalism, aka communism, in America has gone largely unrecognized and undeterred for more than a century. It has metastasized throughout and touches virtually everything that we have taken for granted in this constitutional republic. Benjamin Franklin warned, "We have given you a Republic. It remains to be seen if you will be able to retain it." We have not retained it very well.

I quoted Dr. Jamie Glazov above. He came, with his parents, to America from Russia in 1972 when he was five years old. His book is well worth reading. His parents were astounded when they came to America and attempted to make intellectual friends:

> My father could also now, for the first time, speak out without fear in defense of Soviet citizens who were languishing in the Gulag and in psychiatric hospitals for their political and religious beliefs… While we were cherishing our newfound freedom, we encountered a strange species: intellectuals in the universities who hated my parents for the story they had to tell. For the first time in their lives my father and mother confronted the intelligentsia that was hostile to them. Back in Russia, dissident intellectuals risked their lives when they pronounced one word of truth… In America, most of the intellectuals who surrounded us scoffed at the importance of real intellectual freedom and dismissed my parents' experience; they demonized their own society, wished for its defeat, and supported the communist enemy that muzzled free speech and tortured millions of human beings.[22]

We review now the ten essential tenets of communism that Marx detailed, to show how they have already penetrated our republic. Then I add several related observations. The challenge is, as I have said before, to alert all truth seekers to the imminent threat, so we'll join together and *buy into* salvaging Christian civilization while we still have some chance. We won't succeed "selling" this. No one wants to be sold.

WHAT'S WRONG WITH CENTRAL BANKING?

The preeminent resource here is the book by G. Edward Griffin, *The Creature from Jekyll Island*.[23] I cannot improve beyond briefly reviewing what he reveals about the Federal Reserve System.

Two national banks in America had initially been in operation. In 1781, the first was engineered by Robert Morris in Philadelphia to emulate the English mercantile system. It was a dismal failure. Under Hamilton's influence, the Bank of the United States was chartered in 1791. It also failed, and the charter's renewal was defeated in 1811. But wildcat banks picked up on loans for the war of 1812, tripling the money supply. This led to the Second Bank of the United States.

Andrew Jackson removed federal deposits from the bank, dissolving the bank. The opposition deliberately triggered a national depression, resulting in Jackson's impeachment effort.

This brings us to Lincoln and the Civil War. As I noted in our discussion of slavery, I have a slightly different emphasis than that of Griffin regarding Lincoln's motivation for the war. It is true that there were significant financial motivations for the war, the North taking advantage of the South in terms of trade with Europe. In discussing Thomas Jefferson I noted that Lincoln would have striven to preserve the Union but couldn't tolerate the expansion of slavery into the western territories. Strong Republican economic pressure for the war is not denied.

The war resulted in enormous debt and another national banking system erected to convert government bonds into fiat money, costing the American people half their assets because of inflation and locking the nation into perpetual debt. The House of Morgan profited from the Civil War and partnered with the House of Rothschild, leading to the first governor of the Federal Reserve Bank of New York, which deliberately created inflation in the United States to shift investment money to England and to save that economy from depression.

Fast-forward to today. Central banks manage the money supply around the globe. The Federal Reserve System, also known as the Fed, was established by an act of Congress in 1913. It is America's central bank, making it the most powerful single actor in the US economy and thus the world. It is complicated and deceitful and controls the world's money.

The Board of Governors of the Federal Reserve System directs monetary policy. Its seven members, who are nominated by the president and confirmed by the Senate, are responsible for setting the discount rate and the reserve requirement for member banks. Staff economists provide all analyses. The Federal Open Market Committee (FOMC) oversees open market operations and meets eight times a year. There is a Fed bank located in each of their twelve districts. Thus, the Fed is a "hybrid," one foot in politics and the other in banking.

The platform for the Fed was laid in 1910 by six persons. Nelson Aldrich was the Senate whip and also an investment associate of J. P. Morgan. His son-in-law was John D. Rockefeller Jr. The other five, including Paul M. Warburg, who represented the Rothschilds and Warburgs in Europe and masterminded the enterprise, together controlled a quarter of all the money in the world. They met, under the elaborate cover of secrecy, at the private resort of Morgan, who owned Jekyll Island, "going duck hunting." Thus, the ruse could not have been more obvious from the onset.

So the stage is set for the creature from Jekyll Island, the name "Federal Reserve System" being carefully chosen to hide its nature as a central bank, still modeled after the Bank of England. Woodrow Wilson had publicly declared his allegiance, and the associate of Morgan and Warburg, Colonel House, moved into the White House and became the unseen president. It was adopted in 1913 and has been revised 195 times and counting.

Griffin provided "the Rothschild formula," which, he said, "reveals a personality profile, not just of the Rothschilds, but of that special breed of international financiers whose success typically is built upon certain character traits. These include cold objectivity, immunity to patriotism, and indifference to the human condition."[24]

This is the formula, "in a nutshell," which has been adopted or adapted almost universally: War is the ultimate discipline of any government, and governments cannot survive without meeting this challenge. The greater the threat is, the greater is the need for government to expand its debt; therefore, it must be perpetually involved in war or the threat thereof. To maintain this threat, enemies must have credible military might. Lacking this, it is necessary to provide them with sufficient monies. This may require *creating* an enemy by financing the rise of a hostile regime.

Should a government refuse to go into debt, encouraging political opposition or revolution is required to replace that government with one that is cooperative. Assassination for this purpose is advantageous. A balance of power is necessary to avoid peace; neither side can be allowed to have a decisive victory over the other so as to maintain perpetual war. Therefore, both sides of the conflict need to be financed.

Morgan controlled the news media and demonized Germany to draw the United States into WW I. Griffin shows that Winston Churchill deliberately set up the sinking of the *Lusitania*, carrying American passengers, by a German U-boat, to incite the United States to join in the war. With the declaration of war, Congress voted one billion dollars in credit for England and France. He also shows that the Bolshevik Revolution was orchestrated by foreign financiers, including the United States, using the Rothschild formula.

Griffin then showed how the new Federal Reserve depressed interest rates and massively expanded the money supply, causing investors to get better returns by moving their money to England, thus supporting Great Britain to pay for its socialist programs. This caused the Great Depression.

There is circumstantial evidence that the Bank of England and the Federal Reserve had concluded, at a secret meeting in February of 1929, that a collapse in the market was inevitable and that the best action was to let nature take its course. Immediately after that meeting, the financiers sent advisory warnings to lists of preferred customers—wealthy industrialists, prominent politicians, and high officials of foreign governments—to get out of the stock market [before the October crash]. Meanwhile, the American people were being assured that the economy was in sound condition.[25]

The Founders insisted that money had to be in commodities—in fact, silver, a dollar at 371.25 grains of pure silver. Harry Dexter White, Roosevelt's communist spy in 1944 at Bretton Woods, eliminated the gold-exchange standard in order to promote world communism.

On to the International Monetary Fund (IMF) and the World Bank milking industrialized nations on the pretext of helping underdeveloped nations but actually buying off those dictators. Now the mechanism was in place to build a true world communist government within the framework of the United Nations. Governmental interference with the money supply has always the same effect: inflation (the hidden tax), economic chaos, booms and busts, and political upheaval.

All money earned in the banking system is created out of nothing by making loans. If the loans default, the federal government is expected to cover them. As a last resort, the Fed simply prints more fiat money, creating hidden inflation. For example, in 1982, Chicago's Continental Illinois bank went broke, so the FDIC assumed $4.5 billion in bad loans and essentially nationalized the bank. This was later seen in the savings and loans insolvencies.

How goes the Federal Reserve System today? By 1992, there were already more people receiving government checks than there were paying income tax. As I write, the total national debt is $23,305,297,151,134—*trillions* of dollars—and counting. Americans work half the year working for the government, and as I write, the Democratic nominee, Joe Biden, and his democratic platform assert that they will raise taxes, apparently by four trillion dollars.

The Council on Foreign Relations (CFR), an extension of the Fed, is actually the hidden government of the United States. In fact, now the International Monetary Fund (IMF) / World Bank is established in conjunction with the Fed to exhaust the American economy and bring the system down to weaken the United

States both economically and militarily, handing over our nuclear arsenal to the communist United Nations.

Griffin stated that this same Rothschild formula is in play between the United States and Russia: "Lets you and him fight." We have a more menacing player in the arena: China. We see that money interests and the Pentagon, which is seeded with communists, have been sanguine about China continuing to steal intellectual property from the US, maintaining their unfair balance of trade and supplying our medications and items we need for our national defense. And China has moved this up a notch with the worldwide Wuhan virus.

WHAT ABOUT GOVERNMENT-CONTROLLED EDUCATION?

The founders were staunchly opposed to state-controlled education, comparing it to the state-controlled Church of England from which they had fled. America spends more on public education than virtually every other tier 1 country and yet ranks at the very bottom in terms of actual education. The priorities that the founders specified as "education" have been eliminated by the communist agenda. This has spawned generations of adult children, so many still dependent and living with their parents today, trained to dream of a Socialist utopia where they never have to grow up. Coming up: examining the communist infiltration of public education in detail.

WHAT ABOUT GOVERNMENT-CONTROLLED LABOR?

The Communist Manifesto says, "Workers of the world, unite." Vladimir Lenin said, "Trade unions are a school of communism." Actually, communist countries do not allow labor unions because the state has become the corporate executive for the entire nation and will destroy any resistance. Meanwhile, however, communist unions will do just fine and "organized labor" was actually mandated in the Soviet Union initially. This, of course, resulted in "wholesale corruption, forced inequality and grotesque injustice. Hmm. Sounds a lot like what unions have inflicted upon the United States: wholesale corruption as many union chapters have historically acted as fronts for organized crime; forced inequality…gross injustice as greedy unions strong-armed lavish salaries and benefits for themselves."[26]

An easy read that outlines the development of communist labor unions in America while Obama was still president is found on the website Red State,[27] written by Dr. Keith C. Westbrook, PhD. He quotes the following communist unions from another source:[28] SEIU, AFL-CIO, UNITE HERE, Blue Diamond Workers Organizing Committee, Coalition of Black Trade Unionists, Change to Win, United Farm Workers of America, United Steel Workers of America, Chicago Teamsters Union, National Health & Human Services Union. He adds, for good measure, the Workers Party of Brazil, as well as the Party of Democratic Socialism of Germany.

He then goes on to chronicle seventy-six communist organizations in America, adding, "This is just the tip of the iceberg, the number of groups and organizations is in the thousands!" He tops the list of communist unions with the Service Employees International Union, whose former president, Andy Stern, recently returned from a trip to China, where he met with "high-ranking" government officials, published in an article dated 2020.[29] Stern is selling the communist model:

> The conservative-preferred, free-market fundamentalist, shareholder-only model—so successful in the 20th century—is being thrown onto the trash heap of history in the 21st century. In an era when countries need to become economic teams, Team USA's results—a jobless decade, 30 years of flat median wages, a trade deficit, a shrinking middle class and phenomenal gains in wealth but only for the top 1 percent—are pathetic.

You can wonder where he is getting his news these days, as our economy was the best ever before the Wuhan virus shut it down. Blue Collar workers' wages were up 16 percent; there was record low unemployment for every segment of the nation; deals had been finalized that correct the trade deficit, etc. For communists, facts are irrelevant; the party line is always right. Of course, unions force members, without their consent, to contribute their money to be lobbied by the communist leaders to promote communist legislators, and the individuals have no recourse, even if they—individuals—have an open mind.

Unions have been around since the days of the revolution. They always tended to be Socialistic. Even at that time, Eugene Debs said, "The earth is for all the people…The machinery of production and distribution for all the people… The collective ownership and control of industry and its democratic management [is] in the interest of all the people."[30]

The Democrats took control of Congress in 1910 and elected the "progressive" Woodrow Wilson in 1912, and he initiated more progressive laws. He was responsible, as we saw, for creating the Federal Reserve.

The full communist orientation got underway with President Herbert Hoover, president during the Great Depression—when unemployment reached 25 percent. For one thing, he signed an act called the Norris–La Guardia Act, which disallowed employers to compel employees to sign a statement that they would *not* form a union. From that time—except during the Cold War—the political ideology of the Democratic Party has been progressive socialism. Almost every law supporting the socialized labor movement was created and passed under Democratic governments from that point for almost a hundred years.

The unions had recently supported the Republican president, Donald Trump. Let's not expect much, as their forced union dues have historically been doled out to buy the Democrats, as I said. Also, in spite of the glaring contradiction, Andy Stern, tied to his powerful Service Employees International Union and recently returned from his trip to China, is selling the communist model. The bottom line is, the government has still not been able to capture the entire workforce, but trade unions are a school of communism and the plan to achieve this through communist unions has been alive and doing well.

WHAT ABOUT CONTROL OF TRANSPORTATION AND COMMUNICATION?

While the government still lacks all the means of production, which Marx required, it has managed to corrupt the Commerce Clause and get away with it. Article 1, section 8, clause 3 states, "To regulate Commerce with foreign Nations, and among the several States, and with the Indian Tribes." These few words have spawned hundreds of lawsuits and are the most contested words of the Constitution. To "regulate" in the language of that Sitz im Leben means "to make regular" (i.e., to facilitate the free flow of goods and not prohibit the free flow of any good—except in cases of danger). The concern then was that states with access to harbors exercised their commercial advantage to the detriment of the inland states. Now "interstate commerce" includes sending your sister in another state a birthday card or wishing her happy birthday over the phone.

James Madison in Federalist No. 51, says, "In framing a government which is to be administered by men over men, the great difficulty lies in this: you must first enable the government to control the governed; and in the next place oblige it to control itself." Case in point:

When Senator Diane Feinstein was asked where Congress gets the authority to require that individuals have health insurance she replied, "Well, I would assume it would be in the Commerce Clause of the Constitution. That's how Congress legislates all kinds of various programs."[31]

Commerce has been defined progressively as (a) trading of economic commodities; (b) the modes of their transportation; (c) any kind of commodity; (d) the movement of any thing or any person and its mode of transportation; (e) economic activity that substantially or causally impacts on the trafficking, trading, or transportation of commodities; (f) any human activity or other phenomenon that has any ultimate impact on activities in more states than one.[32]

In a celebrated case decided by the Supreme Court in 1942, *Wickard v. Filburn*, Filburn planted twenty-three acres of wheat for his personal consumption and for his livestock, including necessary seeds for future plantings. But the Agricultural Adjustment Act of 1938, regulating crops for interstate and foreign trade, only allowed him to raise wheat on eleven acres. (So much for the "land of the free.") The extra acreage gave Filburn 239 extra bushels of wheat, so he was fined for having too much wheat for personal use. The Supreme Court found Filburn guilty, holding that his twenty-three acres of wheat was competing with wheat in commerce by reducing the demand for wheat.

"What if every citizen started growing twenty-three acres of wheat for their personal consumption?" they argued. This would substantially affect interstate commerce. In order to maintain a steady and fair market, the Supreme Court affirmed that Filburn's personal use of his wheat interfered with the national wheat market and decided that Congress has the right to regulate this by using the commerce power granted to them.[33]

As I said, there are hundreds of court cases pertaining to these sixteen words, and I hope you get the point from this brief review. One that particularly raised popular ire was the decision that purchasing a product online from another state required buyers to pay sales tax, nonetheless, in their own state. It is argued that this is, instead, an interstate import tariff. Justice Kennedy argued that persons in state A could go across state lines and buy products in state B, which does not have a sales tax, and get away with *smuggling their purchase in the trunks of their cars* across state lines. We see this happening in Northern Michigan. Many citizens in Sault Ste. Marie, Ontario, routinely fill up their gas tanks in Sault Ste. Marie, Michigan, because gas is much cheaper in Michigan. But I haven't heard of Canadian customs checking their gas tanks and arresting them. A balanced discussion of the Commerce Clause, by Dr. David F. Forte, law professor at Cleveland State University and the senior editor of *The Heritage Guide to the*

Constitution, can be found at Heritage.org Commerce, Commerce, Everywhere: The Uses and Abuses of the Commerce Clause.

Regarding the communications industry, Project Veritas acts as a whistleblower, surreptitiously videotaping and recording incriminating information about companies. An undercover video was released on October 14, 2019, alleging that Jeff Zucker, the president of CNN, has structured this major media outlet to, in effect, overthrow the government by ordering his employees to sabotage the duly elected president of the United States because he has a "personal vendetta" against him.[34] CNN has been widely accused of reporting false and skewed news about President Donald Trump since he ran for the presidency. Other major media outlets have allegedly done the same, all finding the same false "sound bites," which jump from station to station and are repeated over and over. Recall, a lie told a hundred times becomes the truth. I have noted above the strategy of disinformation that is alive and doing well in America.

WHAT ABOUT THE OTHER PLANKS OF MARX'S PLATFORM?

- Governmental ownership of agricultural means and factories
- Total abolition of private property
- Property rights confiscation
- Elimination of rights of inheritance
- Regional planning

These remaining five essential tenets of communism share much and thus are considered together. They concern confiscation of private property or the freedom to make use of private property. Communism prohibits private property.

Mark Steyn is referring to the Environmental Protection Agency (EPA) when he says:

> For more and more Americans, law has been supplanted by "regulation"—governing set of rules not legislated by representatives accountable to the people, but invented by an activist bureaucracy, much of which is well to the left of either political party. As the newspapers blandly reported in 2010, the bureaucrats weren't terribly bothered about whether Congress would pass a cap-and-trade mega-bill into law because, if faint-hearted Dems lose their nerve, the EPA will just "raise" "standards" all by itself.[35]

The Environmental Protection Agency (EPA) now defines *wetlands* as "areas where water covers the soil, or is present either at or near the surface of the soil all year or for varying periods of time during the year, including during the growing seasons."[36] Sen. Rand Paul dove into wetlands:

> Respect and protection of private property rights sets the United States apart from other nations and has fueled the greatest expansion of economic freedom the world has ever known. Indeed, private property rights are among the foundational rights of any democracy, not just ours... For years, the EPA's regulatory jurisdiction has been limited to the "navigable waters" of the United States, a term that has always been understood to include only large bodies of water capable of serving as pathways for interstate commerce. Regulation of all other waters was, rightly, left to the states. Unhappy with the limited scope of the jurisdiction given to it by Congress, the EPA and Army Corps of Engineers have simply redefined the meaning of "navigable waters" in an extraordinary way, to include virtually every body of water in the nation right down to the smallest of streams, farm ponds and ditches.
>
> The result of this startling grab is that virtually every property owner in the nation will now be subject to the unpredictable, unsound and often Byzantine regulatory regimes of the EPA. Worse yet, the states are cut out of the loop altogether, leaving landowners to lobby distant federal bureaucrats when the system wrongs them—and wrong them it will... If we fail [to block this rule], we will all live in a regulatory state where farmers must go before the EPA to seek permission to build a farm pond to keep their livestock alive, where homebuilders must seek EPA approval before beginning construction on a housing development that contains a dry creek bed, and where energy producers are left waiting for months or even years to get permits from the EPA, costing the producers tens, if not hundreds, of thousands of dollars that inevitably will be passed on to consumers.[37]

The attempt by the Congress to pass a law restricting such actions stalled in the judiciary committee and never became law.

By "bailing out" banks or other companies, the federal government acquires equity in those companies. Beyond that, the government acquires property of debtors to the government, sometimes temporarily. The government also nationalizes corporations to protect essential services, such as railroads. This is a list of some federally owned enterprises:[38]

- Commodity Credit Corporation (CCC)
- Corporation for National and Community Service (AmeriCorps)
- Corporation for Public Broadcasting
- Export-Import Bank of the United States
- Federal Agricultural Mortgage Corporation
- Farm Credit Banks
- Federal Crop Insurance Corporation (FCIC)
- Federal Deposit Insurance Corporation (FDIC)
- Federal Financing Bank (FFB)
- Federal Home Loan Banks
- Federal Home Loan Mortgage Corporation (Freddie Mac)
- Federal National Mortgage Association (Fannie Mae)
- Federal Prison Industries (UNICOR)
- The Financing Corporation
- Gallaudet University
- Government National Mortgage Association (Ginnie Mae)
- Legal Services Corporation
- Millennium Challenge Corporation (MCC)
- National Cooperative Bank
- National Corporation for Housing Partnerships (NCHP), Washington, DC
- National Credit Union Administration Central Liquidity Facility (CLF)
- National Endowment for Democracy
- National Fish and Wildlife Foundation (NFWF)
- National Park Foundation
- National Railroad Passenger Corporation (Amtrak)
- Neighborhood Reinvestment Corporation
- Overseas Private Investment Corporation
- Pennsylvania Avenue Development Corporation, Washington, DC
- Pension Benefit Guaranty Corporation
- St. Lawrence Seaway Development Corporation
- Securities Investor Protection Corporation
- Tennessee Valley Authority

Some people assert their independence by creating sustainable living "off the grid." They soon find that their un*alien*able right to their property, so strongly emphasized by the founders, doesn't count. The government steps in with citations for "endangering the lives of others," building without a license, lacking proper codes, or requiring permits that will never be granted.

The people living in the Garden of Eden, located in Arlington, Texas, have been growing their own food, building their own shelters, and producing the necessities of life since 2009. Their goal is to demonstrate how a sustainable community can operate and thrive in harmony with themselves and with nature. It hasn't been so harmonious recently. In 2013, the state of Texas brought several SWAT teams to the quiet and peaceful Garden of Eden community and threatened to shut it down. In what appears to be an intimidation tactic, only a single arrest was made based on unrelated outstanding traffic violations, and a handful of citations were given for city code violations.

Absolutely no drug-related violations were found, and all inhabitants of the community were unarmed. Each of the community members present in the house were initially handcuffed at gunpoint by heavily armed SWAT officers. This included the mother of a twenty-two-month-old and a two-week-old. As part of the raid, the officers destroyed many of the crops, including wild and cultivated plants, such as blackberries, lamb's quarters, and okra. Officers also proceeded to remove a variety of materials the community had planned to use in sustainability projects, like pallets, tires, cardboard, and more.[39]

Landowner Shellie Smith was looking for a peaceful resolution to the matter:

> The City codes are in violation of our natural and Constitutional rights to live freely while causing damage to no one, and since there is no damaged party, there has been no crime committed on our part. Rather, the City of Arlington has trespassed and committed robbery against us, amongst other crimes, and will be held accountable in a court of law in due time. We have been targeted by the system because we are showing people how to live without it. We are growing more than just tomatoes here, we are growing the consciousness that will allow people to live freely and sustainably, and the system doesn't want that to be known."[40]

When I was in Alaska, I knew several trappers who live alone in that vast wilderness ten months of the year. These trappers are totally independent, each typically constructing five tiny cabins a day's walk apart. The federal government spent a great deal of taxpayers' money flying helicopters over that vast territory to burn down their cabins.

This is yet another example of overreach. The idea behind "eminent domain" has always been clear. The government can forcefully purchase property at its full value to construct highways and other necessary *public* projects. The Fourth Amendment of the Constitution states: "The right of the people to be secure in their persons, houses, papers and effects, against unreasonable searches and seizures, shall not be violated." Not so anymore. Cities all over America are seizing people's homes and land for *private* use—for example, if some private developer can make more tax revenue by building on the land. This is the new "public good" (i.e., communalism instead of individualism).[41]

President Trump recently restored the right of inheritance, eliminating the death tax. For example, a farm can now be transferred to the children without bankrupting it with taxation for the "sale" at face value. However, restoring this right is only as good as the next election.

ROOSEVELT AND THE COMMUNIST UNITED NATIONS

The effort to make America a communist state, already well along, got its modern impetus from World War II, under the direction of none other than President Franklin D. Roosevelt, the icon of our heroic defeat of Hitler. In fighting that European war, far from America's shores, Roosevelt was determined to protect Germany's neighbor, Stalin and the USSR, diverting military aid to Russia and depriving our army. His effort saved Stalin. While it is a mortal sin—political "*un*-correctness"—to say so, Roosevelt was a staunch communist.[42] The party refused to award him an official communist card because that would expose him. There are various references to this fact on the internet.

> For all those admirers of Franklin Delano Roosevelt, who believe he was a great president, remove the blinders and face up to the fact that his socialist mindset and administration destroyed the last remnants of the Old Republic. Most of these same cheer leaders for the "New Deal" are in love with big government and seek to empower a federal authority at the expense of the Federalism model that is based upon separations of power and States Rights. With the unholy alliance with the Soviet Union, FDR linked his inner objectives with the greatest autocrat liquidator that fought World War II, as a Commu-

nist expansionist to destroy most of the traditional institutions that make up Western Civilization.[43]

The Russian newspapers during the last election [1932] published the photograph of Franklin D. Roosevelt over the caption, "The first communistic President of the United States." Said Sen. Thomas Schall, a Republican from Minnesota. "Evidently the Russian newspapers had knowledge concerning the ultimate intent of the President, which had been carefully withheld from the voters in this country. In fact, the voters of the United States were meticulously misled as to such intentions."[44]

Two of his top advisors were communist operatives. Harry Dexter White was a member of the Communist Party USA (CPUSA). Directed by FDR, in cooperation with a Russian, Pavlov, he undermined the Japanese efforts to avoid war with America and orchestrated the belligerent acts of FDR against Japan that left it no alternative. This is "beyond dispute."

> Interestingly, one of the most recent admissions concerning White's crucial role in this [i.e., orchestrating war with Japan] comes from Benn Steil, senior fellow and director of international economics at the Council on Foreign Relations (CFR). In the decades since World War II, the CFR's very influential members in government, the media, and academe have been in the forefront of the efforts to debunk factual anticommunist charges of rampant Soviet penetration of the top levels of the American government. The CFR choir could always be counted on to defend Alger Hiss, the Rosenbergs and their fellow "atomic bomb spies," the Red China Lobby, and the many other Communist agents exposed operating in the top echelons of federal agencies. And the same CFR intelligentsia could be just as dependably relied upon to denounce as "McCarthyites" any responsible patriots who attempted to force officialdom to investigate, remove, and/or prosecute traitors in our government, especially those in positions most sensitive to our national security.[45]

Harry Hopkins was another Soviet spy and Roosevelt's closest advisor during World War II.[46] In fact, he was said to be the "shadow president" operating from Lincoln's bedroom for three and a half years. He arranged for planeload after planeload of classified information to go to Stalin, including instructions and materials for making the atomic bomb and yellowcake uranium for that purpose.[47]

Roosevelt's ambitions did not stop with the war. He, together with Stalin, created the catastrophic vehicle for a one-world communist utopia. Roosevelt died before its completion, but it succeeded without him. We are talking about the United Nations, built on the Soviet model. On October 24, 1945, in New York City, the United Nations was formed with the false goal to maintain world peace—in reality a stepping stone for world government.[48] Earl Browder, general secretary of the Communist Party USA (CPUSA) is quoted,[49] "The American Communists worked energetically and tirelessly to lay the foundations for the United Nations."

You may recognize the name Alger Hiss, who was eventually one of the few of the multitude of communists in the federal government to be convicted as a communist spy. It was he who was Roosevelt's executive secretary of the 1944 Dumbarton Oaks Conference, where the UN Charter was drafted. Again, as the director of the State Department's Office of Special Political Affairs, he credentialed everyone who attended the initial San Francisco Conference in 1945, where the UN Charter was finally established. In 1946, he arranged for the Soviets to run UN military activities, the right to run the UN, while the US ran UN financial activities, the right to pay for it.[50]

The Bretton Woods Conference, in July 1944, was as important as the Dumbarton Oaks Conference because it established post–World War II global economic policies, including the International Monetary Fund (IMF) and World Bank group of institutions. This was done by FDR's senior US Treasury Department official, the communist spy, Harry Dexter White,[51] noted above.

Fast-forward to September 1961, our State Department 7277, *Freedom From War, The United States Program for General and Complete Disarmament in a Peaceful World*. It can be obtained with this link. It called for making the United States completely defenseless against communist oppression. These are some of the contents:

> This new program provides for the progressive reduction of the war-making capabilities of nations and the simultaneous *strengthening of international institutions* to settle disputes and maintain the peace. It sets forth a series of comprehensive measures which can and should be taken in order to bring about a world in which there will be freedom from war and security for all states... A strenuous and uninterrupted effort must be made toward the goal of general and complete disarmament; at the same time, it is important that specific measures be put into effect as soon as possible... There is an insepa-

rable relationship between the scaling down of national armaments on the one hand and the building up of international peace-keeping machinery and institutions on the other. Nations are unlikely to shed their means of self-protection in the absence of alternative ways to safeguard their legitimate interests. This can only be achieved through the progressive strengthening of international institutions under the United Nations and by *creating a United Nations Peace Force* to enforce the peace as the disarmament process proceeds... independent states adhering to common standards of justice and international conduct and subjecting the use of force to the rule of law; a world which has achieved general and complete disarmament under effective international control; and a world in which adjustment to change takes place in accordance with the principles of the United Nations.

The disbanding of all national armed forces and the prohibition of their reestablishment in any form whatsoever other than those required to preserve internal order and for contributions to a United Nations Peace Force; [d]isarmament must proceed as rapidly as possible, until it is completed, in stages containing balanced, phased, and safeguarded measures.

States would give advance notification of space vehicle and missile launchings... [This includes] dismantling or the conversion to peaceful uses of certain military bases and facilities wherever located... *The manufacture of armaments would be prohibited* except for those of agreed types and quantities to be used by the U.N. Peace Force and those required to maintain internal order. All other armaments would be destroyed or converted to peaceful purposes. (Emphasis mine)

The following are but a few of the many advantages that the communists expected to realize from the creation of the UN:[52]

- Economic assistance through the vast array of UN agencies
- Enormous potential for expansion of espionage, subversion, and terrorism through the diplomatic immunity offered to UN officials
- Use of the UN podium for communist propaganda purposes

- Use of UN diplomatic and propaganda machinery to attack and under-
mine anticommunist countries and to support procommunist regimes
and organizations
- Transfer of tremendous sums of money from the American producers to
corrupt, collectivist projects and potentates throughout the world
- Steady erosion of US sovereignty through a myriad of UN treaties and
agreements
- Depletion and weakening of US military resources in UN operations
worldwide
- Gradual subordination of US military command to international authority (UN, NATO, SEATO, CENTO, OAS, etc.).

WHAT IS SUSTAINABLE DEVELOPMENT?

A major emphasis of the United Nations is Sustainable Development, known as
Agenda 21, later amended to the Sustainable Development Group,[53] which is
a plan to create a one-world Communist government by attacking civilization.
Remember Karl Marx: everything that exists deserves to perish.

Agenda 21 is a master plan to disembowel America. Since I attended the
Freedom Action Conference in 2010, sponsored by Tom DeWeese[54], I had been
active in lecturing and developing a group of patriots to call attention to this
menace to life in America. Tom DeWeese is a truth seeker, and he devoted his life
to saving America. He is still sounding the alarm after half a century. His organization is the American Policy Center. Tom wrote a novel, *Erase*,[55] in 2016, which
depicts the way that life in America will fall apart if Sustainable Development
succeeds.

The Wuhan virus pandemic that was unleashed by China and has com-
promised virtually every nation on earth was hidden and allowed to proliferate
by the World Health Organization (WHO) colluding with China. This has been
documented. The WHO is part of the United Nations Sustainable Development
Group.

We cannot cover this sufficiently here. I am merely alerting you to the basic
parameters. Many communities across America are already "Sustainable Development" communities, having been sold on the Agenda 21 concept. If you google
"Agenda 21 map," you will see many maps like the one we had then. Dr. Michael
Coffman and his research team tracked this projection by using GPS coordinates
and whatever information they could find.[56] They printed this out on a four-by-
six board and delivered it to the US Senate at 3:00 p.m. when the Senate was to

vote, an hour later, on the USA Wildlands Project. This map caused the vote to be tabled—permanently, so it appears.

It depicts a United States covered in red and yellow. Hard to detect are some clustered black dots, around the New York City area for example. The dots are the only places in America where humans may live. The red areas are reserved for grizzly bears and other fauna. The yellow areas are where authorized humans may trespass to look after the red areas. Families are clustered in high-rise structures, living quarters less than a two-stall garage.

The vice president of the World Socialist Party directed the United Nations World Commission on Environment and Development.[57] This Agenda 21 effort was initiated by the United Nations Earth Summit—initially developed in 1970—at its conference in Rio de Janeiro, attended by multilateral organizations and world governments in 1992.[58] This came to be called *Our Common Future*. That meeting was conducted by Maurice Strong, formerly an entrepreneur in the Alberta oil patch, and president of Power Corporation of Canada until 1966. By the early 1970s, he was secretary-general of the United Nations Conference on the Human Environment. He had already stated in 1990:

> What if a small group of world leaders were to conclude that the risk to the earth comes from the actions of rich countries? In order to save the planet, this group decided isn't the only hope for the planet that the industrial civilizations collapse? Isn't it our responsibility to bring this about?[59]

Its purpose was literally to close the world's resources to human beings, under the guise of pursuing "sustainable development." At least 178 countries bought into this program. This became the official policy of the United States in both Republican and Democrat administrations. President Bill Clinton created the President's Council on Sustainable Development in 1993. Its goal is to abolish private property, create a collective society, deny individual rights, and drastically reduce the human population. The Communist government will dictate everything: what food you may have; what kind of work you will do; how many children you may have, if any; what type of education will be afforded the children; and whether you will be kept alive at all. For example, the late Stephen Hawking—a wise, creative scientist—would have been euthanized since he had Lou Gehrig's disease. As I have said, the communist mind considers us the equivalent to cows and chickens, morally disposable.

The 1996 report of the President's Council on Sustainable Development was endorsed when Bill Clinton was president:

> Sustainable Communities encourage people to work together to create healthy communities where natural resources and historic resources are preserved, jobs are available, sprawl is contained, neighborhoods are secure, education is lifelong, transportation and health care are accessible, and all citizens have opportunities to improve the quality of their lives.[60]

Of course, such a plan is *not* sustaining. Being compacted together more tightly than the worst slum of Bombay is extremely unhealthy. Education is government "retraining." Work is enslavement. Our experience with "projects" is that they spawn crime. There would be no quality of life whatsoever.

The map I mentioned was the brainstorm of Dave Foreman's The Wildlands Project and was quickly adopted by Agenda 21. He had been a lobbyist for the Sierra Club. He started with Earth First! in 1983, on the plan that "we must create wilderness in large regions: move out the cars and civilized people, dismantle the roads and dams." This land management policy was defined by Dr. Reed F. Noss in 1992:

> At least half of the land area of the 48 conterminous states should be encompassed in core reserves and inner corridor zones (essentially extensions of core reserves) within the next few decades... Nonetheless, half of a region in wilderness is a reasonable guess of what it will take to restore viable populations of large carnivores...assuming that most of the other 50 percent is managed intelligently as buffer zone. Eventually, a wilderness network would dominate a region...with human habitations being the islands. The native ecosystem and the collective needs of non-human species must take precedence over the needs and desires of humans.[61]

The Sierra Club has been entrusted with arranging this, with one hundred housing units per acre of 1,000 square feet each on fourteen floors, with supplies at the base so no transportation is required. The red areas comprise 50 percent of the landmass in the lower forty-eight states. The Sustainable Development goal is to exterminate at least one billion human beings on earth, so the places for humans need not be that extensive.

Among prominent Americans, Bill Gates has many ideas for exterminating human beings: sterilization programs; devious, toxic vaccination programs; "death panels"; and even dumping millions of tons of chalk dust into the atmosphere to dim the sun.[62]

The federal Congress passed two bills, most recently in February 2019, HR 1111: Department of Peacebuilding Act of 2019,[63] essentially awarding the United Nations power to impose Sustainable Development in America. It must be understood that *peace* means, in Marxist language, the annihilation of opposition—everything that exists deserves to perish. This entire bill is "politi-speak." Here are several quotations:

Sec. 2. Findings. Congress finds the following:

(10) The United Nations recognizes that promotion of peace is vital for the full enjoyment of all human rights and the *United Nations Declaration on the Right of Peoples to Peace* mandates that preservation of the right to peace is a fundamental obligation of each country. In 1999, the United Nations adopted a Programme of Action on a Culture of Peace… The United Nations declared the years 2001 through 2010 an International Decade for a Culture of Peace and Non-Violence for the Children of the World, and the United Nations supports a culture of peace. In 2015, *the UN adopted 17 sustainable development goals,* including promotion of peaceful and inclusive societies.

(11) Peacebuilding is defined by the United Nations as a range of measures targeted to reduce the risk of lapsing or relapsing into conflict by strengthening national capacities at all levels for conflict management and to *lay the foundations for sustainable peace and development.*

(12) In 2000, the Earth Charter Commission released the Earth Charter, an international declaration of fundamental values and principles created to build a just, sustainable, and peaceful global society. (Emphasis mine)

Sustainable Development/Agenda 21 is depicted as three interlocking *E* circles:

- *Environment.* Eliminating private property and making earth unsustainable for most human beings. Dave Foreman actually envisioned having only 100,000 humans on earth.
- *Equity.* Karl Marx called it social justice instead of "equal justice;" the "common good" of the police state. There are open borders and the ability for anyone to use anyone's resources.
- *Economy.* World government seizing power over the engines of wealth. This was the goal of the North Atlantic Free Trade Agreement (NAFTA), which Donald Trump recently replaced with the USMCA trade arrangement.

Of course this seems like some virtual reality horror movie. One would think such a fantasy hasn't a chance. But as I pointed out above, those who are not psychopaths cannot get their heads around the communist mind, which is analogous to psychopathy. You understand the Rothschild formula: central banking is a communist plank. They are "the elites." Communists have already murdered at least one hundred million innocent citizens in the last century. According to Marx, everything that exists deserves to perish. "It is not wrong to cheat, lie, violate oaths or even destroy human life if it is for a good cause."[64]

We need to wake up those communities dreaming of Sustainable Development. Remember, 178 countries have signed on. We have seen what is already in place. Like the image of the frog in the tepid water, we haven't seen what's coming. Does your city have a bicycle lane? That's an Agenda 21 bicycle lane. There is a great deal to learn, but doing it justice would be the tail wagging the dog. If we simply consider the goal and the plans that are gradually being implemented, we pick the brains of many smart, diabolical people dedicated to wrecking America and making Karl Marx proud.

WHAT ABOUT OUR INCOME TAX?

The colonists revolted against the most powerful army in the world, in large part because they had to work "two weeks out of the year" to pay taxes to King George, to which they had not consented. Americans work, on average, "six months out of the year," to feed the voracious appetite of our king, the federal government. As I write, the Democratic platform advocates a greatly *increased* income tax. Marx understood that by crippling and demoralizing a population, they will likely accept anything you offer them. There is a story about Stalin standing in front of the Politburo with a live chicken, plucking it of all its feathers, dropping it to the ground, and throwing down some corn, which the chicken "gratefully" pecked at. The moral, he explained, is to pluck the people, and then they will appreciate whatever you offer them. Consider yourself getting plucked.

Actually, income tax is illegal. The attorney, Tom Cryer,[65] did research to show his law partner that he was obliged to pay income tax. After two years of research, he also refused to file. Well, the government destroyed his practice. He lost all his belongings and was jailed. But in 2007, he convinced a jury that his right to earn a living is not taxable by the US government, and he was acquitted. Thereafter, he dedicated his life to exposing the truth about the unconstitutional tax laws, restoring our constitutional republic.

Before you also refuse to file, however, consider the fate of American libertarian, Allen Schiff,[66] who argued publicly that the income tax in the United States is unconstitutional and, therefore, illegal. However, in his case, judges in several civil and criminal cases ruled against him. He was serving a 162-month prison term beginning in 2006. At eighty-seven years of age, he died while shackled to a hospital bed in a guarded room. The referenced article concludes:

> Events like this will keep happening until people put a stop to it. The life and death of Irwin Schiff show us how far government agents are willing to go to enforce their edicts upon those whom they have subjugated. There are only three options when dealing with government agents: obey, be victimized, or defend yourself. The question now is, how far will we go to prevent such atrocities from happening in the future?

The new Congress, already in 1798, had managed to corrupt the First Amendment with four Alien and Sedition Acts. The Federalist Party of John Adams and Alexander Hamilton was in power, warring with the Democratic-Republican Party of Thomas Jefferson and James Madison. These acts outlawed "false, scandalous and malicious writing against Congress or the President," as well as "opposing any measure or measures of the government." Well, Jefferson and Madison simply nullified these acts. Jefferson wrote,

> The several states who formed that instrument [the Constitution], being sovereign and independent, have the unquestionable right to

judge of its infraction; and that a nullification, by those [states], of all unauthorized acts…is the rightful remedy[67]

The federal income tax also violates the Constitution, and much of what the federal government is doing is unconstitutional. Thomas Woods has also proposed a rightful remedy. His book is *Nullification*.[68] The federal government makes no money. It takes away the citizens' money. So the states should simply keep their money and dole it out to the federal government for those purposes that are authorized in the contract, the Constitution. Only individual human beings have unalienable rights (more on this below). We *consent* to lend (never to give away) some of our rights to the government, which is in place merely to maintain order in society. We don't consent to the government violating our contract with them. The Tenth Amendment states, "The powers not delegated to the United States by the Constitution, nor prohibited by it to the States, are reserved to the States respectively, or to the people."

The devil is always in the details. Currently, the federal government receives all the money and buys the states off with federal grants. Checking the federal government would likely require the Convention of States.

ARE WE DESTINED FOR REVOLUTION?

Porter Stansbury is an economist and investment guru. He has been warning about a coming debt-fueled revolution that he refers to as a Jubilee, from the book of Leviticus, chapter 25, and he even wrote a book about it, *The American Jubilee*.[69] This notion from Leviticus has been taken up by others as well. A Jubilee is essentially the redistribution of wealth every fifty years. Stansbury recalls other quasi-Jubilees in history.

He marks the Great Depression as a Jubilee, when President Roosevelt took everyone's gold and eliminated the "gold clause" in all financial instruments. The fiat money that replaced it cost people 69 percent of their wealth. Stansbury fast-forwards to the 1960s, with the Black Panthers, union and campus violence, assassinations, and uprisings in more than 120 cities, requiring the National Guard. His statistics tells him that this coming Jubilee will be much worse.

He considers this to be inevitable when the interest on debt grows faster than the economy and can't be managed in normal ways. "Sooner or later, debt begins to grow geometrically, far faster than income. And then… it simply can't be managed. That's when the crisis hits."[70]

He doesn't close his eyes to the national debt, but that isn't his focus. It is US total debt, particularly the debt of those with the least income. Their debt stands at 250 percent of income—$13 trillion in 2017. Student loan debt is more than 10 percent of this total, and these frequently unemployed graduates have no collateral and, at best, insufficient income. What truck dealership would give a young man a new truck with the understanding that he can make money with it and pay for it sometime in the future?"The federal government is free to print all the money it needs to pay government debts. Private households are different. The only ways out of private debt are to pay it, to default, or to have it forgiven with a Debt Jubilee."[71]

A century ago, one in thirty high school graduates went to college. Then they actually got an education. Now in spite of spiraling college costs, nearly half attempt it—owing to marketing—and are subjected to a Marxist brainwashing instead. Yet 5 percent of independent business owners in America never even got a GED, while 56 percent do not have a college degree.[72] Dr. Keith Ablow[73] sees other dynamics in play:

> According to a new study by the Pew Research Center, men and women between the ages of 18 and 34 are now more likely to be living with their parents than living on their own or in any other living situation [such as sharing an apartment]… I think the trend is a calamity that reflects the erosion of real self-determination in young people, fueled by their unfounded, rocketing, wafer-thin self-esteem.

> We have created a nation filled with too many perpetual children— Peter and Patty Pans—who were brought up getting trophies for participating in sports, instead of winning, protected from the supposed horrors of being ranked by grades and scores and sold corrosive messages by the likes of Barack Obama and Hilary Clinton that everyone deserves every kind of support, regardless of the level of education they have or the work they put forward. We have hobbled a generation, or two.

> These Peter and Patty Pans are so addicted to drugs like Facebook and Twitter that blow up their egos and make them into fake celebrities that they can feel pretty good for a long time, even when their lives are going pretty badly… This is Barack Obama's America. A super-strong central government, inhaling more and more power,

while our young people are hobbled and inhaling more and more weed. I see the fallout in my psychiatry office.

So the debt crisis raised by Stansbury is complex, but it is real. These millennials and Generation Z youth are the most violent segment of the population. Stansbury thinks the riots showcase hopelessness. These people have no hope of being able to afford the American dream. What Dr. Ablow sees is similar—demoralization. Antifa and the Marxist Black Lives Matter well organized anarchists are destroying businesses and burning down sections of Democratic cites as I write, with the de facto acquiescence of their elected officials. More violence is threatened should they not get their way.

Putting on my psychology hat, fear and anger are two sides of the same coin: flight and fight, responses to threat. Stansbury links this to the opioid crisis, and I would add the homelessness crisis on the West Coast and elsewhere. It doesn't help that even prominent Democratic politicians have been encouraging physical violence against Republicans.

Of course, politicians can't let a crisis go to waste, so the Democrat Party is detouring hard left, offering free college tuition and free everything—a debt Jubilee, as I write. Recall the Tytler cycle: "The majority always votes for the candidates who promise the most benefits from the public treasury." Bernie Sanders, the honest Communist, had been dumped once again, but he notes that his tenants that once were considered radical are now in the Democratic mainstream.

They can't risk honesty. Congress had a new starlet, Alexandria Ocasio-Cortez, and she talks the party line in spades. I think it's not a coincidence that she was a bartender, picking up the chatter of the millennials in the bar. The "dumbing down" of public education, which we are about to examine, leaves these millennials insecure and ill-prepared to take personal responsibility for themselves, so they take cover in communism.

WHAT IS THE REPORT FROM IRON MOUNTAIN?

This information was "leaked" by John Doe, one of fifteen handpicked and highly esteemed experts from a selected variety of disciplines. They began meeting in earnest in 1963 and completed their work in 1965. The report was transcribed, with an introduction by Leonard C. Lewin, in 1966.[74] These fifteen experts met first and last at Iron Mountain but deliberately at different unsuspecting locations bimonthly thereafter. They never kept minutes of their meetings. Although beginning with many different perceptions, in the end, they had unanimous consensus.

Though John Doe felt compelled to share the information, he agreed with all the conclusions.

The starting premise was to avoid any moral or cultural considerations in their "pure" deliberations. Even in their day, they were able to develop a computer model that factored, for an example, what effect a moon landing by US astronauts would have on an election day in Sweden.[75]

The root topic they deliberated was the issue of war and whether peace could be sustainable. They planned a transformation of American society in a world totally unprepared for it. They argued that nations relate to other nations on the basis of the risk of warfare—life and death— and this gives nations their identity and unity. Their premise was that war is the foundation of society and that it is doubtful if anything can replace it without eliminating nationhood and destabilizing society. Recall the Rothschild formula: "War is the ultimate discipline of any government and governments cannot survive without meeting this challenge."

The war industry amounts to one-tenth of the world's economy, and the United States tops all other nations in the proportion of its GNP devoted to it. This "wasteful" additional expenditure, being outside the normal economic system, is thus an adjustable tool needed to stabilize politics and economics. They concluded that, were peace to actually be established, specialized job skills could not simply be reapplied elsewhere, and there would be no call for them. There would be housing relocations and much more.

But even considering the high cost of all these dislocations, they could never cover the 10 percent of "wasteful spending" considered necessary to maintain society. He stated that "it is the incorrect assumption that war, as an institution, is subordinate to the social systems it is believed to serve." Instead, war itself is the basic social system, "which has governed most human societies of record."[76]

Various substitutes for war are explored and found inadequate. War, as was said, serves economic stability— that is, it is a way to organize and *keep governments in power*, preserve sufficient poverty, *restrain antisocial elements*, diminish overpopulation, etc. War stimulates scientific research as well. "[The first function of war] is an essential *element of social control*; the second is *the basic mechanism for adapting individual human drives to the needs of society*"[77] (emphasis mine).

I challenge this philosophy. Humans, joining together in groups, require some form of organization to maintain order and protect the rights of the individuals. Therefore, one or more members of the group acquire the role of managers, called the government. The American constitutional republic finally clarified that un*alien*able rights reside solely in the individuals who have the un*alien*able rights by their nature. Therefore, the managers only draw upon the rights *shared* by the *consenting* individuals in the group who never give up their rights: "That to secure these rights, Governments are instituted among Men, deriving their *just* powers from the *consent* of the governed." The product cannot dominate its creator.

And then only *just* powers apply. The people could not share what they don't have. So governments are not empowered to "restrain antisocial elements." That is, the people have every right to protest and nullify abuses. Society is individual people joined together to improve the rights of the individuals. They are not the slaves of society. There is no just mechanism for "adapting individual human drives to the needs of society." The individuals in the group are not the communists' herd of cows and flock of chickens.

So from here on, the wisdom of these eminent paragons goes astray. I do not question that their IQs were significantly above my own. But I am a psychologist-neuropsychologist. There is this saying that goes, "If everyone is thinking the same way, somebody isn't thinking." This egotistic fifteen-member club became utterly inbred for over two and a half years without any check and balance. For them, human beings are digits in a computer model. Human beings, for them, have no intrinsic nature or un*alien*able rights.

Neuropsychology shows how this incestuous mental inbreeding establishes "templates" in the brains of each, which unconsciously steer and shape viewpoints and do, indeed, over time, create unanimous but skewed consensus. There is the saying that goes, "That idea is so ridiculous only an intellectual could have thought it."

So they propose a mandatory draft into the Army for the "unemployables." In fact, the Army rejects many willing recruits and takes only those with solid qualifications. They think the only reason to allow highway speeds above 20 mph is to kill off more people.[78] I have no claim to be an art expert, but I can't grasp how Shakespeare's, Beethoven's, Bach's music, Goya's, Dante's, and Rembrandt's works were only valuable art to the extent that they advocated war in their art.

They are of the opinion that "a sophisticated form of slavery may be an absolute prerequisite for social control in a world at peace." They note a universal requirement where "procreation [should] be limited to the products of artificial insemination" to control population levels and allow eugenic management. They do acknowledge that "deliberate environmental poisoning could be implemented in a politically correct manner" and that "it is more probable, in our judgment, that such a threat will have to be invented." They even call into question the "unlimited search for knowledge," stating that "a substantial minority" feels that "search be circumscribed in any case."

I bring up the *Report from Iron Mountain* for two reasons. The first is to show that brain trusts are out there that would degrade us to expendable slaves in their macabre fantasy. The second is to speculate about what other such clandestine elite cabals may be lurking out there today, devising ways to destroy all vestiges of our civilization. This group was aligned with the Rothschild formula, the necessity of endless wars or an equivalent degradation of civilization. That "equivalent degradation" has been concocted by the Club of Rome.

WHAT IS THE CLUB OF ROME?

This elite group first met in 1965 at David Rockefeller's estate in Bellagio, Italy. It is still alive and well. It officially got this name under the direction of Aurelio Peccei in 1968. An alternative to endless wars, promoted by the bankers and their Rothschild formula, would be to create an equivalent threat. From his 1970 Club of Rome Project manuscript, we find the plan to create such a threat, turning mankind against itself:

> In searching for a new enemy to unite us, we came up with the idea that pollution, the threat of global warming, water shortages, famine and the like would fit the bill… All these dangers are caused by human intervention… and thus the real enemy, then, is humanity itself… [We] believe humanity requires a common motivation, namely a common adversary in order to realize world government. It does not matter if this common enemy is a real one or… one invented for the purpose.[79]

We see how these endeavors are interconnected. These ideas were presented both in Moscow and Rio de Janeiro in 1971. The publication, *Limits to Growth*, in 1972 called for population reduction and "consigning billions to poverty," in the words of Yale economist Henry Wallich.[80] In 2012, another publication by the Club of Rome was *2052: A Global Forecast for the Next Forty Years*[81] to follow the 1972 book. This book backs away from blatant doomsday alarmism and attempts to predict trends. It is deceptive in now predicting an eventual *decline* in world population. The secret is, well, secret. The state must become more involved. It is noted that the internet will expand knowledge but not alter behavior, so there must be a "greenkeeping force" like the blue berets peacekeeping forces of today. Many names among the members and supporters of the Club of Rome are well known. Among them are the ubiquitous George Soros, well known for making his millions managing a hedge fund and manipulating currencies. He bankrupted England and other countries and has been sowing chaos throughout his life, funding such disruptive organizations recently as Black Lives Matter and Antifa and is proud that he owns the Democratic Party in the United States. Another is Maurice Strong (Sustainable Development/Agenda 21) and, of course, Al Gore.

In fact, Al Gore led the US delegations to the Earth Summit and Kyoto Protocol and chaired a meeting of the full Club of Rome held in Washington, DC, in 1997. Global warming, promoted by Gore's film, *An Inconvenient Truth*, proved not to be "inconvenient" for Gore, who used it to accumulate $175,000,000 along the way.

In 2005, Sen. Jim Inhofe confronted the global warming hoax on the Senate floor.[82] Since then, many scientists who are actually climatologists have debunked this costly hoax (i.e., costing $1.75 *trillion* annually). Among the more recent is John Casey, a consultant at NASA Headquarters and president of the Space and Science Research Corporation. In his book, *Dark Winter*[83], he explains, in his relational cycle theory, with careful mapping of the history of the gentle waxing and waning of the sun, that we are actually in a phase of solar hibernation and headed for a dangerous *cold* period. He is supported by other scientists who note that the sun primarily provides our heat. This is not—pardon the pun—rocket science. He debunks the climate change hysteria.

Another source of information, in case this is not already obvious, is *The Politically Incorrect Guide to Climate Change* by Marc Morano[84]. He began with Senator Inhofe, and he has exhausted this topic in 322 readable pages, followed by 72 pages of references. Of course, whoever dares to expose this threat to our civilization will be blackballed.

WHAT ABOUT ISLAM IN AMERICA?

I have chosen only to glance at the Islamic threat to Christianity in America. It is clearly tangential to our topic and a dire threat to Christian civilization on its own. As I write, communism and the one-world-government agenda are the more pressing threats, at least on the surface.

According to the Pew Research Center, there are at least 1.8 billion Muslims in the world.[85] Books have been written about this threat, if the reader desires to learn more. One is by Brigitte Gabriel in *They Must Be Stopped: Why We Must Defeat Radical Islam and How We Can Do It*.[86] According to Brigitte Gabriel,[87] radical jihadists are estimated to be between 15 to 25 percent of Islamists, based on all intelligence services. "You're looking at 180 million to 300 million people dedicated to the destruction of Western civilization."

The previous American president, Obama, a Muslim himself, encouraged Muslim immigration to America. As a cynic, I assume this was to degrade the Christian character of America more rapidly. He decreed that America is not a Christian nation. The Islamic presence in localities in America is already such that areas are effectively off-limits to non-Muslims. Detroit—notably the suburb, Dearborn—and Minneapolis are sufficiently Muslim as to have elected their representatives to the federal Congress, Rep. Rashida Tlaib (D-MI) and Rep. Ilhan Omar (D-MN). They have already made their mark, disrupting "business as usual" in Congress.

WHO WAS MUHAMMAD?

He was born in 570 AD and began receiving his "revelations" at age 40.[88] In his travels, he had learned about the Jewish and Christian beliefs, and these were intertwined in his teachings. I merely want to point out that he taught that the goal of Islam is to conquer, kill, or enslave Christians and to use any means to trick them in order to overcome them. The word *al-Taqiyya* means "to conceal or disguise one's beliefs, convictions, ideas, feelings, opinions, and strategies."[89] The word *makara* means "cunning, guile, or deceit."[90]

ARE ISLAMIC TEACHINGS ABHORRENT?

These facts, among many others, are commonly known. Muslim women have, on average, eight children. Since first generation marriages are encouraged, the result is many genetically defective Muslims. Husbands are tacitly encouraged to beat their wives. Women have clitoral "circumcision." Sharia law—tacitly practiced in some areas in America—is barbaric, archaic law. Winston Churchill characterized Mohammedanism thus: "The influence of the religion paralyzes the social development of those who follow it. No stronger retrograde force exists in the world."[91]

DO OTHER NATIONS HAVE PROBLEMS WITH ISLAM?

As an example, in Sweden, Muslim children have told their classmates they will cut their throats while showing them beheadings on their mobile phones.[92] If a cashier at the store is not veiled, Muslims take what they want without paying, call the cashier a "Swedish whore," and spit on her. One in four women is afraid to leave home in fear of being accosted and raped, and Swedish police in numerous cities have advised women to not walk alone at night and to go home early.[93] Since the 1990s, one-third of the three hundred Swedish Muslims who joined ISIS in Syria and Iraq came from the city of Gothenburg, a core of Wahhabism, a virulent form of Islam.

CHAPTER 9

WHAT ABOUT PUBLIC EDUCATION?

THE SIGNIFICANCE OF PUBLIC EDUCATION

It has been said that "the hand that rocks the cradle rules the world." Those who socialize and train the younger generation create the future. Throughout human history this has been the job of parents, preparing their offspring for fulfilling lives. To support parents, our founding fathers saw the need for schools to instill Christian virtue, as well as teaching readin', writin', and 'rithmetic. They were convinced that this experiment in governance "as the first free people of modern times" can only work if We the People continue to practice responsible Christian virtue and are also knowledgeable and discerning.

In 1787, the very year the Constitution was written and approved by Congress, that same Congress passed the famous Northwest Ordinance. In it they emphasized the essential need "to teach religion and morality in the schools." This included the three important subjects:[94]

1. *Religion*, which might be defined as a "fundamental system of beliefs concerning man's origin and relationship to the cosmic universe as well as his relationship to his fellowmen";

2. *Morality*, which may be described as a "standard of behavior distinguishing right from wrong";

3. *Knowledge*, which is "an intellectual awareness and understanding of established facts relating to any field of human experience or inquiry."

THE TRANSFORMATION IN PUBLIC EDUCATION

John Adams, in 1765, could boast about America:

> A native of America who cannot read and write is as rare…as a comet
> or an earthquake. It has been observed that we are all of us lawyers,
> divines, politicians, and philosophers. And I have good authorities
> to say that all candid foreigners who have passed through this coun-
> try…will allow that they have never seen so much knowledge and
> civility among the common people in any part of the world… Lib-
> erty cannot be preserved without a general knowledge among the
> people.[95]

The "virtue" that is the focus of public education today, however, is not "Do unto
others as you would have them do unto you," "Honor thy father and mother," "A
penny saved is a penny earned." It is the antithesis of Christian virtue. As we shall
see, it is the progressive agenda to deliberately dumb down future citizens and
program them to be dependent on a Communist world government.

The hand that rocks the cradle today, to a large extent, is the (unconstitutional) federal Department of Education. Rather than supporting parents, our
society has allowed it to capture that role. In fact, it has flip-flopped the socialization our founders envisioned. Today children only learn what they derisively
"need to know," not how to be independent thinkers, so they can get a job and
become dependent cogs in society's wheel. They also learn a lot of things their
parents don't want them to.

To survive and thrive, all living things must be free to develop their innate
capabilities—to do things the right way according to their nature. A good example could be wolves. They are marvelous hunters. In the summers, they are pretty
much on their own, but in winter, when they need to feed on larger animals, they
band together. But they are still independent individuals. Some are the chasers,
and some, the catchers, each doing what it does best. But if wolf pups are penned
and kept from expressing their natural potential, they never convert to become
authentic wolves. Placed in the wild as adults, they are utterly helpless and will
always depend on their masters to feed them.

THE CORROSION OF PUBLIC EDUCATION

Seventy-five percent of American taxpayer dollars never get past the bureaucracy to actually educate the children.[96] Among the twenty-one tier-1 nations, America ranks dead last in the quality of its public education by at least one statistic, even though more of these taxpayer dollars are spent on it by Americans than are spent by almost every other country. Tragically, 20 percent of dropouts in high school have been the *gifted* students.[97] They just don't fit in. Franklin D. Roosevelt is quoted to have said, "In politics, nothing happens by accident. If it happens, you can bet it was planned that way." Benjamin Franklin said, "We have given you a Republic. It remains to be seen if you will be able to retain it." How could this betrayal have eluded us for a century?

John Rockefeller, the communist-leaning oil magnate, was represented at Jekyll Island. He was also a principal agent in undermining education. In 1902, he established the General Education Board, which morphed into the federal Department of Education. This is a quote from its first newsletter:

> In our dreams we have limitless resources and the people yield themselves with perfect docility to our molding hands. The present education conventions fade from their minds, and unhampered by tradition, we work our own good will upon a grateful and responsive rural folk. We shall not try to make these people or any of their children into philosophers or men of learning, or men of science. We have not to raise up from among them authors, editors, poets, or men of letters. We shall not search for embryo great artists, painters, musicians, nor lawyers, doctors, preachers, politicians, statesmen, of whom we have an ample supply. The task we set before ourselves is very simple as well as a very beautiful one, to train these people as we find them to a perfectly ideal life just where they are. So we will organize our children and teach them to do in a perfect way the things their fathers and mothers are doing in an imperfect way, in the homes, in the shops, and on the farm.[98]

Andrew Carnegie, the steel magnate, funded the Carnegie Foundation for the Advancement of Teaching (CFAT) in 1905, fronted as a pension fund for college professors but run by progressives. It has morphed, through Democratic and Republican administrations, to become the primary think tank for government policy on education. CFAT and their proxies in federal and state governments co-control educational research, and their "findings" are consistently taken as gospel. Its members head the most prestigious review boards, committees, and task forces on education matters.[99]

At the 1914 annual meeting in Saint Paul, Minnesota, a resolution was passed by the National Education Association (NEA). An excerpt stated,

> We view with alarm the activity of the Carnegie and Rockefeller Foundations—agencies not in any way responsible to the people—in their efforts to control the policies of our State educational institutions, to fashion after their conception and to standardize our courses of study, and to surround the institutions with conditions which menace true academic freedom and defeat the primary purpose of democracy as heretofore preserved inviolate in our common schools, normal schools, and universities.[100]

John Dewey (1859–1952), a Fabian communist at Columbia University, is considered the "father of modern, progressive education." He got his backing from Rockefeller and Carnegie. He took his cue from Horace Mann, who in turn copied the educational model developed in Prussia for the purpose of developing unthinking soldiers who would blindly follow orders.[101]

> The Nazi leadership appreciated the difficulty of indoctrinating the older generation…They were all the more determined to mold the new generation along Nazi lines. As the leader of the Nazi Teacher's League, Hans Schemm, put it: "Those who have the youth on their side control the future."

This project was developed where Dewey taught, at the experimental school at Columbia University:

> Unblushing materialism finds its crowning triumph in the theory of the modern school. In the whole plan there is not a spiritual thought, not an idea that rises above the need of finding money for the pocket and food for the belly. It is a matter of instant inquiry, for very sober consideration, whether the General Education Board, indeed, may not with the immense funds at its disposal *be able to shape to its will practically all the institutions in which the youth of the country are trained.*[102] (Emphasis mine)

Dewey's focus was the *socialization* of the child as the appropriate main thrust of all formal education. To Dewey, subject matter was entirely secondary. Dewey stated in 1899: "Children who know how to think for themselves spoil the harmony of the collective society which is coming where everyone is interdependent."[103] Years later, Vladimir Lenin put it this way: "Give me four years to teach children and the seed I have sown will never be uprooted."[104].

B. K. Eakman explains that people in high places have long been aware that their initiatives would not win popular approval if the public had the facts, discovering, among other things, that "the school" is now a clinic or a laboratory and that the term *cognitive learning* is a belief system. They would also learn that these changes in definition permit certain learning experiences to be passed off as hard subject matter when, in fact, they are attitude manipulation exercises and thought control experiments created by psychologists.[105]

PUBLIC EDUCATION IN UNIVERSITIES

The stoned hippies came from Woodstock to become the professors in the universities. Virtually every professor in a university in America is communist leaning and anyone who is not must stay under cover.[106] So the malleable students are in jeopardy, and polls state that as many as 70 percent of millennials and Generation Z youth desire socialism.[107] I would argue that you know more about it than they do, if only in reading this book. Of course, they are the products of John Dewey's "great leap forward."

UNIVERSAL DISINFORMATION IN PUBLIC EDUCATION

In spite of identifying this travesty, we discover the Pied Piper still leading the children astray, monopolizing disinformation in America's high schools and universities and programming the youth to adopt communism. Our founders must be rolling in their graves. The Pied Piper is Howard Zinn, a deceased Harvard professor. This is about one of his believers and Zinn's book, *A People's History of the United States,* first published in 1980:[108]

> In Tacoma, Washington, during the pre-dawn hours of Saturday, July 13, 2019, 69-year-old Willem Van Spronsen attempted to light a propane tank on fire, torched a vehicle, and threw "incendiary devices" at the outbuildings for the Northwest Detention Center and

vehicles in the parking lot. When confronted by police, he pointed his rifle at them and was shot dead before he could fire... Van Spronsen was a member of Antifa (short for "anti-fascist"), a masked domestic "protest" group...

After rambling on about "the forces of evil," "concentration camps for folks deemed lesser," and the ineffectiveness of "the centrist" reformer, [his] manifesto told readers, "see howard zinn, 'a people's history of the united states.'" The book would provide,he alleged, support for Van Spronsen's assertion that "we are living in visible fascism ascendant."

Zinn's book, billed as a textbook, has sold more than 2.6 million copies since it was first published. It is frequently bought with public tax dollars and used in public school classrooms, then and now. His book does not deserve to have "history" in the title. Zinn's book is filled with lies, omissions, distortions of evidence, logical fallacies, and plagiarism from dubious sources.[109]

High school students taking Advanced Placement US History are likely to use the book, especially since the AP guidelines have been rewritten to conform to the Zinn vision of history. Teachers can even download lesson plans from the Zinn Education Project. Beyond AP classes, Zinn's book is used in college education programs and teaching workshops. Today, Zinn's view has become accepted in classrooms across the country, a consequence of its popularity, as well as its match with ideas commonly taught in teacher education classes, which feature some of the farthest-left professors in the academe, according to surveys. The work teaches students to view history through the lens of toxic identity politics. The enslavement of blacks and women, exploitation and murder of workers and Indians, imprisonment of political dissidents, and America's World War II treatment of Japanese-born Americans all get prime billing. For Zinn, America is irredeemable and merits comparisons to Nazi Germany.

The Zinn Education Project is my compass in a sea of corporate textbooks, packaged common core curriculum and standardized testing. My entire curriculum is based on lessons that can be found on the Zinn Education Project." (Chris Buehler, high school social studies teacher, Portland, Oregon)[110]

Mary Grabar has published a book in 2019, entitled *Debunking Howard Zinn: Exposing the Fake History That Turned a Generation Against America*.[111]

A sequel to Howard Zinn is the 1619 Project developed by the New York Times Magazine in 2019, which claims that slavery is the center of America's history. It has already infiltrated public education, although President Trump, as I write, has forbidden these anti-American teachings in public education, offering instead the 1776 Project of the black activist, Bob Woodson. Scholars have been quick to discredit the 1619 Project, and I have shown that the opposite is true. Our founders were the champions of slaves. This is one article that notes how specious this is.[112]

> "So wrong in so many ways" is how Gordon Wood, the Pulitzer Prize-winning historian of the American Revolution, character-ized the New York Times's "1619 Project." James McPherson, dean of Civil War historians and another Pulitzer winner, said the Times presented an "unbalanced, one-sided account" that "left most of the history out." Even more surprising than the criticism from these generally liberal historians was where the interviews appeared: on the World Socialist Web Site, run by the Trotskyist Socialist Equality Party....
>
> A September essay for the World Socialist Web Site called the project a "racialist falsification" of history. That didn't get much attention, but in November the interviews with the historians went viral. "I wish my books would have this kind of reaction," Mr. Wood says in an email. "It still strikes me as amazing why the NY Times would put its authority behind a project that has such weak scholarly support." He adds that fellow historians have privately expressed their agreement. ... Joseph Kishore, the Socialist Equality Party's national secretary, says the "1619 Project" is aimed at legitimizing the politics of the Democratic Party and at "dividing workers" by race. "The interests of a black worker on the line in an auto plant and a white worker," he says, "are fundamentally the same, and a million miles from the interests of an Oprah Winfrey or a Hillary Clinton." He rejects the "pseudo-left politics" of identity.

EXPOSING THIS TRAVESTY

Our republic had given us a platform for sovereign, individual ingenuity and creativity. A day late and a dollar short, more and more authorities are exposing the educational goal to retrograde what is essentially human about human nature and to create a homogeneous herd of unthinking pawns fit for a Marxist Communist state. These are some of the heroes who have revealed this travesty. One of the first of the whistleblowers was Beverly (B. K.) Eakman.[113]

> Shaver explains how attitudes and opinions are assessed using a "cognitive" basis. Notice that it is the so-called "intellectual component" of values which permits psychologically manipulative curricula to be passed off as basic subject matter.

Another is Joel Turtel.[114]

> It turns out that millions of children have good reasons to hate public school, reasons that parents should not ignore. Parents whose children are doing well in their studies often don't see a problem with their local public school. But for these parents, what if the school has been deceiving you? What if school authorities dumb-down the textbooks and manipulate tests and report-card grades to make you believe your children are doing well in school, when in fact they are not?

Another early whistleblower was John Gatto[115], who was a famous Teacher of the Year in New York City:

> I began to wonder, reluctantly, whether it was possible that being in school itself was what was dumbing [the schoolchildren] down. Was it possible I had been hired not to enlarge children's power, but to diminish it?

There is John Stormer:[116]

> Failing academics—the dumbing down of our children—is not the only problem. Some kids do learn and excel. Chapter 10 documents the techniques used to manipulate the thinking and values of the

very smart kids. They are taught to base their thinking and decisions on faulty, humanistic, God-is-not-relevant foundations. They are being trained and prepared to be the leaders of "the new world order" which education 'reformers' say they are working to create.

Connor Boyack[117] has many books aimed at compensating for inferior education:

Part of the problem with industrialization is the classification of education as a product, rather than a service. When I go to the store, I can select from off-the-shelf products that have been made available for purchase. I can't change what is offered… Contrast that experience with getting a haircut, where the stylist is extremely attentive to your needs and desires.

Then there is Dr. Samuel Blumenfeld[118]:

[He] has spent 40 years discovering why US public schools have produced millions of functional illiterates, impaired the brains of countless young Americans, created a black underclass, and are incapable of achieving academic competence… [He] has teamed up with international journalist and educator Alex Newman to expose the architects of the progressive plan to socialize America by dumbing down the population. They reveal how close the utopians have come to achieving final success as the Obama administration works feverishly to nationalize K-12 schooling with Common Core.

And, most comprehensive of all is Charlotte Thompson Iserbyt.[119] She had access to the classified information at the federal Office of Educational Research and Improvement as senior policy advisor. I have her *abridged* edition. It is 465 pages—in tiny type. Her book reveals that changes gradually brought into the American public education system work to eliminate the influence of a child's parents (religion, morals, national patriotism) and mold the child into a member of the proletariat in preparation for a socialist-collectivist world of the future. She says that these changes originated from plans formulated primarily by the Carnegie Foundation for the Advancement of Education and Rockefeller General Education Board and details the psychological methods used to implement and effect the changes.

The substance of the directives under which we operate is that we shall use our grant making power to so alter life in the United States that we can be comfortably merged with the Soviet Union [bank-rolled by the Ford Foundation].[120]

Mary Gabler[121] recently added to the rebuttal of our degraded education system. In her stunning new book, *Debunking Howard Zinn*, she finally exposes Zinn's Marxist disinformation. As we have seen, his totally discredited book still brain-washes American students today. She remarked that "his cultish following contin-ues to grow nearly forty years after the publication." She is a resident fellow at the Alexander Hamilton Institute.

A LAST WORD

I want to acknowledge the many individual teachers who are not consciously a part of this communist takeover. They love children and want what is best for them. We can't stereotype. But even they have been taught by dumbed down teachers who have been taught by dumbed down teachers for many generations, and you don't know *what* you don't know. Federal dollars (i.e., your tax dollars) and a lot of grant money out there are the carrots that insure that all the local school districts march in lockstep.

No government can be allowed to encroach upon the sovereign right of loving parents to freely encourage and promote the full potential of their unique children. Governments are not into education; they are into acquiring power. It is shocking to realize that this fundamental attack on the decision-making capacity of American citizens and the betrayal of the foundations of our nation have been in play for more than one hundred years. It is even more shocking that these termites have eaten away the fabric of our nation so secretly for so many gen-erations. Parents can rescue their children. Homeschooling is an obvious remedy for the toxic effects of American public "education." It enables children to pursue their interests in depth, at their own pace, fulfilling their own curiosities. Children are respected as individuals and empowered to be all they can be. We consider this below.

It requires a courageous effort to thwart the attacks we have explored on our Christian way of life. All truth seekers must join and buy into sustaining whatever it will take. In Section 3, we review our starting point and then tackle how we get there.

RESTORING CHRISTIAN CIVILIZATION

CHAPTER 10

THE GOOD NEWS IN PERSPECTIVE

INTRODUCTION

My commitment to you, throughout, is to be candid in my personal viewpoints. Although they can be controversial, you deserve nothing less. Patrick Henry said, "I wholly disapprove of what you say—and will defend to the death your right to say it." Assertions must accept refutations, and I value constructive alternative insights from readers. Sharing different points of view characterizes the health of a free society, and what I say is surely not "the last word." I introduce ideas that I believe are essential, but I don't claim the infallibility of a pope.

As I said above, if Americans today were almost universally Christian, as in the past, I would have nothing to say about these topics. Until now, they have carried the Christian message and sustained civilization preeminently in our constitutional republic. But traditional Christians in America—and around the free world—no longer have the numbers to sustain our civilized way of life. Think of the animal kingdom. When a species cannot adapt to an ever changing Sitz im Leben, its numbers decline; many have become extinct. If we are to salvage our civilization, traditional Christians must unite with the large percentage of sincere, truth-seeking Americans who are not traditional Christians. We must accommodate one another's point of view. As I show in the appendix, each human mind is incredibly adaptable.

As I observed in the book's introduction, there are issues about which we are likely to disagree, and religion is so important that it is particularly emotional. In this sincere dialogue, truth is refined. What is essential is our allegiance to the Christian message and civilized way of life—aligned with our unchanging human nature. Whatever our conflicting perspectives, we must put them aside and, as a band of brothers, never allow different orientations to deter us from our common cause.

First, I want to recall what was said about understanding the people of primitive Africa:

> The most difficult task that a writer can undertake is to give an intelligent description of a personality whose emotions and mental processes are completely alien to him. The writer is apt to reason, 'If I were in this character's position, how would I think and behave?' This is particularly true of men who write about wild animals and attribute to the animals thoughts and emotions that an animal simply does not possess. It is equally true of authors who write about wild people. A savage does not think along the same lines as a civilized man. In some instances, he may seem extremely shrewd, and in other situations, he may give the impression of incredible stupidity. But in few cases does he go through the same mental processes as his civilized brother.

While the people who lived in the time of Jesus were much better educated and more sophisticated than those people, the point is the same. Our *unconscious* brain (see the appendix) is continually responding to input from our ongoing experiences and forming unconscious "templates" or assumptions from that input. These templates then anticipate how things are most likely. They are valuable shortcuts to keep us up on what is going on, and we would get overwhelmed otherwise. Nonetheless, we can get in trouble making assumptions. And in the case of trying to comprehend a Sitz im Leben two thousand years ago and adapt to that, these assumptions, instead, provide tunnel vision that will cloud all attempts at being objective. That is, our unconscious brain encodes and interprets what we are learning by being programmed by the Sitz im Leben of our daily experiences. The unconscious brain doesn't correct for another Sitz im Leben. In this case, it sets us up. In few cases would a person of that age go through the same mental processes as we do. We must recognize that and consciously do our best to realign our thinking.

WHAT DO WE KNOW ABOUT GOD?

As I have said, if we are literally made in the image and likeness of God, then God is also the mirror image of us, so the old bearded man in the white cloak would not be a stretch. This is anthropomorphizing God—*anthropos* (man) and *morphe* (form)—picturing God as if God were in the form of a human being.

In the ancient Sitz im Leben, God was very active. As darkness descended, all of creation fell back into chaos. With the first light, God put the trees and the hills and everything else back into existence. (I actually had a patient with that delusion.) God surely needed a reliable alarm clock.

In the Sitz im Leben of Saint Thomas Aquinas, the earth was still a pancake floating on water—you can poke a hole and water comes up—and the firmament was still an enormous astrodome to hold the water away, with spigots so rain could come down and a mobile light show for decoration. So by the time of Aristotle and then Saint Thomas, who was guided by him, the Sitz im Leben had moved on.

Since then, we have faced the epistemological problem. The argument is that you cannot get something from nothing. Is everything in the cosmos simply our imagination and nothing actually exists? Does my imagination exist? Do I exist? René Descartes said, *"Cogito, ergo sum"* (i.e., "I know I am real since I am actually thinking"). So he was sure that much existed.

But we are still learning about nature. We know that light travels 186,000 miles a second, faster than a speeding bullet, which can't do better than half a mile. But light is not instantaneous. We know that the radiation from some stars took millions of years, traveling that fast just to get to us; in fact, some may not have reached us yet after billions of years. So we think that there is really a lot of stuff out there, and we are pretty puny in comparison. But how could it get there in the first place? You can't get something from nothing.

So Saint Thomas argued that there had to be a First Cause. Something—someone—was there that created everything, including the astrodome—the un-created Creator. That was his definition of God. But Saint Thomas didn't know about the speed of light, etc. It would be a stretch to figure that God is operating up there in the cosmos somewhere, with an infinite computer, supervising the whole cosmos in minute-to-minute operation. We would still be anthropomorphizing God.

What the creation story tells us is that there are immutable natural laws, and only by obeying those laws can we be true to our nature and live functional lives the right way. In our Sitz im Leben, we are discovering just how true that is as we learn more and more about the laws of nature—even the periodic table of the elements and Nano particles. The devastation of Nagasaki and Hiroshima should convince us that there is really something to the atomic theory. We have now succeeded in whole genome sequencing. As I have said, if you deny the laws of nature, try jumping off a tall building to prove there is no law of gravity, but I don't recommend it.

How did all this stuff and all these laws get there? You can't get something from nothing. The truth is, I don't know, and the point is, *I don't care*. So far as I know, no one has figured out the epistemological problem. But I'll assume that car coming at me is real, and I'll do my best to avoid it.

THE NATURAL GOD

I believe that there are laws—call them God's laws—that direct the right way for me to live. My focus is being intent to obey those laws and to do my part to live a Christian way of life, affirming that Christ is alive as Lord in his living, civilized community. I do not believe in an old man with a long white beard standing guard at the pearly gates. Nor can I fathom the epistemological problem—far above my pay grade as a philosopher— but I'm not going to get stymied trying to decide how many angels can dance on the head of a pin as theologians debated in the middle ages. I don't think we need to sprinkle holy water around with an aspergillum to zap those unseen devils lurking about.

And I can't convince myself that he has a cell phone and answers my call or even texts me back. Saying that does not mean that someone can't get answers by praying. We think in our language and communicate in our language. It is natural and appropriate to pray in our language as though conversing with a loving friend who understands our language.

Even the primitive Africans believed in spirits to explain things about nature they could not understand. They poked holes in people's ears to let out the evil spirit. Trepanning (burring a hole in the skull to let out the evil spirit) was practiced from 4,000 BC until the mid-sixteenth century. We had the Salem witch trials (1692–93) in which women and men were murdered because of demonic possession. The pagans had various gods and spirits as well to give them control— by appeasement—or an explanation for what was beyond their understanding.

Life is not a virtual reality computer game. We only get to do it once. We best get it right. We have the real world. These laws are "in my DNA" as a social animal. As I said, I believe that the kerygma provided by Jesus, the Lord, lives on in his authentic community, which continues to adapt and apply these laws about the right way for human beings to live for each Sitz im Leben. Jesus continues to teach us the smart way to live—the rewarding way to live—in the real world. Isn't that enough? So should we rename God's laws as nature's laws, or should we rename nature's laws as God's laws? By staying true to our nature, obeying these laws, we prosper by living the right way. This is the true Christian way. Doing so together is civilization. This is the gratuitous Good News.

This raises a final question. If we have the innate capacity in our DNA to discern the right way to live, why do we even need scripture? I look at it this way. I want to take my van and drive from Hartford to Phoenix. I have an onboard compass in the vehicle, and I know I must go west-southwest to get there. But I would never set out without consulting MapQuest or AAA and getting road maps for all the states I will travel through. Life isn't a video game; I can't push a button and just start over if I make the wrong turn. I want to be right the first time. Besides, it's a way to avoid disagreements with my sister- and brother-in-law, who will be travelling with us. That is what scripture and the Christian message provide—the road map of virtuous, civilized living and a consensus, so we align with one another about the right way to live. The Lord, alive in the modern Christian community, is always updating our maps.

CLARIFYING CONCEPTS

In the remainder of this chapter, and in Chapter 11, I provide many scriptural quotations, basically categorizing the New Testament. Of course these quotations can be read word for word. They can also be skimmed and used for future reference. The translation of scripture used is the Jerusalem Bible, aligned with our Sitz im Leben.

First, what is meant by *grace* in scripture? The Greek word *charis* means a freely given, unearned favor. Consistently, this is found to mean the gratuitous— freely given—*proclamation of the Good News* to Jews and pagans alike. This is unambiguous in the following passages:

> You have probably heard how I have been entrusted by God with the grace [gratuitous favor] he meant for you, and that it was by a revelation that I was given the knowledge of the mystery, as I have just described it very shortly. (Eph. 3:1–3)

> I have been made the servant of that gospel by a gift of grace [gratuitous favor] from God who gave it to me by his own power. I, who am less than the least of all the saints, have been entrusted with this special grace [gratuitous favor], not only of proclaiming to the pagans the infinite treasure of Christ but also of explaining how the mystery is to be dispensed. (Eph. 3:7–9)

This is to show, for all ages to come, through his goodness toward us in Christ Jesus, how infinitely rich he is in grace. Because it is by grace [gratuitous favor] that you have been saved, through faith; not by anything of your own, but by a gift from God; not by anything you have done, so that nobody can claim the credit. We are God's work of art, created in Jesus Christ to live the good life as from the beginning he had meant us to live it. (Eph. 2:7–10)

Each one of us, however, has been given his own share of grace [i.e., special natural "gifts" or capabilities], given as Christ allotted it. (Eph. 4:7)

Not that I do boast of preaching the gospel, since it is a duty that has been laid on me; I should be punished if I did not preach it! If I had chosen this work myself, I might have been paid for it, but as I have not, it is a responsibility that has been put into my hands. Do you know what my reward is? It is this: in my preaching, to be able to offer the Good News free [as a gratuitous favor], and not insist on the rights which the gospel gives me. (1 Cor. 9:16–18)

We find in scripture various characterizations of Jesus as a human being, a son of God as Christians also are sons of God.

And so the child will be holy and will be called Son of God. (Luke 1:36)

Blessed be God the Father of our Lord Jesus Christ, who has blessed us with all the spiritual blessings of heaven in Christ. Before the world was made, he chose us, chose us in Christ, to be holy and spotless, and to live through love in his presence, determining that we should become his adopted sons, through Jesus Christ. (Eph. 1:3–5)

God overlooked that sort of thing when men were ignorant, but now he is telling everyone everywhere that they must repent, because he has fixed a day when the whole world will be judged, and judged in righteousness, and he has appointed a man to be the judge. And God has publicly proved this by raising this man from the dead. (Acts 17:30–18:1)

Moses, for example, said, "The Lord God will raise up a prophet like yourself for you, from among your own brothers; you must listen to whatever he tells you." (Acts 3:22)

Remember the Good News that I carry, Jesus Christ risen from the dead, sprung from the race of David; it is on account of this that I have my own hardships to bear, even to being chained like a criminal—but they cannot chain up God's news. (2 Tim. 2:8–10)

Jesus the Nazarene was a man commended to you by God by the miracles and portents and signs that God worked through him when he was among you, as you all know. (Acts 2:22)

For there is only one God, and there is only one mediator between God and mankind, himself a man, Jesus Christ, who sacrificed himself as a ransom for them all. (1 Tim. 2:5–6)

Father, may they be one in us, as you are in me and I am in you, so that the world may believe it was you who sent me. I have given them the glory you have to me, that they may be one as we are one. With me in them and you in me, may they be so completely one that the world will realize that it was you who sent me and that I have loved them as much as you loved me. (John 17:21–3)

See also Acts 2:36; Matthew 4:1; Luke 2:41–44, 46–50; Luke 4:1–3; and John 14:28.

Similarly, the conception of Bultmann that Jesus is Lord living on in the living body of Christians finds support in scripture:

Now the Church is his body, he is its head. (Col. 1:18)

Nor is the body to be identified with any one of its many parts. If the foot were to say, "I am not a hand and so I do not belong to the body," would that mean that it stopped being part of the body? If the ear were to say, "I am not an eye, and so I do not belong to the body," would that mean that it was not a part of the body? If your whole body were just one eye, how would you hear anything? If it was just one ear, how would you smell anything? Instead of that, God put all the separate parts into the body on purpose. If all the parts were the same, how could it be a body? As it is, the parts are many but the body is one. The eye cannot say to the hand, "I do not need you," nor can the head say to the feet, "I do not need you."... Now you together are Christ's body; but each of you is a different part of it. (1 Cor. 12:14–21, 27)

If we live by the truth and in love, we shall grow in all ways into Christ, who is the head by whom the whole body is fitted and joined together, every joint adding its own strength, for each separate part to work according to its function. (Eph. 4:15–16)

Though your body may be dead it is because of sin, but if Christ is in you then your spirit is life itself because you have been justified... [and] will give life to your own mortal bodies through his Spirit living in you. (Rom. 8:11)

He has put all things under his feet, and made him, as the ruler of everything, the head of the Church; which is his body, the fullness of him who fills the whole creation. (Eph. 1:23)

For he is the peace between us [uncircumcised and circumcised] and has made the two into one and broken down the barrier which used to keep them apart, actually destroying in his own person the hostility caused by the rules and decrees of the Law. This was to create one single New Man in himself out of two of them and by restoring peace through the cross, to unite them both in a single Body and reconcile them with God. (Eph. 2:14–17)

Bear with one another charitably, in complete selflessness, gentleness and patience. Do all you can to preserve the unity of the Spirit by the peace that binds you together. There is one body, one Spirit, just as you were all called into one and the same hope when you were called. (Eph. 4:2–4)

If you ever experienced viewing a body that had been dead even two days without the services of a mortician, you would be convinced that what was left of the corpse could not be pumped back up and resemble the person before death. But in the Sitz im Leben of Jesus's time, raising the dead to life was said to be not such an unusual endeavor. Metaphorically, in their prescientific myth, this ability apparently identified a respected person, someone of influence, someone to be taken seriously. Not only was Jesus, in their myth, capable of doing so for even someone dead that long but also his disciples and others.

> On arriving, Jesus found that Lazarus had been in the tomb for four days already… Jesus said in great distress, with a sigh that came straight from the heart, "Where have you put him?" They said, "Lord, come and see."… Still sighing, Jesus reached the tomb: it was a cave with a stone to close the opening. Jesus said, "Take the stone away." Martha said to him, "Lord, by now he will smell; this is the fourth day." Jesus replied, "Have I not told you that if you believe you will see the glory of God?" So they took away the stone. Then Jesus lifted up his eyes and said: "Father, I thank you for hearing my prayer, I knew that you always hear me, but I speak for the sake of those who stand round me, so that they may believe it was you who sent me. When he had said this, he cried out in a loud voice, "Lazarus, here! Come out!" The dead man came out, his feet and hands bound with bands of stuff and a cloth round his face. Jesus said to them, "Unbind him, let him go free." (John 11:17, 33–35, 38–44).

> These twelve Jesus sent out, instructing them as follows: "Do not turn your steps to pagan territory, and do not enter any Samaritan town; go rather to the lost sheep of the House of Israel. And as you go, proclaim that the kingdom of God is close at hand. Cure the sick, raise the dead, cleanse the lepers, cast out devils." (Matt. 10:5–8)

> John spoke up, "Master," he said "we saw a man casting out devils in your name, and because he is not with us we tried to stop him." But Jesus said to him, "You must not stop him; anyone who is not against you is for you." (Luke 9:49–50)

> "I tell you most solemnly, whoever believes in me will perform the same works as I do myself, he will perform even greater works, because I am going to the Father." (John 14:12)

Rev. Arthur Fisher was virtually an add-on to the Acts of the Apostles, since he also went about making converts from community to community, adapting the kerygma to their Sitz im Leben. He *gratuitously* brought them the Good News, demonstrating Christian civilization with his good works and by his message. He spent a considerable amount of time *caring* for the sick, including sewing up those spear wounds:

> I soon found that a missionary has more to do than stand under a fig tree and read the Scriptures to a group of natives. In Uganda, he had to be a combination explorer, doctor, carpenter, linguist, big game hunter and with a bit of the politician thrown in too.

To be relevant, everyone's message—the good news—must correspond to their Sitz im Leben. The Good News—the appropriate way to live—is essential to our nature and unchanging, but Jesus lives on in the evolving, living community. His teachings guide us to the right way to live today.

RECONCILING TROUBLING ASSERTIONS

There are statements in the gospels that struggle with a literal implication. They make it blatantly clear that we must glean immutable Christian values and not confabulate them with a very different Sitz im Leben when scripture was written. Here are examples that exemplify the primitive Sitz im Leben that had no problems with logical contradictions—for example, "Why do your disciples break away from the tradition of the elders? They do not wash their hands when they eat food" (Matt. 15:2). "[Jesus] went in and sat down at the table. The Pharisee saw this and was surprised that he had not washed before the meal" (Luke 11:38). Are Christians not to wash their hands before eating?

Scripture says, "Leave your offering there before the altar, go and be reconciled with your brother first" (Matt. 5:24); "Honor your father and your mother and you must love your neighbor as yourself" (Matt. 19:19); "Here are my mother and my brothers. Anyone who does the will of God, that person is my brother and sister and mother" (Mark 3:30). But it also says, "I have come to set a man against his father, a daughter against her mother, a daughter-in-law against her mother-in-law. A man's enemies will be those in his own household" (Matt 10:35–36) and "If anyone comes to me without hating his father, mother, wife, children, brothers, sisters, and his own life too, he cannot be my disciple" (Luke 14:26).

> Brother will betray brother to death, and the father his child; children will rise against their parents and have them put to death. You will be hated by all men on account of my name; but the man who stands firm to the end will be saved. (Matt 10:21–22)

> Do you suppose that I am here to bring peace on earth? No, I tell you, but rather division. For from now on a household of five will be divided: three against two and two against three; the father divided against the son, son against father, mother against daughter, daughter against mother, mother-in-law against daughter-in-law, daughter in-law against mother-in-law. (Luke 12:51–53)

Again, throughout the gospels, Jesus says, "I am telling you not to worry about your life and what you are to eat, nor your body and how you are to clothe it" (Matt. 6:25). "If you wish to be perfect, go and sell what you own and give the money to the poor, and you will have treasure in heaven" (Matt. 19:21). "Anyone who wants to save his life will lose it; but anyone who loses his life for my sake, that man will save it" (Luke 9:24).

One might conclude that we are to join the homeless, clogging the cities, particularly on the west coast, and living without personal responsibility and burdening society. That is not the Christian message.

> I have never asked anyone for money or clothes; you know for yourselves that the work I did earned enough to meet my needs and those of my companions. I did this to show you that this is how we must exert ourselves. (Acts 20:33–34)

> However, we do urge you, brothers, to go on making even greater progress and to make a point of living quietly, attending to your own business and earning your living, just as we told you to, so that you are seen to be respectable by those outside the Church, though you do not have to depend on them. (1 Thess. 4:10–12)

> This does not mean that to give relief to others you ought to make things difficult for yourselves: it is a question of balancing what happens to be your surplus now against your present need, and one day they may have something to spare that will supply your own need. (2 Cor. 8:13–14)

There were no biologists in that Sitz im Leben to explain conception. It was understood that only the male contributed to the ribbon of life, planting seed in the female as in the ground. That is why only males could continue inheritance. Actually, the Christian message elevated women, who were treated more like a man's livestock prior to Christianity. We saw how the primitive Africans saw nothing wrong with beating one's wife to death. Instead, "this is why a man must leave father and mother, and cling to his wife, and the two become one body. They are no longer two, therefore, but one body. So then, what God has united, man must not divide" (Matt. 19:5–6). Again, "the wife has no rights over her own body; it is the husband who has them. In the same way, the husband has no rights over his body; the wife has them" (1 Cor. 7:4–5).

But Paul was a devout Pharisee and imbued with the Law of Moses. It was only with the Nineteenth Amendment in 1920 that women in America were deemed capable of voting, even though the Constitution affirms that "all men are created equal," having the same essence. It took a long time for that to sink in; finally, in our Sitz im Leben.

> As in all the churches of the saints, women are to remain quiet at meetings since they have no permission to speak; they must keep in the background as the Law itself lays it down. If they have any questions to ask, they should ask their husbands at home; it does not seem right for a woman to raise her voice at meetings. (1 Cor. 14:34–35)

> However, what I want you to understand is that Christ is the head of every man, man is the head of woman, and God is the head of Christ. For a man to pray or prophecy with his head covered is a sign of disrespect for his head. For a woman, however, it is a sign of disrespect to her head if she prays or prophecies unveiled; she might as well have her hair shaved off. In fact, a woman who will not wear a veil ought to have her hair cut off. If a woman is ashamed to have her hair cut off or shaved, she ought to wear a veil. A man should certainly not cover his head, since he is the image of God and reflects God's glory. For man did not come from woman; no, woman came from man; and man was not created for the sake of woman, but woman was created for the sake of man. That is the argument for women's covering their heads with a symbol of the authority over them, out of respect for the angels. However, though woman cannot

do without man, neither can man do without woman in the Lord.
(1 Cor. 11:2–12)

John is more truly a gospel—from the Greek *euangelion*, "the good messenger or good news"—than were the Synoptics. It is a liturgical instruction, following and superseding the Jewish liturgy and traditions. The events of Jesus's life are interpreted to be signs. Jesus is portrayed as thoroughly human—simple and humble. He says that Jesus is the Word of God, and this has acquired various interpretations. In Greek, *logos* means "word," but it is the word *going forth*, "the spoken word or a statement." In this way, Jesus is the physical message and messenger of the invisible God the Father. John juxtaposes extremes, dichotomies: light, darkness; good, evil; sons of light, sons of darkness; God, Satan. This style was distorted by Gnostic dualism, which was a heresy.

St. Augustine was converted from Manichaeism, a form of Gnosticism. That religion posited two gods, the spiritual (good) god and the material (evil) god. The gods fought, and the evil god trapped some of the spiritual in matter; this is mankind. Man's goal is to escape in his spirit back from the evil physical body and be saved. The implication would be to commit suicide!

Following his conversion, this matrix in the unconscious mind of Augustine influenced all religious thinking thereafter but is not found in the kerygma, the Good News of Christianity. It implies that God is incompetent and blundered in creating matter and the natural world, making an essentially defective product. It subsequently condemns man, while alive, to be *essentially* an evil sinner, God's mistake, only liberated from this essentially evil material nature by death. This curse is hardly the good news of God's joyous free gift of functional, civilized living.

Actually, humans know how to be good and also how to be evil, but the natural world is not intrinsically perverse and evil, nor is mankind intrinsically dysfunctional in essence. What is defective becomes extinct. We are functional in our nature, our essence, and capable of fulfillment, taking responsibility for our behavior, living in liberty, and pursuing happiness. We are blessed with our natural, un*alien*able rights, in accord with the laws of nature and of nature's God.

CHAPTER 11

BASIC THEMES OF THE GOOD NEWS

INTRODUCTION

As noted above, in this chapter, I have drawn many quotations from scripture, divided according to various themes. This section can, of course, be studied word for word. It can also simply be a reference for you, to skim and move on. The purpose is to demonstrate that the good news of Christianity is clearly conveyed in the New Testament, teaching every truth seeker of whatever persuasion the wise way to live. Putting these teachings to use as a nation, we can salvage civilization.

LOVE OF FELLOW MAN

> If I have all the eloquence of men or of angels but speak without love, I am simply a gong booming or a cymbal clashing. If I have the gift of prophecy, understanding all the mysteries there are, and knowing everything and if I have faith in all its fullness to move mountains, but without love, then I am nothing at all. If I give away all that I possess, piece by piece, and if I even let them take my body to burn it, but without love, it will do me no good whatever. Love is always patient and kind; it is never jealous; love is never boastful or conceited; it is never rude or selfish; it does not take offense, and it is not resentful. Love takes no pleasure in other people's sin, but it delights in the truth; it is always ready to excuse, to trust, to hope, and to endure whatever comes. Love does not come to an end… In short, there are three things that last: faith, hope and love; and the greatest of these is love. (1 Cor. 13:1–8, 13)

Jesus said, "You must love the Lord your God with all your heart, with all your soul, and with all your mind. This is the greatest and the first commandment. The second resembles it: You must love your neighbor as yourself. On these two commandments hang the whole Law, and the Prophets also." (Matt. 22:37–40)

You are God's chosen race, his saints; he loves you, and you should be clothed in sincere compassion, in kindness and humility, gentleness and patience. Bear with one another; forgive each other as soon as a quarrel begins. The Lord has forgiven you; now you must do the same. Over all these clothes, to keep them together and complete them, put on love. And may the peace of Christ reign in your hearts, because it is for this that you were called together as parts of one body. Always be thankful. (Col. 3:12–15)

You know that among the pagans their so-called rulers lord it over them, and their great men make their authority felt. This is not to happen among you. No; anyone who wants to become great among you must be your servant, and anyone who wants to be first among you must be slave to all. For the Son of Man himself did not come to be served but to serve, and to give his life as a ransom for many. (Mark 10:42–45)

Anyone who says, "I love God," and hates his brother, is a liar, since a man who does not love his brother that he can see cannot love God, whom he has never seen. So this is the commandment that he has given us, that anyone who loves God must also love his brother. (1 John 4:20–21)

Then Peter went up to him and said, "Lord, how often must I forgive my brother if he wrongs me? As often as seven times?" Jesus answered, "Not seven, I tell you, but seventy-seven times." (Matt. 18:21–22)

So then, if you are bringing your offering to the altar and there remember that your brother has something against you, leave your offering there before the altar, go and be reconciled with your brother first, and then come back and present your offering. (Matt. 5:23–24)

This is my commandment: love one another, as I have loved you. A man can have no greater love than to lay down his life for his friends. You are my friends, if you do what I command you. (John 15:12–13)

To this day, we go without food and drink and clothes; we are beaten and have no homes; we work for our living with our own hands. When we are cursed, we answer with a blessing; when we are hounded, we put up with it; we are insulted and we answer politely. We are treated as the offal of the world, still to this day, the scum of the earth. (1 Cor. 4:11–13)

"For I was hungry and you gave me food; I was thirsty and you gave me drink; I was a stranger and you made me welcome; naked and you clothed me, sick and you visited me, in prison and you came to see me." Then the virtuous will say to him in reply, "Lord, when did we see you hungry and feed you; or thirst and give you drink? When did we see you a stranger and make you welcome; naked and clothe you; sick or in prison and go to see you?" And the king will answer, "I tell you solemnly, in so far as you did this to one of the least of these brothers of mine, you did it to me." (Matt. 25:35–40)

The scribes and Pharisees brought a woman along who had been caught in adultery; and making her stand there in full view of everybody, they said to Jesus, "Master, this woman was caught in the very act of committing adultery, and Moses has ordered us in the Law to condemn women like this to death by stoning. What have you to say?" They asked him this as a test, looking for something to use against him. But Jesus bent down and started writing on the ground with his finger. As they persisted with their question, he looked up and said, "If there is one of you who has not sinned, let him be the first to throw a stone at her." Then he bent down and wrote on the ground again. When they heard this they went away one by one, beginning with the eldest, until Jesus was left alone with the woman, who remained standing there. He looked up and said, "Woman, where are they? Has no one condemned you?" "No one, sir," she replied. "Neither do I condemn you," said Jesus "go away and don't sin any more." (John 8:3–11)

Pure, unspoilt religion, in the eyes of God our Father is this: coming to the help of orphans and widows when they need it, and keeping oneself uncontaminated by the world. (James 1:27)

See also Matthew 6:25–27, 7:12, 18:32–35, 20:27–28, 23:11–12; Mark 9:37, 12:28–32; Luke 10:25–28; John 13:34–35; and Galatians 5:19–24.

UNIVERSAL ACCEPTANCE

We had to proclaim the word of God to you first, but since you have rejected it, since you do not think yourselves worthy of eternal life, we must turn to the pagans. For this is what the Lord commanded us to do when he said: I have made you a light for the nations, so that my salvation may reach the ends of the earth. (Acts 14:46–47)

[Peter] was hungry and was looking forward to his meal, but before it was ready he fell into a trance and saw heaven thrown open and something like a big sheet being let down to earth by its four corners; it contained every possible sort of animal and bird, walking, crawling or flying ones. A voice then said to him, "Now Peter, kill and eat!" But Peter answered, "Certainly not, Lord; I have never eaten anything profane or unclean." Again, a second time, the voice spoke to him, "What God has made clean, you have no right to call profane." (Acts 10:10–15)

Do not hesitate to eat anything sold in butchers' shops: there is no need to raise questions of conscience; for the earth and everything that is in it belong to the Lord. If an unbeliever invites you to his house, go if you want to, and eat whatever is put in front of you, without asking questions just to satisfy conscience. But if someone says to you, "This food was offered in sacrifice," then out of consideration for the man that told you, you should not eat it, for the sake of his scruples; his scruples, you see, not your own. Why should my freedom depend on somebody else's conscience? If I take my share with thankfulness, why should I be blamed for food for which I have thanked God? (1 Cor. 10:25–30)

We hear that some of our members have disturbed you with their demands and have unsettled your minds. They acted without any authority from us… It has been decided by the Holy Spirit and by ourselves not to saddle you with any burden beyond these essentials: you are to abstain from food sacrificed to idols, from blood, from the meat of strangled animals and from fornication. Avoid these, and you will do what is right. (Acts 15:24–29)

If anyone had already been circumcised at the time of his call, he need not disguise it, and anyone who was uncircumcised at the time of his call need not be circumcised; because to be circumcised or uncircumcised means nothing: what does matter is to keep the commandments. (1 Cor. 7:18–19)

APPROPRIATE ASSOCIATIONS

Do not harness yourselves in an uneven team with unbelievers. Virtue is no companion for crime. Light and darkness have nothing in common. Christ is not the ally of Beliar [i.e. *The Satanic Bible*] nor has a believer anything to share with an unbeliever. The temple of God has no common ground with idols, and that is what we are— the temple of the living God. (2 Cor. 6:13–16)

What I wrote was that you should not associate with a brother Christian who is leading an immoral life, or is a usurer, or idolatrous, or a slanderer, or a drunkard, or is dishonest; you should not even eat a meal with people like that. (1 Cor. 5:11–12)

I am sending you out like sheep among wolves; so be cunning as serpents and yet as harmless as doves. (Matt. 10:16)

Do not give dogs what is holy; and do not throw your pearls in front of pigs, or they may trample them and then turn on you and tear you to pieces. (Matt. 7:6)

TAKING RESPONSIBILITY

You know how you are supposed to imitate us: now we were not idle when we were with you, nor did we ever have our meals at anyone's table without paying for them; no, we worked night and day, slaving and straining, so as not to be a burden on any of you. This was not because we had no right to be, but in order to make ourselves an example for you to follow. We gave you a rule when we were with you: not to let anyone have any food if he refused to do any work. Now we hear that there are some of you who are living in idleness, doing no work themselves but interfering with everyone else's. In the Lord Jesus Christ we order and call on people of this kind to go on quietly working and earning the food that they eat. My brothers, never grow tired of doing what is right. (2 Thess. 3:7–13)

A crowd was sitting round him at the time the message was passed to him, "Your mother and brothers and sisters are outside asking for you." He replied, "Who are my mother and my brothers?" And looking around at those sitting in a circle around him, he said, "Here are my mother and my brothers. Anyone who does the will of God, that person is my brother and sister and mother." (Mark 3:32–35)

I have never asked anyone for money or clothes; you know for yourselves that the work I did earned enough to meet my needs and those of my companions. I did this to show you that this is how we must exert ourselves to support the weak, remembering the words of the Lord Jesus, who himself said, "There is more happiness in giving than in receiving." (Acts 20:33–35)

Be at peace among yourselves. And this is what we ask you to do, brothers; warn the idlers, give courage to those who are apprehensive, care for the weak and be patient with everyone. Make sure that people do not try to take revenge; you must all think of what is best for each other and for the community. Be happy at all times; pray constantly; and for all things give thanks to God, because this is what God expects you to do in Christ Jesus. (1 Thess. 5:14–18)

As for loving our brothers, there is no need for anyone to write to you about that, since you have learnt from God yourself to love one another, and in fact this is what you are doing with all the brothers throughout the whole of Macedonia. However, we do urge you, brothers, to go on making even greater progress and to make a point of living quietly, attending to your own business and earning your living, just as we told you to, so that you are seen to be respectable by those outside the Church, though you do not have to depend on them. (1 Thess. 4:9–12)

It is written in the Law of Moses: You must not put a muzzle on the ox when it is treading out the corn. Is it about oxen that God is concerned, is there not an obvious reference to ourselves? Clearly this was written for our sake to show that the ploughman ought to plough in expectation, and the thresher to thresh in the expectation of getting his share. If we have sown spiritual things for you, why should you be surprised if we harvest your material things? Others are allowed these rights over you and our right is surely greater? In fact we have never exercised this right. On the contrary we have put up with anything rather than obstruct the Good News of Christ in any way... Do you know what my reward is? It is this: in my preaching, to be able to offer the Good News free, and not insist on the rights which the gospel gives me. (1 Cor. 9:8–12, 18)

Ten bridesmaids took their lamps and went to meet the bridegroom. Five of them were foolish and five were sensible: the foolish ones did take their lamps, but they brought no oil, whereas the sensible ones took flasks of oil as well as their lamps. The bridegroom was late, and they all grew drowsy and fell asleep. But at midnight there was a cry, "The bridegroom is here! Go out and meet him." At this all those bridesmaids woke up and trimmed their lamps, and the foolish ones said to the sensible ones, "Give us some of your oil: our lamps are going out." But they replied, "There might not be enough for us and for you; you had better go to those who sell it and buy some for yourselves." They had gone off to buy it when the bridegroom arrived. Those who were ready went in with him to the wedding hall and the door was closed. The other bridesmaids arrived later. "Lord, Lord," they said "open the door for us."

But he replied, "I tell you solemnly I do not know you." So stay awake, because you do not know either the day or the hour. (Matt. 25:1–13)

There is a variety of gifts, but always the same Spirit; there are all sorts of service to be done, but always to the same Lord; working in all sorts of different ways in different people, it is the same God who is working in all of them. The particular way in which the Spirit is given to each person is for a good purpose. (1 Cor. 12:4–7)

See also Matthew 22:8–14, 24:11–13; Luke 16:5–9; and Ephesians 4:25–28.

PERSISTENCE

Our one desire is that every one of you should go on showing the same earnestness to the end, to the perfect fulfillment of our hopes, never growing careless, but imitating those who have the faith and the perseverance to inherit the promises. (Heb. 6:11–12)

You will have in you the strength, based on his own glorious power, never to give in, but to bear anything joyfully, thanking the Father who has made it possible for you to join the saints and with them inherit the light. (Col. 1:11–12)

Work for the Lord with untiring effort and with great earnestness of spirit. If you have hope, this will make you cheerful. Do not give up if trials come; and keep on praying. (Rom. 12:11–12)

We must never get tired of doing good because if we don't give up the struggle we shall get our harvest at the proper time. (Gal. 6:9)

And he said to her, "The children should be fed first, because it is not fair to take the children's food and throw it to the house-dogs." But she spoke up: "Ah, yes sir," she replied "but the house-dogs under the table can eat the children's scraps." And he said to her, "For saying this, you may go home happy: the devil has gone out of your daughter." So she went off to her home and found the child lying on the bed and the devil gone. (Mark 7:27-8)

USING COMMON SENSE

At that time Jesus took a walk one Sabbath day through the corn-fields. His disciples were hungry and began to pick ears of corn and eat them. The Pharisees noticed it and said to him, "Look, your disciples are doing something that is forbidden on the Sabbath." But he said to them, "Have you not read what David did when he and his followers were hungry—how he went into the house of God and how they ate the loaves of offering which neither he nor his followers were allowed to eat, but which were for the priests alone?… For the Son of Man is master of the Sabbath." (Matt. 12:1–8)

When he had gone back into the house, away from the crowd, his disciples questioned him about the parable. He said to them, "Do you not understand either? Can you not see that whatever goes into a man from outside cannot make him unclean, because it does not go into his heart but through his stomach and passes out into the sewer?" (Thus he pronounced all foods clean.) And he went on, "It is what comes out of a man that makes him unclean. For it is from within, from men's hearts, that evil intentions emerge: fornication, theft, murder, adultery, avarice, malice, deceit, indecency, envy, slander, pride, folly. All these evil things come from within and make a man unclean." (Mark 7:14–23)

Or again, what king marching to war against another king would not first sit down and consider whether with ten thousand men he could stand up to the other who advanced against him with twenty thousand? If not, then while the other king was still a long way off, he would send envoys to sue for peace. (Luke 14:31–32)

See also Mark 2:23–28.

SINGLE-MINDEDNESS

No servant can be the slave of two masters: he will either hate the first and love the second, or treat the first with respect and the second with scorn. You cannot be the slave both of God and of money. (Luke 16:13)

He who is not with me is against me; and he who does not gather with me scatters. (Luke 11:23)

Every kingdom divided against itself is heading for ruin, and household divided against itself collapses. (Luke 11:17)

Where are all the philosophers now? Where are the scribes? Where are any of our thinkers today? Do you see now how God has shown up the foolishness of human wisdom? If it was God's wisdom that human wisdom should not know God, it was because God wanted to save those who have faith through the foolishness of the message that we preach. And so, while the Jews demand miracles and the Greeks look for wisdom, here are we preaching a crucified Christ; to the Jews an obstacle that they cannot get over, to the pagans madness, but to those who have been called, whether they are Jews or Greeks, a Christ who is the power and the wisdom of God. For God's wisdom is wiser than human wisdom, and God's weakness is stronger than human strength. (1 Cor. 1:20–25)

See also Matt. 6:24 and Matt. 12:30.

UNPRETENTIOUSNESS

So when you give alms, do not have it trumpeted before you; this is what the hypocrites do in the synagogues and in the streets to win men's admiration. I tell you solemnly, they have had their reward. But when you give alms, your left hand must not know what your right is doing; your almsgiving must be in secret, and your Father who sees all that is done in secret will reward you. (Matt. 6:3–4)

Anyone who welcomes this little child in my name welcomes me; and anyone who welcomes me welcomes the one who sent me. For the least among you all, that is the one who is great. (Luke 9:48)

No, the greatest among you must behave as if he were the youngest, the leader as if he were the one who serves. (Luke 22:26)

DANGERS FROM WEALTH

People who long to be rich are a prey to temptation; they get trapped into all sorts of foolish and dangerous ambitions which eventually plunge them into ruin and destruction. The love of money is the root of all evils and there are some who, pursuing it, have wandered away from the faith, and so given their souls any number of fatal wounds. (1 Tim. 6:9–10)

Warn those who are rich in this world's goods that they are not to look down on other people; and not to set their hopes on money, which is untrustworthy, but in God who, out of his riches, gives us all that we need for our happiness. Tell them that they are to do good, and be rich in good works, to be generous and willing to share—this is the way they can save up a good capital sum for the future if they want to make sure of the only life that is real. (1 Tim. 6:17–19)

My brothers, do not try to combine faith in Jesus Christ, our glorified Lord, with the making of distinctions between classes of people. Now suppose a man comes into the synagogue, beautifully dressed and with a gold ring on, and at the same time a poor man, and say, "Come this way to the best seats"; then you tell the poor man, "Stand over there" or "You can sit on the floor by my foot-rest." Can't you see that you have used two different standards in your mind, and turned yourselves into judges, and corrupt judges at that? Listen, my dear brothers, it is those who are poor according to the world that God chose, to be rich in faith and to be the heirs to the kingdom which he promised to those who love him. (James 2:1–6)

"You know the commandments: You must not kill; You must not commit adultery; You must not steal; You must not bring false witness; You must not defraud; Honor your father and mother." And he said to him, "Master, I have kept all these from my earliest days." Jesus looked steadily at him and loved him, and he said, "There is one thing you lack. Go and sell everything you own and give the money to the poor, and you will have treasure in heaven; then come, follow me." But his face fell at these words and he went away sad, for he was a man of great wealth. (Mark 10:19–22)

He sat down opposite the treasury and watched the people putting money into the treasury, and many of the rich put in a great deal. A poor widow came and put in two small coins, the equivalent of a penny. Then he called his disciples and said to them, "I tell you solemnly, this poor widow has put more in than all who have contributed to the treasury; for they have all put in money they had over, but she from the little she had has put in everything she possessed, all she had to live on." (Mark 12:41–4)

Yes, I tell you again, it is easier for a camel to pass through the eye of a needle than for a rich man to enter the kingdom of heaven. (Matt. 19:24)

CIVIL OBEDIENCE

"Hand me a denarius and let me see it." They handed him one and he said, "Whose head is this? Whose name"? "Caesar's" they told him. Jesus said to them, "Give back to Caesar what belongs to Caesar—and to God what belongs to God." (Mark 12:15–17)

For the sake of the Lord, accept the authority of every social institution: the emperor, as the supreme authority, and the governors as commissioned by him to punish criminals and praise good citizenship. God wants you to be good citizens, so as to silence what fools are saying in their ignorance. You are slaves to no one except God, so behave like free men, and never use your freedom as an excuse for wickedness.

Have respect for everyone and love for our community; fear God and honor the emperor. (1 Pet. 2:13–17)

See also Matthew 22:21.

JESUS ON THE OFFENSIVE

Just before the Jewish Passover Jesus went up to Jerusalem, and in the Temple he found people selling cattle and sheep and pigeons, and the money changers sitting their counters there. Making a whip out of some cord, he drove them all out of the Temple, cattle and sheep as well, scattered the money-changers' coins, knocked their tables over, and said to the pigeon-sellers, "Take all this out of here and stop turning my Father's house into a market." (John 2:13–17)

He said to them, "But now if you have a purse, take it; if you have a haversack, do the same; if you have no sword, sell your cloak and buy one, because I tell you these words of scripture have to be fulfilled in me: He let himself be taken for a criminal. Yes, what scripture says about me is even now reaching its fulfillment." "Lord," they said, "there are two swords here now." He said to them, "That is enough." (Luke 22:35–38)

See also Matt. 21:13 and Mark 11:15–17.

THE PHARISEES AND SADDUCEES

Alas for you, scribes and Pharisees, you hypocrites! You who shut up the kingdom of heaven in men's faces, neither going in yourselves or allowing others to go in who want to… Alas for you, scribes and Pharisees, you hypocrites! You who pay your tithe of mint and dill and cumin and have neglected the weightier matters of the Law—justice, mercy, good faith! These you should have practiced, without neglecting the others. You blind guides! Straining out gnats and swallowing camels! Alas for you, scribes and Pharisees, you hypocrites! You who clean the outside of cup and dish and leave the inside full of extortion and intemperance. Blind Pharisee! Clean the inside of cup and dish first so that the outside may become clean as well. (Matt. 23:13–26)

They asked him, "Is it against the law to cure a man on the Sabbath day?" hoping for something to use against him. But he said to them, "If any one of you here had only one sheep and it fell down a hole on the Sabbath day, would he not get hold of it and lift it out? Now a man is far more important than a sheep, so it follows that it is permitted to do good on the Sabbath day." Then he said to the man, "Stretch out your hand." He stretched it out and his hand was better, as sound as the other one. At this time the Pharisees went out and began to plot against him, discussing how to destroy him. (Matt. 12:10–14)

But when he saw a number of Pharisees and Sadducees coming for baptism he said to them, "Brood of vipers, who warned you to fly the retribution that is coming?" (Matt. 3:7–8)

"Alas for you lawyers also," he replied "because you load on men burdens that are unendurable, burdens that you yourselves do not move a finger to lift." (Luke 11:46)

Then the disciples came to him and said, "Do you know that the Pharisees were shocked when they heard what you said?" He replied, "Any plant my heavenly Father has not planted will be pulled up by the roots. Leave them alone. They are blind men leading blind men; and if one blind man leads another, both will fall into a pit." (Matt. 15:12–14)

See also Matthew 28:12–14, Luke 4:29–30, Luke 11:39, and Galatians 2:16.

WHAT ABOUT MEN?

While he was still a long way off, his father saw him and was moved with pity. He ran to the boy, clasped him in his arms and kissed him tenderly. Then his son said, "Father, I have sinned against heaven and against you. I no longer deserve to be called your son". But the father said to his servants, "Quick! Bring out the best robe and put it on him; put a ring on his finger and sandals on his feet. Bring the calf we have been fattening, and kill it; we are going to have a feast, a celebration, because this son of mine was dead and has come back to life; he was lost and is found." (Luke 15:21–24)

Let these words of mine remain in your heart and in your soul; fasten them on your hand as a sign and on your forehead as a circlet. Teach them to your children and say them over to them, whether at rest in your house or walking abroad, at your lying down or at your rising…so that you and your children may live long in the land. (Deut. 11:18–21)

The man who fails to use the stick hates his son; the man who is free with his correction loves him. (Prov. 13:24)

Parents, never drive your children to resentment or you will make them feel frustrated. (Col. 3:21)

You can remember how we treated every one of you as a father treats his children, teaching you what was right, encouraging you and appealing to you to live a life worthy of God, who is calling you to share the glory of his kingdom. (1 Thess. 2:11–12)

Husbands should love their wives as Christ and sacrificed himself for her… In the same way, husbands must love their wives as they do their own body; for a man to love his wife is for a man to love himself. (Eph. 5:25–28)

WHAT ABOUT WOMEN?

Then, if there are some husbands who have not obeyed the word, they may find themselves won over, without a word spoken, by the way their wives behave, when they see how faithful and conscientious they are. Do not dress up for show: doing up your hair, wearing gold bracelets and fine clothes; all this should be inside, in a person's heart, imperishable: the ornament of a sweet and gentle disposition—this is what is precious in the sight of God. (1 Pet. 3:1–5)

A perfect wife—who can find her? She is far beyond the price of pearls. Her husband's heart has confidence in her, from her he will derive no little profit. (Prov. 31:10–12)

She puts her back into her work and shows how strong her arms can be. She finds her labour well worth while; her lamp does not go out at night. She sets her hands to the distaff, her fingers grasp the spindle. (Prov. 31:17–19)

She holds out her hand to the poor, she opens her arms to the needy. Snow may come, she has no fears for her household, with all her servants warmly clothed. (Prov. 31:20–21)

She is clothed in strength and dignity, she can laugh at the days to come. When she opens her mouth, she does so wisely; on her tongue is kindly instruction. (Prov. 31:25–26)

Many women have done admirable things, but you surpass them all! Charm is deceitful, and beauty empty; the woman who is wise is the one to praise. (Prov. 31:29–30)

When a woman is giving birth, she has sorrow because her hour has come, but when she has delivered the baby, she no longer remembers the anguish, for joy that a human being has been born into the world. (John 16:21)

Counseling King David

David said to Abigail, "Blessed be Yahweh, the God of Israel, who sent you to meet me today! Blessed be your wisdom and blessed you yourself for restraining me today from the crime of bloodshed and from avenging myself with my own hand!" (1 Sam. 25:32–34)

The Weaker Sex?

Jael came out to meet Sisera and said to him, "My Lord, stay here with me; do not be afraid! He stayed there in her tent, and she covered him with a rug… Then he said to her, "Stand by the tent door, and if anyone comes and questions you—if he asks, 'Is there a man here?' say 'No.'" But Jael the wife of Heber took a tent-peg, and picked up a mallet; she crept up softly to him and drove the peg into his temple right through to the ground. He was lying fast asleep, worn out; and so he died. And now Barak came up in pursuit of Sisera. Jael went out to meet him and said, "Come in, and I will show you the man you are looking for." He went into her tent; Sisera lay dead, with the tent-peg through the temple. (Judg. 4:18–22)

Businesswoman

> We sat down and preached to the women who had come to the meeting. One of these women was called Lydia, a devout woman from the town of Thyatria who was in the purple-dye trade. She listened to us, and the Lord opened her heart to accept what Paul was saying. After she and her household had been baptized she sent us an invitation: "If you really think me a true believer in the Lord," she said "come and stay with us;" and she would take no refusal. (Acts 16:13–15)

Husband and Wife, Business Partners and Witnesses

> After Paul left Athens and went to Corinth, where he met a Jew called Aquila whose family came from Pontus. He and his wife Priscilla… were tentmakers of the same trade as himself [so] he lodged with them, and they worked together… After staying on for some time, Paul took leave of the brothers and sailed for Syria, accompanied by Priscilla and Aquila… When Priscilla and Aquila heard [Apollos] speak boldly in the synagogue, they took an interest in him and gave him further instruction about the Way. (Acts 18:1–3, 18, 26)

> My greetings to Prisca and Aquila, my fellow workers in Christ Jesus, who risked death to save my life. I am not the only one to owe them a debt of gratitude, all the churches among the pagans do as well. My greetings also to the church that meets at their house. (Rom 16:3:4)

WHAT ABOUT CHILDREN?

> Children, obey your parents in the Lord, for this is right. "Honor your father and mother" (this is the first commandment with a promise), "that it may go well with you and that you may live long in the land." Fathers, do not provoke your children to anger, but bring them up in the discipline and instruction of the Lord. (Eph. 6:1–4)

> God is treating you as sons. For what son is there whom his father does not discipline? If you are left without discipline, in which all have participated, then you are illegitimate children and not sons.

Besides this, we have had earthly fathers who disciplined us and we respected them. (Heb. 12:5–11)

Listen, my son, to your father's instruction, do not reject your mother's teaching: they will be a crown of grace to your head, a circlet for your neck. (Prov. 1:8–9)

But you know that he has proved himself by working with me on behalf of the Good News like a son helping his father. (Phil. 6:21–2)

A wise son is his father's joy, a foolish son his mother's grief. (Prov. 10:1)

A wise son loves discipline, a mocker will not listen to reproof. (Prov. 13:1)

Even at play a child reveals whether his actions will be pure and right. (Prov. 20:11)

It is always my greatest joy to hear that my children are living according to the truth. (3 John 1:4)

My son, if you take my words to heart, if you set store by my commandments, turning your ear to wisdom, and applying your heart to truth: yes, if your plea is for clear perception, if you cry out for discernment, if you look for it as if it were silver, and search for it as for buried treasure, you will then...discover the knowledge of God... He keeps his help for honest men, he is the shield of those whose ways are honourable. (Prov. 2:1–8)

And they were bringing children to him that he might touch them, and the disciples rebuked them. But when Jesus saw it, he was indignant and said to them, "Let the children come to me; do not hinder them, for to such belongs the kingdom of God. Truly, I say to you, whoever does not receive the kingdom of God like a child shall not enter it." And he took them in his arms and blessed them, laying his hands on them. (Mark 10:13–16)

He said to his disciples, "Obstacles are sure to come, but alas or the one who provides them! It would be better for him to be thrown into the sea with a millstone put round his neck than that he should lead astray a single one of these little ones." (Luke 17:1–2)

But Saul answered David, "You cannot go and fight the Philistine; you are only a boy and he has been a warrior from his youth." David said to Saul, "Your servant used to look after the sheep for his father and whenever a lion or a bear came out and took a sheep from the flock, I used to follow him up and strike him down and rescue it from his mouth." (1 Sam. 17:33–35)

A VIRTUOUS PARADIGM

In searching for a paradigm of Christian virtue that would be universally embraced, I thought of my Boy Scout Oath, which I can still recite. Here it is:

Trustworthy—behaving honorably, fulfilling a promised task, being honest.

Be the shepherds of the flock of God that is entrusted to you: watch over it, not simply as a duty but gladly, because God wants it; not for sordid money, but because you are eager to do it. Never be a dictator over any group that is put in your charge, but be an example that the whole flock can follow. (1 Pet. 5:2–3)

These are the things that you must do. Speak the truth to each another; let the judgments at your gates be such as conduce to peace; do not secretly plot evil against one another; do not love false oaths; since all this is what I hate. (Zech. 8:16–17)

You are not to keep two different weights in your bag, one heavy, one light. You are not to keep two different measures in your house, one large, one small. You must keep one weight, full and accurate, so that you may have a long life. (Deut. 25:13–15)

Loyal—loyal to anyone to whom loyalty is due.

Wherever you go, I will go, wherever you live, I will live. Your people shall be my people, and your God my God. Wherever you die, I will die and there I will be buried. (Ruth 1:16–17)

Do not abandon friend, or father's friend; when trouble comes, do not go running to your brother's house. Better a friend near than a brother far away. (Prov. 27:10)

At this, Peter said, "Though all lose faith in you, I will never lose faith." Jesus answered him, "I tell you solemnly, this very night, before the cock crows, you will have disowned me three times." Peter said to him, "Even if I have to die with you, I will never disown you." And all the disciples said the same. (Matt. 26:33–35)

There are no devout men left, fidelity has vanished from mankind. All they do is lie to one another, flattering lips, talk from a double heart. (Psalms 12:1–2)

Helpful—prepared to save life, help injured persons, attend to duties and do "good turns."

A man was once on his way down from Jerusalem to Jericho and fell into the hands of brigands; they took all he had, beat him and then made off, leaving him half dead. Now a priest happened to be travelling down the same road, but when he saw the man, he passed by on the other side. In the same way a Levite who came to the place saw him, and passed by on the other side. But a Samaritan traveler who came upon him was moved with compassion when he saw him. He went up and bandaged his wounds, pouring oil and wine on them. He then lifted him on to his own mount, carried him to the inn and looked after him. Next day, he took out two denarii and handed them to the innkeeper. "Look after him," he said "and on my way back I will make good any extra expense you have." (Luke 10:30–36)

Is there a poor man among you, one of your brothers, in any town of yours in the land that Yahweh your God is giving to you? Do not harden your heart or close your hand against that poor brother of yours, but be open-handed with him and lend him enough for his needs… Of course there will never cease to be poor in the land; I command you therefore: Always be open-handed with your brother, and with anyone in the country who is in need and poor. (Deut. 15:7, 11)

Friendly—offering friendship to all.

This is my commandment: love one another as I have loved you. A man can have no greater love than to lay down his life for his friends. (John 15:13)

The news of all the disasters that had fallen on Job came to the ears of three of his friends. Each of them set out from home—Eliphaz of Teman, Bildad of Shuah and Zophar of Naamath—and by common consent they decided to go and offer him sympathy and consolation… They sat there on the ground beside him for seven days and seven nights. (Job 2:11–13)

A friend is a friend at all times, it is for adversity that a brother is born. (Prov. 17:17)

Courteous—polite to everyone out of generosity.

Remind them that it is their duty to be obedient to the officials and representatives of the government; to be ready to do good at every opportunity; not to go slandering other people or picking quarrels, but to be courteous and always polite to all kinds of people. (Titus 3:1–2)

She waited behind him, at his feet, weeping, and her tears fell on his feet, and she wiped them away with her hair; then she covered his feet with kisses and anointed him with the ointment. When the Pharisee who had invited him saw this, he said to himself, "If this man were a prophet, he would know who this woman is that is touching him and what a bad name she has."… Then [Jesus] turned to the woman. "Simon," he said "you see this woman? I came into your house, and you poured no water over my feet, but she has poured out her tears over my feet and wiped them away with her hair. You did not anoint my head with oil, but she has anointed my feet with ointment. For this reason I tell you that her sins, many sins, must have been forgiven her, or she would not have shown such great love." (Luke 7:38–9, 44–47)

[Jesus] got up from the table, removed his outer garment and, taking a towel, wrapped it round his waist; he then poured water into a basin and began to wash the disciples feet and to wipe them with the towel he was wearing… When he had washed their feet and put on his clothes again he went back to the table. "Do you understand," he said "what I have done to you? You call me Master and Lord, and rightly; so I am. If I, then, the Lord and Master, have washed your feet, you should wash each other's feet. I have given you an example so that you may copy what I have done to you." (John 13:4–5, 12–15)

Kind—caring for all living things.

Kindly words are a honeycomb, sweet to the taste, wholesome to the body. (Prov. 16:24)

What the Spirit brings is very different: love, joy, peace, patience, kindness, goodness, trustfulness, gentleness and self-control. There can be no law against things like that, of course. (Gal. 5:22–23)

Never have grudges against others, or lose your temper, or raise your voice to anybody, or call each other names, or allow any sort of spitefulness. Be friends with one another, and kind, forgiving each other as readily as God forgave you in Christ. (Eph. 4:31–32)

You are God's chosen race, his saints; he loves you, and you should be clothed in sincere compassion, in kindness and humility, gentleness and patience. Bear with one another; forgive each other as soon as a quarrel begins. (Col. 3:12–13)

Love your enemies and do good, and lend without any hope of return. You will have a great reward, and you will be sons of the

Most High, for he himself is kind to the ungrateful and the wicked. (Luke 6:35)

Obedient—obeying the laws of nature and cooperating with all lawful authority.

This is what Yahweh our God has commanded you. Stray neither to right nor to left. Follow the whole way that Yahweh has marked for you and you shall live, you shall prosper and shall live long in the land you are to possess. (Deut. 5:32–33)

If anyone loves me he will keep my word, and my Father will love him, and we shall come to him and make our home with him. (John 14:23)

For the sake of the Lord, accept the authority of every social institution: the emperor, as the supreme authority, and the governors as commissioned by him to punish criminals and praise good citizenship. God wants you to be good citizens, so as to silence what fools are saying in their ignorance. You are slaves to no one except God, so behave like free men, and never use your freedom as an excuse for wickedness. (1 Pet. 2:13–16)

Obey your leaders and do as they tell you, because they must give an account of the way they look after your souls; make this a joy for them to do, and not a grief—you yourselves would be the losers. (Heb. 13:17)

Cheerful—willingly completing tasks; never shirking responsibility.

A glad heart is excellent medicine, a spirit depressed wastes the bones away. (Prov. 17:22)

Each one should give what he has decided in his own mind, not grudgingly or because he was made to, for God loves a cheerful giver. And there is no limit to the blessings which God can send you. (2 Cor. 9:7–8)

Finally, brothers, fill your minds with everything that is true, everything that is noble, everything that is good and pure, everything that we love and honour, and everything that can be thought virtuous or worthy of praise. (Phil. 4:9)

Whatever your work is, put your heart into it as if it were for the Lord and not for men, knowing that the Lord will repay you by making you his heirs. (Col. 3:23–24)

Thrifty—making the best use of money, goods, and opportunities.

Idler, go to the ant; ponder her ways and grow wise; no one gives her orders, no overseer, no master, yet all through the summer she makes sure of her food, and gathers her supplies at harvest time. (Prov. 6:6–8)

Seven years are coming, bringing great plenty to the whole land of Egypt, but seven years of famine will follow them, when all the plenty in the land of Egypt will be forgotten, and famine will exhaust the land… Pharaoh should take action and appoint supervisors over the land, and impose tax of one-fifth on the land of Egypt during the seven years of plenty… This food will serve as a reserve for the land during the seven years of famine. (Gen. 41:29–30, 34, 36)

The slack hand brings poverty, but the diligent hand brings wealth. (Prov. 10:4)

If in a wise man's dwelling there is precious treasure and oil, the fool will gobble it up.(Prov. 21:20)

An open town and without defences: such is the man lacking self-control. (Prov. 25:28)

Brave—courageously overcoming fear to stand up for what is right.

Then David said to his son, "Be strong, stand firm be fearless, be dauntless and set to work, because Yahweh God, my God, is with you. (1 Chron. 28:20)

Among the churches of God we can take special pride in you for your constancy and faith under all the persecutions and troubles you have to bear. It all shows that God's judgment is just, and the purpose of it is that you may be found worthy of the kingdom of God; it is for the sake of this that you are suffering now. (2 Thess. 1:4–5)

God's gift was not a gift of timidity, but the Spirit of power, and love, and self-control. So you are never to be ashamed of witnessing to the Lord, or ashamed of me for being his prisoner; but with me, bear the hardships for the sake of the Good News. (2 Tim. 1:7–8)

But Saul answered David, "You cannot go and fight the Philistine; you are only a boy and he has been a warrior from his youth." David said to Saul, "Your servant used to look after the sheep for his father and whenever a lion or a bear came out and took a sheep from the flock, I used to follow him up and strike him down and rescue it from his mouth; if he turned on me I seized him by the hair at his jaw and struck him down and killed him. Your servant has killed both lion and bear, and this uncircumcised Philistine shall be like one of them." (1 Sam. 17:33–36)

Clean—clean in thought, speech, sport, and habits, as well as having honorable friends.

Ah, how happy those of blameless life who walk in the Law of Yahweh! How happy those who respect his decrees, and seek him with their whole heart, and, doing no evil, walk in his ways. (Psalm 119:1–3)

So as we go in, let us be sincere in heart and filled with faith, our minds sprinkled and free from any trace of bad conscience and our bodies washed with pure water. (Heb. 10:22)

Alas for you, scribes and Pharisees, you hypocrites! You who clean the outside of cup and dish and leave the inside full of extortion and intemperance. Blind Pharisee! Clean the inside of cup and dish first so that the outside may be clean as well. (Matt. 25:25–26)

No one who has taken a bath needs washing, he is clean all over. You too are clean. (John 13:11)

God, create a clean heart in me, put into me a new and constant spirit. (Psalm 51:10)

What I wrote is that you should not associate with a brother Christian who is leading an immoral life, or is a usurer, or idolatrous, or a slanderer, or a drunkard, or is dishonest. (1 Cor. 5:11)

Reverent—faithful in his social obligations and obeying the commandments.

We have been given possession of an unshakable kingdom. Let us therefore hold on to the grace that we have been given and use it to worship God in the way that he finds acceptable, in reverence and fear. (Heb. 12:28)

"I will give you all these, he said, if you fall at my feet and worship me." Then Jesus replied, "Be off, Satan! For scripture says: You must worship the Lord your God, and serve him alone." (Matt. 4:9–10)

Do all you can to present yourself in front of God as a man who has come through his trials, and a man who has no cause to be ashamed of his life's work and has kept a straight course with the message of the truth. (2 Tim. 2:15)

Brothers, if one of you misbehaves, the more spiritual of you who set him right should do so in a spirit of gentleness, not forgetting that you may be tempted yourselves. You should carry each other's troubles and fulfil the law of Christ. (Gal. 6:1–2)

Expound to me the way of your statutes, Yahweh, and I will always respect them. Explain to me how to respect your Law and how to observe it wholeheartedly. (Psalm 119:33–34)

CONCLUSION

These scripture quotations illustrate the kerygma—the Good News—about the right way for human beings to live, in accord with our true nature. Like a tiny seed in that original Sitz im Leben, with a precarious start, this Good News has grown through the centuries into a splendid tree, with branches spreading throughout the Western world, even to our own Sitz im Leben. It is now our destiny to keep it alive and bearing fruit.

On the Jefferson Memorial is written: "As that becomes more developed, more enlightened, as new discoveries are made, new truths discovered and manners and opinions change, with the change of circumstances, institutions must advance also to keep pace with the times. We might as well require a man to wear still the coat which fitted him when a boy as civilized society to remain ever under the regimen of their barbarous ancestors."

To fulfill this mission, then, we must stay true to the message and yet secure it within our own Sitz im Leben, so it continues to fit. This is the challenge for our generation and succeeding generations. Losing this pearl of great price would condemn us to the regimen of the barbarians at our gate.

CHAPTER 12

WHAT WILL IT TAKE?

MEETING THE CHALLENGE

For a while, as a psychotherapist, I had a magic wand. You could push a button and the star at the end would light up. But it wasn't very effective. If we are going to salvage Christian civilization, it will require transforming our Sitz im Leben, and we are going to have to go all out. Band-Aids are out. You heard it said: insanity is doing the same thing over and over and expecting different results. We are seeing the insane results.

The colonists, in their Sitz im Leben, confronted challenges unimaginable in ours. Think of Washington's fledging army crossing the river as best they could, battered by sleet and snow, marching to fight the Hessian forces in Trenton, New Jersey, on December 26, 1776. Many of the troops did not have boots, so they were forced to wear rags around their feet. Some of the men's feet bled, turning the snow dark red. They were determined to do whatever it took: Washington's catchphrase was "Victory or death." In the end, those dedicated patriots who had set aside their plowshares had taken on the most powerful army in the world and beat it twice.

They wouldn't consent to the British crown taxing them two weeks out of their year. Americans who earn a living work for the federal "king" six months of the year. Our freedoms are in much worse shape than theirs were then. The threat of communism is far worse than anything King George could have imagined. Yes, we are up against it. It can seem overwhelming. What can you and I do as individuals against this enormous communist encroachment metastasized across our society and so well locked in place? Here's an interesting story.

Twenty years ago, virtually none of the students in Baldwin, Michigan, a town of 1,200 in one of Michigan's poorest counties, attended college. Today virtually all do graduate and are going to a four-year college, a community college, or a technical school, and kindergarteners plan to go to college. What happened? The citizens had a *goal* to find a way to get their children out of poverty.[1] They also had a *plan*. They pooled their meager assets and offered to pay up to $5,000 a year toward higher education after the student applied for Pell Grants and possible scholarships.

One person, Rich Simonson, a career politician, retired in his hometown and got his fellow citizens to set a goal of raising $140,000. They got $160,000. They made other adjustments. They adjusted the school calendar to schedule time off for the deer hunting season, for example. They made sure their curriculum provided quality education. The entire attitude in the community changed—the greatest contributor of all. This is just one example of what one person can accomplish with a goal and an action plan.

This is another. Early in 2009, an email between two housewives went viral. They discussed the need to organize a *Taxed Enough Already*, Tea Party, group to fight oppressive taxation. This was picked up by CNBC reporter, Rick Santelli, in February. On September 12, 2009, I was standing on the Capitol lawn, listening to the speakers. The Fake News said there were perhaps seventy-five thousand Tea Party marchers. The police estimated two million. The entire city was gridlocked. People walked miles from their stranded buses. Every state, including Hawaii and Alaska, marched together. There were groups of physicians marching in their white coats.

Looking back toward the Washington Monument, a mile away, is an image—forever burned in my memory—of a tight-packed mass of humanity, and everywhere you looked was a sea of marchers. We all yelled in unison: "Can you hear us now!"

Later, looking for supper, people got up to shake my hand. It took but a spark in that dry tinder forest to ignite a conflagration. Seven years later, this emboldened silent majority painted the map of America red and elected Donald Trump to be their president. What it takes is someone with American self-confidence, commitment, and a goal. Take the initiative, develop a plan, and take action. Donald Trump became wealthy building skyscrapers. The secret, he said, was having a solid foundation. Everything rests on the foundation. So we must start from the bottom up.

Salvaging Christianity begins with the family. The foundation of society from early times has been the family. People look out for their children, protecting them from communist indoctrination and empowering them to develop their potential. Think homeschooling. We will explore that shortly.

In the early years of our republic, it was customary for families to read a passage of scripture at dinner and to discuss it. This also empowered the children to think for themselves and talk about their ideas. Dinnertime in our Sitz im Leben may not work, but a regular time could become customary to turn off the TV and spend twenty minutes most nights doing something like that, either with a selected scripture passage or perhaps identifying a current news item, in order to clarify it and refocus it from a perspective of Christian values. When something interferes, there's always tomorrow. Kids grown? Adults should regularly get their heads together about issues of the day and think about making a difference.

Family discussions should have some structure applied to everyone's personal experiences to draw conclusions from. There are no bad suggestions. Build on what is said. Don't preach. Be sure to show appreciation for all ideas: "That's interesting," "That's something to think about," "Boy, that says it all," etc. Certain scriptural passages or other topics may become favorites and merit repetition.

Then we must start linking families together. Getting like-minded people together today is a lot easier than it was in the colonists' day. We have social media, for better and for worse. We have to discover like-minded truth seekers and link up with them and build a coalition. Those who homeschool will support one another, make social plans, etc.

In the early days of our republic, Americans had a way of life that was unique, and it has typified the American personality ever since. The Frenchman Alexis de Tocqueville is often referenced about his observations when he studied Americans in 1831. He said,

> Americans of all ages, all conditions, and all dispositions constantly form associations. They have not only commercial and manufacturing companies, in which all take part, but associations of a thousand other kinds, religious, moral, serious, futile, general or restricted, enormous or diminutive... If it is proposed to inculcate some truth or to foster some feeling by the encouragement of a great example, they form a society.[2]

In other words, Americans have traditionally been do-it-yourselfers. Americans didn't look to the government for help; they got together and did it themselves. Compared to other nations, Americans still have the distinction of being the world's most "internal" people, to borrow a psychology word. We are confident we can make things happen and feel it is up to us to take responsibility for getting it done. This attitude spurred on America's inventors and entrepreneurs.

CONFRONTING BUSINESS AS USUAL

Our Sitz im Leben took a drastic turn in the 1960s, when the federal government assumed the role of interpreter and enforcer of ethical codes, as Christopher Caldwell explains:

> The changes of the 1960s, with civil rights at their core, were not just a major new element in the Constitution. They were a rival constitution, with which the original one was frequently incompatible— and the incompatibility would worsen as the civil rights regime was built-out. Much of what we have called 'polarization' or 'incivility' in recent years is something more grave—it is the disagreement over which of the two constitutions shall prevail: the de jure constitution of 1788…or the de facto constitution of 1964.[3]

In order to save civilization, we must keep our self-determination. President Reagan said, "The most terrifying words in the English language are: I'm from the government and I'm here to help." We must start from the bottom up and do it ourselves.

We can't turn a blind eye to that "helpful" government. We must do whatever we can to keep our so-called representatives in check. You have to first of all accept that they do not represent you. They are not your friend. Don't kid yourself. They want you to befriend them and especially vote for them. They go in poor and leave millionaires. Their priority is staying there long enough to get the big bucks. As Thomas Sowell said, they don't ever think beyond Stage 1: getting reelected.

First, we must link all dedicated truth seekers together and take a stand against politically correct speech and identity politics. We must identify those who are willing to be sincere representatives, starting with roles like county commissioner, for example. This must build in strength until self-serving politicians can be replaced in the primaries by sincere, genuine state and federal representatives.

That is going to take a while, and linking all sincere Americans working together must include the millennials and Generation Z youth. Public education has indoctrinated them to think that freedom means getting everything free, and they will vote for communism, though they know nothing about it. Three organizations reaching out to them are #Walkaway, Young Americans Against Socialism, and Young Americans for Liberty. You can google them. We will look into approaching our millennials as well. We start now with a remedy for the communist indoctrination of our children. The hand that has been rocking the cradle is guilty of child abuse.

Having mobilized Americans who have in common the awareness of this crisis and the commitment to confront it, we then must figure out what we have to do. Plans to make this happen are proposed below.

CHAPTER 13

WHAT TO DO ABOUT PUBLIC EDUCATION?

INTRODUCTION

Young children are persistently curious. They would be investigating everything in my office, and it would need some straightening after they left. I'm thinking about my own girls. A walk would stop so they could pursue a strange bug. We visited a museum in Edinburgh. Kids in a museum? I couldn't get them to leave, knowing they would be tired for the evening's plans. Just one more display. If you have children, you know what I mean. Curiosity makes human beings human beings. Public education dehumanizes human beings. We need to foster this human curiosity, so it can develop into a lifelong love affair with learning.

The goal of education is for children to become more and more knowledgeable and desirous of discovering more and more. It doesn't mean getting a paper diploma that certifies that the child jumped through a special series of hoops and came out alive, bumping along on the assembly line until dropping off at the end and being stamped Certified. It surely does not mean "going to school."

John Taylor Gatto, in his book, *Dumbing Us Down*,[4] introduces himself by saying, "I don't teach English; I teach school—and I win awards doing it." He goes on to say, "The first lesson I teach is confusion. Everything I teach is out of context... The second lesson I teach is class position. I teach that students must stay in the class where they belong... The third lesion I teach is indifference. I teach children not to care too much about anything... The fourth lesson I teach is emotional dependency. By stars and red checks, smiles and frowns, prizes, honors, and disgraces, I teach kids to surrender their will... The fifth lesson I teach is intellectual dependency. Good students wait for a teacher to tell them what to do." There are two more to come; you get the idea.

Dr. Ben Carson is an esteemed neurosurgeon. He specialized in children. He currently serves as Secretary of the Department of Housing and Urban Development. His mother, Sonya, married at thirteen but was soon divorced and left raising her two sons. She worked as domestic help and noticed that the people she worked for watched little TV but read a lot. Living in Detroit, she made her sons go to the library each week, pick out a new book, and write a report about it, which she carefully checked. Only later did Ben realize that she was illiterate. He stated that at first, he resented this but soon couldn't wait to satisfy his next curiosity. It paid off for him.

This approach to education sets homeschooled children apart. They don't have to begin to get interested in something only for a bell to ring and kill their curiosity. They are self-motivated. They crave learning and have learned how to learn meaningful information efficiently rather than how to pass tests. Once something starts to get boring, they put it aside and go to something interesting. Conrad Boyack has a small book, *Passion-Driven Education*,[5] which explains well the educational crisis we are in and shows how many subjects can be connected to what the child is most passionate about learning.

We must confront this threat to Christian civilization in America. Clearly, the goal must be to provide a way for our children to find the right way to live. The inborn curiosity in each human being craves to be enhanced, not stymied. They must be empowered to be virtuous, self-responsible, freedom-loving, knowledgeable adults. Throughout human history, this has been the sovereign responsibility of parents. Now no more. Communist indoctrination has taken over.

Jon Rappoport[6] addressed literacy. He distinguished three levels of illiteracy. In the first, sophomores read at a fourth-grade level and couldn't read a sign warning them of the danger of swimming. At the second level, they read words at their age level but don't really know what the author is saying; they can't explain the paragraph. And at the third level, they can also tell you something about what it means, but they can't figure out what the point is, what the argument is all about. They can't grasp the logic the author is using to arrive at a conclusion. These latter two illiteracies often go unnoticed.

> Now if you, as a parent, want to go even deeper, if you understand the article about foreign policy is driven by an agenda and the author is biased…what chance do you have? The students can't even grasp what the author is *saying*.

According to one report, 80 percent of high school graduates in New York City are said to be illiterate, but they apparently can read at the lowest levels.[7] Rappoport concludes, "Any person who has looked into the history of education in America soon learns—from authors John Taylor Gatto and Charlotte Iserbyt, for example—that the system has been intentionally rigged and degraded."

Wendy Lecker[8] focuses on math. Science demonstrates that "rote learning and memorization at an early age are necessary [and] are critical to developing math skills."

> They conducted brain scans of children, adolescents, and adults and found that hippocampus plays a critical but time limited role in the development of memory based problem solving skills. The hippocampus helps the brain encode memories in children that as adults they can later retrieve efficiently when working on more complex math concepts. The hippocampal system works a certain way in children to help develop memory-based problem solving skills [helping the development of this critical brain system so essential for later more complicated math work]. Once the children pass a certain age, the processes change.

She states that Common Core "ignored" brain research. We know better. As FDR famously stated, "in politics, nothing happens by accident. If it happens, you can bet it was planned that way." This is a substantial article. You get the point.

ARE THERE MORE REASONS TO HOMESCHOOL?

Beyond training children in Christian virtue and saving them from the corruption of communist public education and bad example, there are many more advantages to homeschooling. Homeschooling knits the family together—the bedrock of Christian civilization. You will find that you don't need a full school day to achieve your daily plan, so children have more time to pursue their curiosities and share family activities. They learn practical skills by helping out at home. Children discover that they can find ways to teach themselves and satisfy their curiosities independently, leading to lifelong learning. Classes are not chopped up into class hours, so a curiosity can be pursued and satisfied. Older children teach younger siblings. The best way to learn is to teach.

You will find that you can get ahead, so children can move on to higher education in less than twelve years, and research shows that homeschooled children do better in higher education. Children are not trapped into age herding. By getting involved in the community, children associate with persons of various ages and backgrounds. They network with others who have similar interests. Older children can even get part-time jobs and thus get educated in being good, productive citizens. In this way, they can gain self-confidence, contribute to pay for their own projects and expenses, and learn to be realistic and goal oriented. They may get involved in causes they espouse in fundraisers, etc. This teaches them to contribute to society as adults. The list goes on. These ideas are expanded in a book by Cafi Cohen, *Homeschooling: The Teen Years: Your Complete Guide to Successfully Homeschooling the 13- to 18- Year-Old.*

Here is one more argument for homeschooling children in America.[9] A rather new FBI initiative instructs high schools across America to report students to them who express antigovernment and anarchist political beliefs: "High school students are ideal targets for recruitment by violent extremists." Such as by their extremist Marxist teachers, perhaps? It calls for public school educators to be "observing and assessing concerning behaviors and communications" of students embracing extremist ideologies. According to the FBI, "some adults embrace domestic violent extremist ideologies [and] their beliefs can permeate family norms, oftentimes influencing their children."

The FBI and federal and local law enforcement groups categorize many libertarian, constitutionalist, and other groups and individuals as "sovereign citizens" who may refer to themselves as constitutionalists or freemen, including [conspiracy theories of] the formation of global government and a police state as indicators of extremist or sovereign citizen ideology. The document attempts to persuade law enforcement that sovereign citizens are a direct threat to them.

"In January 2015 a delegation of Sam Adams Associates for Integrity in Intelligence—which included ex-officers from the NSA, CIA and British MI5—visited the Stasi museum in Berlin. As the former intelligence officers-turned whistleblowers walked among the well-preserved offices and conference rooms of a former totalitarian state's internal spy apparatus," writes Elizabeth Murray, who served as deputy national intelligence officer for the Near East in the National Intelligence Council, "the sense of deja vu and irony of what the United States of America has become was clearly not lost on any of them."

Additionally, school social workers chronicle all sorts of information about each child, and this information is fed into a public database. When they grow up, the government has an ample dossier on each citizen. You may say, "Well, my child is not a criminal." It's all in the eye of the (socially correct) beholder.

HOW IS HOMESCHOOLING POSSIBLE?

In spite of considerable opposition from the powerful federal public education machine, it is legal to exercise your un*alien*able natural right as parents to teach your children. However, the laws vary from state the state, and you have to learn what they are. Just don't expect your Department of Education to provide you with the truth. By googling "homeschooling state laws/your state," you should be able to download these requirements. Have a friend do it for you if you don't have the internet.

There are many trustworthy resources, and the first one to advocate is the Home School Legal Defense Association, which states, "Homeschool with confidence! You're steps away from experienced legal protection, personalized educational support, and cutting-edge homeschool advocacy." You can easily become a member: HSLDA.org, at PO Box 3000 Purcellville, VA 20134-9000, 540 338 5600. They provide advice and will defend you in case anyone gives you grief.

Even the state forms you may be "required" to complete may not be legally required. Typically, your claim for a religious reason to homeschool trumps the bulk of these regulations, such as the educational credentials of the parents.

There is an ever-growing body of information and resources available for advice on the internet and in multiple books and publications. Your challenge is picking which of the thirty-nine flavors to choose. Just searching "homeschool" or "home education" can overwhelm you.

WILL I ENCOUNTER CRITICISM?

Unfortunately, yes. In fact, it may come from communal, organized religion. It may also come from relatives or neighbors who are certain you would ruin your children forever. Forgive them. Their brainwashing has been in play more than one hundred years. But don't take them seriously.

One common criticism is that homeschooling isolates children from society. This is, of course, the reverse. Homeschooling opens up many opportunities to get involved in the community: 4-H, co-op classes, scouts, volunteer activities, community projects, etc. These activities provide quality socialization and encourage self-confidence, build maturity, and escape the negative influence of bullies, cliques, endorsed sexual promiscuity, and LGBTQ promotion in public education. Children make contact with like-minded homeschoolers and often network with one another and develop book clubs or inventive enterprises, etc. with others. They are safe from those murder magnets called gun-free zones, which is a good thing.

HOW MUCH WILL THIS COST?

Well, you don't get something for nothing. Raising children costs money no matter what. Initial expenditures usually diminish after the initial start-up. This must work into the family budget. You might want to add dance classes, for example, even if the child is in public school, or join Future Farmers of America. Joining various community organizations is often the cost of gas for the family "taxi."

Most everyone already has a computer nowadays, and this is an overwhelming resource—like trying to drink from a fire hose. For the most part, any information is out there for the taking. As kids get older, researching their interests that way becomes captivating.

As children get into high school, you may need more resources, even a special tutor, for example, when you get into advanced calculus. *Gasp!* Online classes are offered. This is where networking with other homeschoolers is particularly beneficial. Everyone has individual strengths and weaknesses.

With the Internet Reformation, linking up with like-minded people in your community should be relatively easy. This initial association with like-minded citizens will expand and link to other such associations, as we discussed above. In an energized Christian community, everyone supports everyone else. This also enables children—and yourselves—to develop quality friendships that endure for life. You'll discover community resources you didn't know existed and may be free.

CAN PARENTS AND CHILDREN ADAPT?

Good question. Children adapt more readily than their parents, but if they have been conditioned by public education for a number of years, learning in a new way will take time, perhaps considerable time. Expect this to happen. One day at a time. Learning via homeschooling is also learning homeschooling. Measure progress rather than set hard benchmarks. Recognizing progress is always reassuring. Failing to meet an arbitrary deadline is demoralizing.

Is it worth the effort? Conrad Boyack tells of an eighteen-year-old valedictorian who spoke to her graduation class:

I cannot say that I am any more intelligent than my peers. I can at-test that I am only the best at doing what I am told and working the system. Yet, here I stand, and I am supposed to be proud that I have completed this period of indoctrination… But I contest that I am a human being, a thinker, an adventurer—not a worker. A worker is someone who is trapped within repetition—a slave of the system set up before him. But now, I have successfully shown that I was the best slave… While others sat in class and doodled to later become great artists, I sat in class to take notes and become a great test-taker. While others would come to class without their homework because they were reading about an interest of theirs, I never missed an as-signment… So, I wonder, why did I even want this position? Sure, I earned it, but what will come of it?… I have no clue about what I want to do with my life; I have no interests because I saw every sub-ject of study as work, and I excelled at every subject just for the pur-pose of excelling; not learning. And quite frankly, now I'm scared."[10]

My point is that this adaptation period, long or short, will pay off. Recall what Jon Rappaport said about literacy, being able to be a critical reader—a philosoph-ical reader, if you will—getting the point and catching disinformation. That's the difference provided in homeschooling: true learning, not enslavement. And parents need to go easy on themselves and give themselves all the time they need to adapt. They likely have been in the "education" rut themselves.

SO WHAT ABOUT NUTS AND BOLTS?

One of the blessings of homeschooling is that it is a do-it-yourself project. People can test out which way will work best, evaluating progress. Some find that setting aside special times and creating a school environment suits them, whether in a study room or at the kitchen table. Others are more adventuresome and creative. Perhaps some of each. Children have their own best learning style, and homes-chooling is tailor-made. Home economics is helping Mom fix dinner or working with Dad's latest project. Conrad Boyack shows how the readin', writin', and 'rithmetic can creatively be tied into each child's passionate curiosities.[11]

Finding "boots on the ground" to make this work is often the greatest hur-dle to homeschooling. In our day, often both parents have full-time jobs. Who will be primarily responsible for teaching? Maybe Dad and Mom can team teach. School serves as the daytime babysitter, but who babysits in the summer? I am thinking that, with our population growing older, there are often grandparents with time on their hands and often a need to continue to feel useful. Would serve to keep them sharper. If you don't use it, you lose it. As the children get older, homeschooling becomes more and more self-directed, and basic supervision is all that is needed. Avoiding technology addiction is one supervising responsibility. Where there's a will, there is often a way. By the time the next generation comes around, we may have created local one-room neighborhood schools or even quality public schools, such as were envisioned by our founders, so children can get much of their education there.

If nothing can be worked out, don't feel like second-class parents. Just supplement with home teaching of Christian values, such as the nightly discussions mentioned above. Talk with your children about their school experiences on a regular basis to block the disinformation that will be coming from school. Guide them to think for themselves and stick up for themselves. Linking up with like-minded citizens, do protest when you have to. With the internet, children can learn to get curious again at home, like happened with Dr. Ben Carson. Just get them started. Maybe your situation will improve.

WHAT ABOUT GOING TO COLLEGE?

As children get close to higher education, if they desire it and are not self-sufficient already, adapting to what they will be required to know must be investigated. Among academic records, typical homeschooling community involvement puts your thumb heavily on the scales with top universities. From a search of various internet sources,[12] these appear to be standard requirements. You can go to College Search on the internet to find the requirements of a specific college.

- English: four years (not necessarily chronological years but competence years)
- Foreign language: two to three years (ideally, find a homeschooler who speaks another language; would be fun to learn a language together)
- Math: three years (two years algebra, geometry, trigonometry. Calculus may be excused.)
- Science: two to three years, with laboratory experience (This latter requirement may be excused)
- Social studies /history: two to three years

I would add to this list cursive writing, which has been largely discontinued in public education. College students may rely on laptop computers, but there are times when cursive writing is liberating. Presentations morph more and more into video presentations instead of written presentations. I view this as enslavement. The learner is the captive of the creator of the video. One can reread a part of the article that was in doubt, write down notes about it, highlight it for future reference, and compare sections of the topic. The creator of the video allows none of this and is controlling the pace. One is in control of written information, not video information.

You can get information on getting into college from www.khanacademy. org. The question always arises about accreditation to get into college. The fact is that accreditation is not required to get into college. Getting a decent score on an SAT or ACT will do it, and there are many workbooks to help prepare for these tests. Here are two websites that address homeschooling accreditation:

- https://howdoihomeschool.com/2019/02/06/ dont-need-homeschool-accreditation-college

- https://www.thehomeschoolmom.com/what-is

Another question is, why go to college? Why would young persons who have escaped the "every child left behind" public school brainwashing want to subject themselves to line the pockets of Marxist snobs to be brainwashed in the college industry that is grossly overcharging for its third-rate product?

Some of our most successful leaders are self-educated. Homeschooled adolescents have learned how to learn and how to acquire the knowledge that is relevant to them. Being competent, inner-directed learners pays off in learning on the job, always required anyway. Of course there are resources that even an "internet university" can't provide, such as sophisticated laboratories, so there are exceptions.

Over time, alternative quality education that incorporates the purposes our founders intended will deplete public schools and universities. Supply and demand economics will create new products to satisfy this new market. As I write, President Trump has ordered colleges and universities that receive taxpayer support to stop teaching anti-American distortions and to begin teaching the true history of American exceptionalism. As it is said, you can't change the stripes on a tiger—turn Marxist professors into enlightened professors, imbued with a respect for the constitution they are by oath committed to uphold.

WHAT RESOURCES ARE THERE?

There are various homeschooling "schools" on the internet. One is the Ron Paul Curriculum.[13] It offers free PDFs K-12 but does not offer accreditation. It is intended to work in conjunction with other resources. There are ways you can test online for competence. Conrad Boyack has written thirteen (and growing) short booklets, grouped as *The Tuttle Twins*, https://tuttletwins.com, which teach basic virtue, self-reliance, and respect for the Constitution. He also offers one for high school students.

When you explore internet curricula, let the buyer beware. Some offer solid accreditation but are public school wolves in homeschooling sheep's clothing. You can pick and choose what information you wish to study. Virtually everything that one might be curious about is only a couple clicks away.

This is but an introduction to homeschooling. Rather than replicate here what you can learn from various quality references, read one or two that seem responsive to your concerns, more if you still have unanswered questions. They provide ideas about the knack of homeschooling. What I hope you gain from this is that homeschooling is clearly doable and, at least at the present time, the chance to protect your children. The hand that rocks the cradle rules the world.

As I said, in the future, nondenominational local schools that teach Christian virtue and teach individuals to think for themselves and take responsibility for their lives, as well as provide a quality academic education, may relieve parents of some of this responsibility, as the founders intended. Meanwhile, creative neighborhood homeschooling co-ops might develop. For now, do-it-yourself education seems to be the remedy.

ARE CHARTER SCHOOLS THE ANSWER?

As Donald Trump began his presidency, he appointed Betsy DeVos as Secretary of the Federal Department of Education[14] who espouses the expansion of charter schools to improve the quality of education in America, and she has been known for crusading for better education. The esteemed Dr. Thomas Sowell recently published a book, *Charter Schools and Their Enemies*, in support of charter schools. Truly, some provide a quality alternative to standard public education. Is that the answer? Sadly, it seems often to be an illusion, painting lipstick on the pig. You will recall that, in the very year the Constitution was written and approved by Congress, the Congress passed the Northwest Ordinance, spelling out the essential need to teach religion and morality in the schools. This included the three important subjects:

1. *Religion*, which might be defined as a "fundamental system of beliefs concerning man's origin and relationship with the cosmic universe as well as his relationship to his fellowmen"
2. *Morality*, which may be described as a "standard of behavior distinguishing right from wrong"
3. *Knowledge*, which is an intellectual awareness and understanding of established facts relating to any field of human experience or inquiry.[15]

Prayer is currently permitted in public schools, but they surely will not be teaching Christian morality any time soon. Charter schools are still considered federal public schools. They must employ certified teachers and meet the state's requirements for hours and days of instruction. They must also comply with federal "[*un*]constitutional provisions against the establishment of religion."

Equally troubling, charter schools are a politician's gold mine. Under the cover of saving education, they are a sinkhole for taxpayer dollars, and politicians are quick to get their fingers in that lucrative pie and corrupt the enterprise. Peter Schweizer wrote a book, *Profiles in Corruption*[16], in which he exposes the way politicians use the cover of charter schools to put taxpayer dollars in their pockets. The secret is real estate. "Ravenel Boykin Curry IV of Eagle Capital Management told the *New York Times* that charter schools are 'exactly the kind of investment people in our industry spend our days trying to stumble on.'"[17]

Schweizer gives examples: interest-only monthly payments of nearly $16,700; paying $1.75 million dollars in five years on a school building valued at $1.2 million dollars; over twelve billion dollars of taxpayer money to finance two hundred charter schools built and operated in Florida. "By 2014, the Mavericks schools had received more than $70 million in state money. Nine million of that went to the management company."[18] Was the education superior? "In Largo, the graduation rate was 7.2 percent; in Homestead, it was an incredible 4.5 percent."[19] And the schools ranked at the very bottom in the quality of the education.

WHAT ABOUT SOCIALIST MILLENNIALS?

The hand on their cradle is guilty of child abuse, and we find ourselves trying to play catch-up. Those Marxist templates in the unconscious brain (see the appendix) blind the millennials, blocking them so they view everything in that mindset.

Learning discernment was never part of their curriculum, so their chronological age and their maturity age don't match. They lack the tools for adult discourse. But of course, we can't write them off. Our civilization will be guided by them, the blind leading the blind.

You've heard the expression "My mind's made up; don't confuse me with facts." Setting them straight is pushing a rope. Thomas Sowell, in his book, *Applied Economics: Thinking Beyond Stage One*,[20] tells on himself,

> When I was an undergraduate studying economics under Professor Arthur Smithies of Harvard, he asked me in class one day what policy I favored on a particular issue of the times. Since I had strong feelings on that issue, I proceeded to answer him with enthusiasm, explaining what beneficial consequences I expected from the policy I advocated. "And then what will happen?" he asked… It became clear that the situation I described would lead to other economic consequences, which I then began to consider and spell out.

> "And what will happen after that?" Professor Smithies asked. As I analyzed how the further economic reactions to the policy would unfold, I began to realize that these reactions would lead to consequences much less desirable than those at the first stage, and I began to waver somewhat.

> "And *then* what will happen?" Smithies persisted. By now I was beginning to see that the economic reverberations of the policy I advocated were likely to be pretty disastrous—and, in fact, much worse than the initial situation that it was designed to improve.

Professor Smithies used the Socratic teaching method, aptly named after the Greek philosopher Socrates. He taught by asking questions. Why do you think this could be such and such? The disciples taught themselves and, in doing so, bought into the answers. We avidly buy, but nobody likes to be sold or lectured to. These brainwashed young people will close their eyes forever if their thinking is challenged. But somewhere in that dark recess of gray matter is the hamstrung ability to think. After all, they do still qualify as *Homo sapiens*. The Socratic approach may be the only way.

Well, you know, you have a point about the wealth of the top 1 percenters in America. I was checking it out, and they together have a whopping twenty-five trillion dollars. Almost no country even makes that much altogether in a whole year. Jeff Bezos alone is worth $140 billion dollars and counting. So if you took that money, you could wipe out the one-and-a-half trillion dollars in student loan debts and pay off the national debt as well, which will be on the backs of you young people. Sounds tempting.

But I was thinking. They don't just keep their money in a big cave somewhere. They use it to make even more money. They are funding a lot of the businesses in America in the stock market. If you take away that money, almost every major business in America would go out of business, and nobody would have a job anymore. Then nobody pays taxes, and the government is broke. How are *we* going to make up for that?

If it got too hard for these wealthy folks, wouldn't they just move somewhere else where they got a good tax break? That's how this country got started, people getting away from England so they could have it better. If that happened, their tax dollars would follow them. I wonder if that could happen here. If it did, what could *we* do about it?

You can come up with better ideas, but the first step is to have them "teach" you about their ideas, so they feel respected and you figure out their level of understanding. Learn what they have to say but also listen for openings. Maybe they had a bad experience or feel powerless to get out of student loan debt. That gives you a clue to the best line of questioning, to help them think beyond Stage 1.

Or ask questions like these: "When you were little, what did you think your life would be like?" "If a rich uncle came along and said, 'Pick what you'd most enjoy doing and I'll pay your way for two months to do it,' what would you do?" "Well, if there's a will there's a way. How could *we* actually make that happen?" Such questions reorient the dialogue to get them to take charge of their lives. "If it's to be, it's up to me."

CHAPTER 14

GETTING ALL THIS TOGETHER

Still, if you will not fight for your right when you can easily win without bloodshed… if you will not fight when your victory is sure and not so costly, you may come to the moment when you will have to fight with all the odds against you, and only a precarious chance for survival. There may be a worse case! You may have to fight when there is no chance of victory, because it is better to perish than to live as slaves.

—Winston Churchill

WHERE DO THINGS STAND?

In 1914, the Minnesota Teachers' Union called out the Carnegie and Rockefeller Foundations for menacing true academic freedom and defeating the primary purpose of democracy in education. The communist John Dewey has the distinction of being the Father of American Public Education, stating that children who can think for themselves spoil the harmony of the communal society that is coming, where everyone is interdependent. But we were complacent.

The First Red Scare coincided with the unrest in America that followed the Russian Revolution in 1917. There was alarm about communist labor unions and anarchist bombings. Several hundred radicals were deported. But all that was soon forgotten. America was once again complacent.

We saw how Roosevelt triggered our war with Japan, fostered Stalin, and solidified the foundation for American communism. He gave Stalin the atomic bomb and, together with Stalin, went about establishing a communist United Nations. We didn't see this coming, but Sen. Joseph McCarthy picked up on it quickly in what was known as the Second Red Scare. Communism won; we lost.

McCarthy is associated to this day with unfair allegations and investigations, and he probably missed the mark at times. Communism captured Hollywood. We were playing chess with Russia, but we hadn't learned how to play. And we were complacent.

With the civil rights movement in the sixties, all of the country's institutions were brought under the scrutiny of the expanding federal government. Add to this the War on Poverty and the War on Drugs, creating, as Christopher Caldwell said, the de facto "second constitution of 1964," endorsed by our judicial elites and civic educators. But we were complacent.

Move on to the 1993 destruction of the World Trade Center, about which more evidence continues to emerge that challenges the official narrative. What is certain is that it gave us expansive and intrusive new encroachments on our liberty, the Department of Homeland Security and Big Brother spying on you. We tolerate full-body groping at airports. But we have still been complacent.

President Obama proclaimed his goal of a radical transformation of America, but We the People turned a deaf ear. We were once more complacent.

Donald Trump is a person not affiliated with "the swamp," the political establishment. As we have since learned, even as he took office, the swamp leaders of our nation's most powerful agencies—the CIA, the FBI, and the Department of Justice, fueled by Hillary Clinton and the Democratic National Committee—colluded and connived to overthrow the will of the electorate, with their insurance policy to remove him from office. As he so often said, "They are not after me; they are after you. I'm just standing in the way." In spite of overwhelming evidence of these crimes, pried piecemeal from the deep state bureaucracy, there have been no prosecutions as I write. Are we still complacent?

George Soros has boasted for years that he owns the Democratic Party, and another millionaire, Michael Bloomberg, in his flawed debate for the Democratic nomination in 2020, bragged that he had bought forty Democrats himself. Soros and Bloomberg are right, as the socialist Democrats vote without exception to echo the party line—not We the People's line—both in the House of Representatives and in the Senate. Voters put a majority of these socialist Democrats in the House of Representatives in 2018, and they all vote the party line in unison.

For example, although it was already proven that charges were untrue, taxpayers spent thirty-five million dollars or more to pursue a dirt-digging investigation conducted by Democrat activists, ruining the lives of innocent Americans and generating mountains of documents, only to admit, after two years and in spite of it all, that Trump had done nothing wrong.

Undeterred, having control of the House, they set about overriding the choice of the people who elected him president by following up with their insurance policy, all the while ignoring their Constitutional responsibilities. With the playbook straight out of Communist Russia, they sequestered themselves, locked out the Republicans, cherry picked witnesses, and didn't allow Republicans even to hear the testimony, cross-examine them, or call other witnesses. They leaked juicy tidbits to the complicit press. They scorned mankind's basic jurisprudence dating to the Magna Carta in 1215. They came up with nothing, and their testimony backfired.

So they impeached the president for fulfilling his Constitutional role under Article 2 of the Constitution. A narrow Republican majority in the Senate stopped this farce from being prolonged indefinitely—mindless of the threat of the Wuhan virus that emerged—while all the Democrats stuck to the party line. Without that slim majority, the next coup could succeed and the nation would be in chaos.

In Communist countries, the media are tightly managed. Anyone who would stray from the party line "disappeared:" the euphemism for being murdered. With few exceptions, we have, as well, similar party line media in America. Whistleblowers disappeared. The Voice of America broadcasts in more than forty languages. It attempts to get accurate information—with an American edge—to countries where the truth is suppressed. We need it to broadcast to America for everyone with an interest in truth seeking.

So we face the fact that there are powerful forces intent on seizing power at any cost (their end justifies any means), whose goal is to eradicate civilization and replace it with an insane communist Armageddon. Karl Marx said, "Everything that exists deserves to perish; I shall stride through the wreckage a creator." From the wreckage, communism has already "created" the murder of more than a million innocent citizens in the last century. It is racking up more victims with this Wuhan virus. This can be labeled the Third Red Scare. We say three strikes and you're out. There is no reasoning with them. Their replacement of individuality with the movement drives them to collectively hate the world and does not accommodate reason. With them, there can be no compromise.

Our complacency must end now. Anything that hints of politically correct attacks on the First Amendment, or identity politics, striving to turn neighbor against neighbor, must be, instead, eradicated. Either we or they will be left standing. As I write, organized Marxist rioters have been destroying many Democrat-run cities for many days, uncontrolled by their complacent mayors and governors, and more riots are foretold with the November election.

According to Wikipedia, "Sedition is overt conduct, such as speech and organization, that tends toward rebellion against the established order. Sedition often includes subversion of a constitution and incitement of discontent toward, or rebellion against, established authority. Sedition may include any commotion, though not aimed at direct and open violence against the laws. Seditious words in writing are seditious libel." According to FindLaw, "Sedition is a serious felony punishable by fines and up to 20 years in prison and it refers to the act of inciting revolt or violence against a lawful authority with the goal of destroying or overthrowing it."

Having studied the threat to civilization that communism poses and the many advances it has already made in America and now witnessing this frontal assault, there is no time left for complacency. Insanity is doing the same things over and over and expecting different results. Well, our complacency over and over has gotten us nowhere. More of the same seems insane.

Focusing on progress is always encouraging and optimistic. Setting a goal we can't meet is discouraging and implies defeat. Recall the words of Winston Churchill: "You may come to the moment when you will have to fight with all the odds against you." He sounds so fatalistic. Dr. Martin Seligman[21], on the contrary, made his reputation researching optimism, and he found that even unrealistic optimism beats pessimism and promotes both physical and emotional health. He makes the case for Pollyanna. I hope Churchill spoke too soon. There's got to be a middle ground.

Are there such people as realistic optimists? Henry Ford put it this way. There are those who think they can and those who think they can't. And they're both right. Henry Ford was a realist. Americans are traditionally known as the most optimistic people on earth. And like Ford, we are a can-do nation. We have confidence that we can make things work out, and we make things work out. We make our optimism authentic. But we have to take a stand.

WHAT'S THE PLAN?

It's in our Constitution. Dr. Edwin Vieira Jr. is recognized as the world's foremost authority on the Constitution. Among many writings, he published a 2,400-page e-book, *The Sword and Sovereignty*, and a shorter one, *Constitutional "Homeland Security."*[22] He has much to say about the Militia in the Second Amendment, but for him, the Militia is every one of We the People, and the goal is citizen-based homeland security. In fact, he emphasizes that a core group of those that he calls gun people is not desirable "because of the many matters in which firearms have no place." His plan, to borrow President Kennedy's words, is to get the citizens to "ask not what your country can do for you – ask what you can do for your country."

We should view this in stages. As I noted in Chapter 12, which focused on the first step of strengthening the family and safeguarding the children, Donald Trump built tall skyscrapers. He emphasized that the secret is having a solid foundation. We are at the stage of digging the foundation. As with any new project, solutions are created along the way. We first need to find who we are and to unify around our common values and purpose—everyone who is concerned about the danger to our civilized way of life. The division in our nation is stark, and We the People must come down, practically speaking, to every one of us who buys in to salvaging Christian civilization.

It is "the inside of the cup" that matters, not churchgoing or labels. Feeling a responsibility to push back against communist barbarism matters. The criteria must be whether individuals aspire to a civilized, right way to live, accept everyone of goodwill, and work together. Think of a band of brothers—soldiers from diverse backgrounds, bonded together to make it happen.

Love of neighbor is an active verb. It isn't a feeling but a commitment to be response-able, that is willing and able to respond. Yet while being inclusive, we cannot compromise our mission with bad apples. The Tea Party movement tapped national goodwill. The Wuhan virus brought our nation together. There are many concerned truth seekers out there. In order to have the impact necessary to actually change our American Sitz im Leben and restore civilization, we must get these truth-seeking people to buy in.

These citizens must recognize how extensively communism has already enveloped this nation, so they will speak out against politically correct mind control, confront those who would pit one group of Americans against another, and buy into salvaging Christianity. Boarding an airplane, when the stewardess explains where the exits are, and "in case the cabin loses pressure, this mask will drop down," etc., most people have their minds on other things. But when the pilot announces, "Buckle your seat belts. We have lost an engine and will be making an emergency landing," everyone is all ears about what the stewardess has to say. We must all recognize what we are dealing with in order to confront it.

It is unrealistic to think that everyone will read this book. Being a Paul Revere and spreading the word by social networking is a starting point. This is today's basic platform for connecting with truth seekers and growing our network. So begin by talking to several friends who are also concerned. Ideally, one of them has read this book as well. Then get together. Psychologists say that more than half of communication is nonverbal—face to face. It's the best way to get on the same page with one another. Having simple meetings builds encouragement—at McDonalds or Big Boy, perhaps. Be sure everyone shares their ideas. Share some of the things you have learned and start thinking of plans. Quiet folks are often those who think deepest but may need to be invited to share their ideas. Network Marketers know they should "book a meeting from a meeting," marking a definite date to get together again. So we begin by linking together those we know who want to buy in to salvaging civilization. Have friends reach out to those they know. Success won't work by trying to *sell* the idea to those who don't recognize the crisis, and we don't need pessimists.

When people are working together, those who are good communicators can schedule meetings and, with friends, line up interested people to come to a meeting. Some folks will already be aware of what we face and may be willing to share their insights if they have the opportunity. If they are considered (not yet invited) to "team teach" at a meeting, learn first how much they actually know, so the speaker(s) are not contradicted. They may have some wake-up stories to share. Then plan how the issues will be presented. Ask for sufficient contributions to cover the cost of a local hall, including coffee and munchies. Invite dialogue and show appreciation for everyone's ideas.

Stick to the basic concerns, how the basic tenants of communism have a foothold in America already. Point out the threat of public "education" and the values of homeschooling. Print out a basic handout for them with the points of what is taught and the way to stay in touch. Always brainstorm about what we can do about it. Try to use the Socratic method, so people figure out for themselves that we can no longer be complacent. Get those in attendance to sign up with their phone and email address, so you can follow up and keep them involved. Then follow up, thank them for coming, and encourage their involvement.

Should somebody at the meeting be a naysayer and try to capture the meeting, the leader must politely cut the person off, saying, "Well, that isn't why these folks are here. Why don't you schedule your own meeting?" If you are confronted by those who have been brainwashed by media disinformation, don't try to dissuade them. Their mind is made up; don't confuse them with facts. Trying to argue their case simply grants them the chance to reinforce their prejudices since they lack meaningful issues to debate. Being good examples of Christian values will have more of a chance to persuade them. They might end up wanting what you have when they see that love of neighbor beats the hatred of identity politics. If you encounter "intellectual" Marxist atheists, it is pointless to debate them. As explained, their reward would be feeling exceptional by talking down to the "deplorable" lower castes in society. Like Karl Marx, they know everything. "There is none so blind as he who will not see." Simply detour around them. They relish the attention.

The amount of motivation, available time, special interests, experience, and many other factors determine what role each will fit into. Some may be willing to phone or email a representative or send a postcard that is supplied, with the representative's address printed on it, when notified. These are printed for you at Staples or OfficeMax. Some may have bones to pick with schools or have some other cause or interest. Some may be willing to keep tabs on what is going on in their state government and keep everyone in the loop. Some are already scouring the internet for the latest threats, as well as any reassurance out there, and can share this with the group. Eventually, some may be willing to run for some office.

We need to find out what suits everyone. The more diversity, the better. Everyone can make a contribution. *Together Everyone Achieves More*. Leaders and organizers will emerge in time, but as scripture says, they must be the servants of the group rather than self-centered individuals, whose real mission is recognition and power. They would overtake the group's mission. Keeping an eye on clear objectives is the only way to succeed.

Try to get folks to choose how they feel most comfortable being part of the team. Suggest choices. If they start on the lowest rung, they may find higher rungs to stand on. Potential activists tend to identify one another at meetings, from what they contribute to the discussions, and you may find them talking together afterwards or at a break.

Homeschoolers will benefit from our networking, discovering other aware homeschooling families. As children find ways to meet up with one another, their parents will also find that they are making lasting friendships. Where you live determines your public resources, such as community sports, dance classes, art or pottery classes, those "soccer mom" clubs, etc. Or perhaps Future Farmers of America and 4-H. These are also opportunities to network with adults as well.

The Boy Scouts of America seems to have succumbed to political correctness—not resembling what it was in my day—and is now in bankruptcy because of homosexual predators in the organization. I believe something will replace it if need be, because it contributed significantly to building American character. It appears that the Girl Scouts of America is still stable.

Nothing compares with actual physical activities, but once relationships are established, the younger generation is far more wired than yours truly, so the problem is really *limiting* their social networking. The website, www.homeschooling.com suggests 100 homeschooling sites that it ranks as the best. There are many homeschooling co-ops to explore. Active parents might want to start their own, from basic to elaborate. Figure out a location and get a consensus among the parents about what the plan will be. Diversity is educational but rules must be in place, with someone authorized to enforce them, to lock out bullying or children with un-Christian behavior. Where there's a will, there are multiple ways.

I'm not big on what I call "white middle-class discussion groups," folks who meet monthly and *talk* about problems. What we need are action plans. Once people sign up to do something, they can meet if purposeful but not out of habit. On the other hand, at the right time, arrange fun get-togethers instead, especially to celebrate some success.

If you know atheists who seem sincere, by all means find out where they stand and tell them about Rudolf Bultmann. Clearly distinguish the business of organized religion from the authentic Christian Good News. Invite them to join in salvaging our civilization.

Among the universal Militia, Vieira is looking for activists: "only enough Americans" to be a good example for others to want to follow. He notes the personal characteristics of members of these groups: idealists of the strongest moral principles; realists who see the pressing need; "and especially pragmatists who can devise ways and means to accomplish their goal." These subgroups must reassure everyone that they are nothing more than a group of local citizens exercising their "freedom to engage in association for the advancement of beliefs and ideas" in line with the First Amendment.

As we grow confident in our power to make a difference and show a good example, our groups will grow. In due time, we will find candidates with civilized Christian values among us who are willing to run for public office, even County Commissioner. Of course, if there is someone running for public office who demonstrates our values and is not simply less bad, assisting the campaign offers the added benefit of meeting other motivated people and expanding the groups. The erosion of civilization caused by self-serving government (mis)representatives must come to an end.

In fact, Vieira envisions a day when:

the Militia will provide immediate, massive, comprehensive, and thoroughgoing responses, specifically designed for and directed to each affected Locality by citizens who always reside near the scene, have personal ties with and sympathy for Local inhabitants, and are intimately familiar with Local needs and resources.[23]

That will be the top floor of our skyscraper, and we are still digging our foundation. It is very important, as we grow in strength, to only focus on progress and never set specific goals. Dr. Vieira addresses this in his second book, *Developing Homeland Security*. When we get to that stage, buying his book would be helpful as it provides precise directions to make this homeland security happen.

As I said, through all of this, serious and urgent as it is, make it fun. When someone scores a victory, have a party. We all need kudos. Celebrate the fact that we still have more freedom than most humans in history and still live in a nation that is redeemable.

Economics drives politics. By uniting in sufficient numbers, we can use our purchasing power to influence policy. If we let it be known that we will patronize businesses and enterprises that support our Bill of Rights and Christian values and that we will refuse to do business with those who do not, the pendulum will swing. If we, united, let it be known that we will not watch news outlets that propagandize disinformation, they will either report the truth or perish. If we, united, refuse to watch a movie if the actor is publicly undermining our civilized way of life, we will send a message at the box office. Together, we can salvage civilization.

THE SECURITY OF A FREE STATE

I don't want to gloss over the Second Amendment because it is the foundation for securing our constitutional republic and is under continuous attack these days. The Second Amendment states in full, "A well regulated Militia, being necessary to the security of a free State, the right of the people to keep and bear Arms, shall not be infringed." In article 1, section 8 of the Constitution, Congress must provide for "organizing, arming, and disciplining, the Militia, and for governing such Part of them as may be employed in the Service of the United States."

To make "regular," then, is to organize, arm, and discipline the Militia. To make regular "such part" of We the People, as the Constitution requires—organized, armed, and disciplined as an army—would not merely be buying a gun for a man who didn't have one. Given all the equipment of modern combat today, this would be extremely expensive, and we might consider it unnecessary since only such part would be employed militarily. Thus the National Guard, a part of We the People, would arguably fulfill that role. That part of the "homeland security" Militia has multiple roles and is deployed to help with the Wuhan virus crisis.

But there is a risk in this logic, which was recently exposed by the managers of the state of Virginia. The government of Virginia threatens to pass laws nullifying—alienating—the un*alien*able right of self-protection recognized in the Second Amendment. The governor in Virginia allegedly threatened to call forth the National Guard to attack We the People in that state, who recently protested peacefully en masse and who have firewalled their counties against such an attempt. This crisis is precisely what Dr. Vieira has devoted his life to preclude. Thomas Jefferson said, "The strongest reason for the people to retain their right to keep and bear arms is a last resort to protect themselves against tyranny in government." Thus, "such part" of We the People is to be made "regular" to, among other duties, *repel* tyranny. Instead, the tyrant would attempt to control "such part" of We the People to *enforce* tyranny, threatening to pit the Militia against the Militia—that is, We the People against one another, neighbors in the Guard against their neighbor.

Understand that the Guard are not all Green Berets; they are secretaries, cooks, truck drivers, mechanics, helicopter pilots, etc., not in sufficient numbers to thwart even the twenty-five thousand armed but peaceable protesters that showed up. Psychological research has shown, particularly that of Dr. Stanley Milgram[24] that most ordinary citizens would blindly "obey orders." Yet Guard members take an oath to support the Constitution as the supreme law of the land and personally support the Second Amendment. This is a formula for chaos.

This is the second consideration. George Washington allegedly said, "Firearms stand next in importance to the Constitution itself." That is because those fourteen words—"the right of the people to keep and bear arms shall not be infringed"—validate We the People as a republic and thus are the backbone of the Constitution. It is not without reason that Edwin Vieira, the world's foremost authority on the Constitution, devoted so much of his life writing about the Second Amendment.

I need to make a philosophical distinction. The laws of nature express nature—that is, the *essence* of something. That is an important word in philosophy. It is simply what makes things what they actually are. The essence of something is immutable, unchangeable. So when the Declaration of Independence says, "We hold these truths to be self-evident, that all men are created equal," it is stating that all human beings have the same essence. Our essence has immutable characteristics and fulfilling those characteristics is our unalienable right and responsibility. Human beings have an un*alien*able right to be human beings. This is self-evident. Our un*alien*able natural rights only come from essence. So the only sources of the rights are the individuals in the group.

Well, some people have brown eyes and some blue eyes; some have straight hair and some, curly hair. These are "accidental" to what our human essence is. The term in philosophy is *accidents*. Whatever is changeable and not essential are accidents. Social arrangements are like accidents. They have no essence, but they are "beings of reason," reasonable arrangements created by real human beings that have an immutable essence.

Okay. Since human beings began gathering in groups, it became clear that some form of organization was necessary, a common force to protect the rights of everyone in the group. So one or more members of the group acquired the social arrangement of managers of the group. We saw how each primitive tribe in Africa had a king. Having power makes people feel secure, so they crave it. Throughout history these group managers have been dictators, claiming some special, un*alien*able right on their own to be autonomous and boss everyone else around, a "right" which they obviously didn't possess.

We call these managers "government," and governments throughout history have seized power. Human beings who happen to have the role of government do not thereby become some special creatures with their own unique essence. They are just members of the group who have become the social managers. Un*alien*able natural rights only come from essence. So the only sources of the rights are the individuals in the group. Only to the extent that the individual members of the group consent to share some of their individual rights with the group managers— which we call government—can the "government" legally have any governmental rights at all.

For example, say George steals Pete's car and sells it to Bill, who then sells it to Sally. Now whose car is it? It is still Pete's car since he alone has the valid title. Unalienable rights may be consensually shared but can never be given up. Human beings can't give up being human beings. Thus, a communist dictatorship cannot steal governmental control from We the People, since the people alone retain their rights. A communist "government" is invalid.

So the Declaration of Independence states "to secure these rights [among which are life, liberty, and the pursuit of happiness] Governments are instituted among Men, deriving their just powers from the consent of the governed." Anything else would be *un*just. It was our founders who finally got it right. Our federal government only exists as a social contract, drafted, and consented to by the separate states. It has no essence (the technical word is that it is an *ens rationis*, "a being of reason," something reasoned about and designed by the people) and thus bestows no intrinsic rights. The only essential rights remain the un*alien*able rights of the people themselves, some of which are consensually shared or *delegated* to it in the contract.

This is an example. In 2017, Rep. Steve Scalise was shot while playing second base. At that time, he was unable to defend himself. But he had shared his right to self-protection with two security guards, and they exercised that right on his behalf and saved him.

So governments cannot simply make up laws. Governments simply explain or interpret and apply the laws of nature embodied in the individuals in the group, rights which are consensually shared. And even if they wanted to, the individuals in the group could obviously not share with the government a make-believe "right" they did not have in their essence. Any law is only a pretend law, a bogus law, which does not faithfully interpret the basis of all law: the laws of nature and of nature's God.

The laws governments make are called Positive Laws—that is, "posited" as spelling out and matching the essential basis of all law, the natural law, to situations that come up. Following Cicero, we say this is "right reason." If they misinterpreted the true laws, these positive laws would have no effect. Were they to outlaw an innocent person's right to life or, for that matter, outlaw gravity, such "laws" would be unjust laws and have no effect. They should not be obeyed.

So we come back to these fourteen words. They attest that we hold true that We the People retain all the rights and hold all the power; thus, these words validate this constitutional republic. We will not allow anyone to infringe on our self-evident and un*alien*able rights, the expressions of our essence as human beings. The people in government with whom we consent to share some of our power can never impose themselves on We the People as if the government we create were the creator, with an essence of its own.

We say there are those who talk the talk and those who walk the walk. There's the story of the mice that got together and unanimously voted that the house cat must have a bell for their protection. But no mouse could be found to bell the cat. Talk is meaningless without the wherewithal to back it up.

This declaration clarifying the security of a free state is unique among the nations of the world. It is the keystone unalienable right that underpins all our essential rights. We mean it. We are freemen. The power remains in the hands of We the People of this republic. Its proclamation of our individualism and our resolve to affirm and back up our self-determination has inspired the inventors and entrepreneurs who have made this nation so exceptional, the envy of the world. It has sustained our Christian civilization.

So it should come as no surprise that the communists in America and the globalists who seek a one-world communist government—denying that humans are self-determining and have any un*alien*able rights—are so rabid in their attacks on our Second Amendment. Some would even say false flag attacks. The Second Amendment stands as our firewall against them.

Our brave police officers, in their dangerous work, inevitably kill innocent citizens every year. At least sixteen million American law-abiding citizens legally carry concealed firearms, not counting those in states that do not require licensing. It is virtually unheard of that any one of them kills an innocent citizen, while—contrary to the incessant drumbeat of disinformation—irrefutable research by Dr. John Lott Jr. and others has shown that crime is thereby reduced. From their research, guns stop crime two million times a year in America. The propaganda news media cover up all this information.

Traditionally, Americans are a do-it-yourself nation. We the People don't wait for government to take care of us; we shoulder responsibility to do it ourselves. We are tool-using animals, and thus our DNA demands that we find the best tool for self-protection. Since colonial days, the only tool everyone can have to adequately defend this unalienable right is a firearm. Only a firearm puts a 120-pound woman on the same playing field with O.J. Simpson. Our soldiers could not protect us as a society without firearms.

Almost without exception, those intent on mass murder target gun-free zones. In the first place, gun-free zones are prima facie unconstitutional as would be a "free speech–prohibited zone" or any other prohibition alienating an un*alien*able right. If sufficient numbers of the whole Militia are trained, with minimal effort and expense, to safely and competently bear firearms and thus were likely present, it is argued that these murderers would be deterred, realizing that they could not achieve their goal. Moreover, *all* crimes of assault would be deterred.

SHOULD WE AFFILIATE?

Time is limited and putting what time we can to the most effective use, so we don't get burned out, is always a priority. That said, there are national organizations of conservative-thinking people, and getting involved with one or more of them can be instructive and, again, be a way of joining others with a common cause. I look to "conservative" groups because the Democratic Party has been captured by the communists at this time. Descriptions are copied from the respective websites. These are a few of them.

- The American Conservative Union (https://www.conservative.org)
  We believe that the Constitution of the United States is the best political charter yet created by men for governing themselves. It is our belief that the Constitution is designed to guarantee the free exercise of the inherent rights of the individual through strictly limiting the power of government.
- American Family Association (https://www.afa.net)
  The American Family Association shines the light of scripture nationwide on social, moral, and public policy issues impacting the family, but the moral climate in local communities will change only as citizens get involved. This association has affiliates in Illinois, Indiana, Kansas, Missouri, Michigan, New York, and Pennsylvania.
- Americans for Prosperity (https://americansforprosperity.org)
  Through broad-based grassroots outreach, Americans for Prosperity (AFP) is driving long-term solutions to the country's biggest problems. AFP activists engage friends and neighbors on key issues and encourage them to take an active role in building a culture of mutual benefit, where people succeed by helping one another. We recruit and unite concerned citizens in thirty-five states to advance policies that will help people improve their lives.
- Citizens United (https://www.citizensunited.org)
  Citizens United is an organization dedicated to restoring our government to citizens' control. Through a combination of education advocacy, and grass roots organization, Citizens United seeks to reassert the traditional American values of limited government, freedom of enterprise, strong families, and national sovereignty and security. Citizens United's goal is to restore the founding fathers' vision of a free nation, guided by the honesty, common sense, and goodwill of its citizens.
- Eagle Forum (https://eagleforum.org)
  Our mission is to enable conservative and pro-family men and women to participate in the process of self government and public policy-making so that America will continue to be a land of individual liberty, with respect for the nuclear family, public and private virtue, and private enterprise.
- Freedom Works (https://www.freedomworks.org)
  We are over six million Americans who are passionate about promoting free markets and individual liberty. Our members all share three common traits: a desire for less government, lower taxes, and more economic freedom. Freedom Works has identified, educated, and actuated citizens

who are enthused about showing up to support free enterprise and constitutionally limited government. Freedom Works trains volunteers, assists in campaigns, and encourages them to mobilize, interacting with both fellow citizens and their political representatives. It is widely associated with the Tea Party movement.

LEARNING THE POLITICAL GAME

When the nationwide Christian coalition attains a sufficient quantity of leaders and maturity, the focus can turn to reversing the corruption rampant in our governing class. That would benefit from professional training in political activism. There are online courses available, for example:

- American Majority (https://www.americanmajority.org/training/activism-training)
- Heritage Action for America (https://heritageaction.com/activist-training)
- Conservative Political Activism (https://conservativepoliticalactivism.zippycourses.com/course/fightback)

The Foundation for Applied Conservative Leadership (https://facl-training.org) is an organization that provides actual workshops. They will provide clear and copious instructions, so that you can arrange for a day of activist training, and the trainer is financed by FACL. An honorarium would be thoughtful. They require a minimum of sixteen registered participants—let me say twenty, so you're sure of having sixteen there—and hopefully, many more. If you're secure with the number, you request a form at least six weeks before your chosen date: http://www.requestfaclclass.com/1day.

You would need to get a group of people together to spread the word and pull this off. Many hands make light work. Your staff has to find a suitable venue and arrange for munchies and lunch.

At this time, their early bird rate is forty dollars for adults and their student rate is twenty-five dollars. General admission is fifty or thirty dollars. This covers your venue, food, and other expenses. FACL has been at this a long time. Their instructions for making this happen are ample and clear. They walk you through it and leave no stone unturned.

PSYCHING OUT THE POLITICIAN

What makes a politician? We put on our psychology hat and try to analyze this special subspecies of *Homo sapiens*. Don't imagine we are alike. Stereotypically, politicians are self-serving. They may start poor, but they will come out rich if they can stay at it long enough. If that isn't enough, they can then get more money as a lobbyist. Besides, that is an easy job—at least between elections—with multiple perks from folks who have money and vested interests.

We saw what Thomas Sowell had to say about thinking beyond Stage 1. Politicians are not leaders. They don't think beyond Stage 1. Stage 1 is getting elected and getting elected again. The concerns of their constituents are publicly acknowledged before elections to get votes. Whether the concerns really have any intrinsic value—or, in fact, may have disastrous long-term consequences—isn't relevant. Anything that can get publicity, so long as it is not absolutely scandalous, is good. Actually, it doesn't so much matter what people say about politicians—whether praiseworthy or critical. What matters is that their name is out there. It's a mental billboard that prompts an X in the voting booth. Of course, they must be politically correct. Their voting record is of marginal interest because most voters aren't that interested in details. They are likely to pay more attention to the politician's hairstyle and whether they like our identity politics persona and appear like one of us.

They'll let you know that they value you as their friend, but they are never your friend. They are professionals at their job—that is, getting reelected. They have devised many ways to get you to be their friend, at least if you are likely to contribute to their campaign and, even better, if you buy a yard sign. They are highly skilled at talking around the issues to get you to believe they see things your way but without actually getting trapped into having to vote for your interests. If you persist, they could ignore you, so you give up. They could say, "You don't understand. We have to be reasonable." They could whine, "Well, those cuts would kill us." They could explain, "That's just not how things are done," "The governor won't sign it," "Well, we have to wait until such and such," "You're the only one talking about this," or "You might end up getting something worse." If they think you control some votes, they could put you on an advisory committee, thereby muzzling you. I'm telling you, they're good at what they do. They could even get threatening (if you are playing hardball) or have others threaten you or threaten your organization and your career: "You'll never work here again." We need not belabor this further. You get the idea.

If you attend a workshop for activists, most likely the approach you will hear is "Inflict pain." Now that doesn't sound particularly Christian, but they know what they are talking about. You must force politicians to act appropriately if they want to be reelected. There you have it.

Let me put it this way. What works better? (a) You and your two friends study the issues and write thoughtful two-page letters to your representative, explaining why it is very important to vote a certain way on a bill or even cosponsor it. (b) You use social media and get 150 folks—who think the way you do—to each send the representative a postcard, telling them how to vote. (You can make copious preaddressed postcards at Staples or OfficeMax.) Obviously, they won't waste the time it takes to read your letters, but when those postcards pile up on their desk, they grab attention. The vote ciphers are spinning in their head.

Your group might print up some leaflets and pass them around in key areas of their district. That will get their attention and maybe get some votes. If someone in your group could get on talk radio, it would get their attention and that of the voters as well. Even letters to the editor might be worth it.

Hold them accountable. If they actually cosponsor the bill, give them an A. A written promise is next best. Do they make a promise in public that gets on the record? That's okay as well. That's it.

Dealing with politicians is a tough business. Replacing them with genuine, civilized leaders has to be the goal. As I said, we can start out small: county commissioner. Get the whole group behind such leaders, those idealists of the strongest moral principles, realists who see the pressing need, and especially pragmatists who can devise ways and means to accomplish their goal. The hairstyle should be secondary. Get them to the finish line.

THE COMMUNIST VIRUS, DANGER AND OPPORTUNITY

The Chinese word character for *crisis* is the combination of two characters: *danger* and *opportunity*. And so it is. The cliché is to never let a crisis go to waste. This gave the socialist Democrats in America an opportunity to try to poison urgent crisis relief legislation by inserting their communist position under the table and then to begin yet another investigation of Donald Trump, this time for his management of the crisis, in league with a media propaganda campaign.

For example, upon news of the virus, Trump had acted immediately—deciding alone, against unanimous opposition—to close the border with China before any deaths in America and thus saved many lives. The echo chamber media are lying to gullible Americans, claiming that he "acted too slowly."

As I write, there has been nationwide home detention/imprisonment, thirty days and counting. The virus has devastated metropolitan areas, but large areas of America are unscathed yet nonetheless had been in this extended lockdown, not permitted to work or go about their lives. Murderers are being released from prison, adding to the crisis. Several have already murdered again.

Yet citizens are fined and sentenced, in one case put in jail for running a nail salon out of their house with all safeguards in place. A lone surfer is arrested, a minister for holding a service with the required social distancing, a family playing all by themselves in the park. A woman with asthma watching her son on the sports field is tasered and handcuffed for taking off her mask. People cannot earn their livelihood or even protest unless the protests are joined by the anarchists and rioters. Liquor and cannabis stores are deemed essential, but church worship has been prohibited. The situation is chaotic already. Communalism and the police state got yet another upturn.

The Chinese Communist leadership—in collaboration with the World Health Organization, part of the communist United Nations Sustainable Development Group—deliberately muzzled and murdered the doctors who tried to warn us. More revealing information continues to trickle out. As I write, Chinese virologist Li-Meng Yan, who escaped from China, and three colleagues claim in a peer-reviewed paper to show evidence the virus did not originate in nature, but was deliberately created in the Wuhan laboratory.

They allowed Wuhan, an international gateway, to proliferate the virus for more than a month while protecting their metropolitan areas until it could no longer be hidden and has now poisoned virtually every nation on earth, furthering their goal of world domination. They have prohibited world experts from learning the facts and expelled the reporters.

We recall the words of Karl Marx: "Everything that exists deserves to perish; I shall stride through the wreckage a creator." Again, Roosevelt said, "In politics, nothing happens by accident. If it happens you can bet it was planned that way." The communists view humans as expendable, equivalent to the farmer's herd of cows or flock of chickens, and they have people to spare in China.

Contrast this characteristic evil of communism with the inspiring response in America, the socialist politicians notwithstanding. The private sector responded with an all-out public-private partnership; businesses rose to the occasion and contributed whatever they could; essential stores and supply chains had been open, at personal risk; churches organized to care for the needy; the public safety and public health providers had been working long hours, again at personal risk; and individuals volunteered to sew masks in their homes and organized brigades to shop for the elderly. The nation came together and practiced love of neighbor when the chips were down. I doubt all these heroes had been attending church services—indeed, some would identify as atheists—, but labels are irrelevant in a crisis. What matters is a personal commitment of truth seekers to demonstrate love for our neighbor. It's in our DNA. The crisis is an opportunity to reaffirm our human nature as social animals, energized by our Christian roots. Jesus still lives in us.

But we've slipped down this slippery slope, and now we must dig in and climb back up. And I'm optimistic that we can. There have been mounting demonstrations against this imposed lockup. The Supreme Court in Michigan found the governor's orders unconstitutional. And as Governor Northam in Virginia threatened to eradicate the un*alien*able Second Amendment, twenty-five thousand armed citizens showed up to peacefully protest. It would appear that the frog, by now in hot water, may finally be thinking of jumping out. This communist crisis has given America a spine and made us less complacent. With the opportunity that this crisis has provided to bring together truth-seeking Americans, finding no time for identity politics, many more citizens appear to be concerned about closing that barn door, even though the horse is already in the pasture. Can we get it back?

This is yet another opportunity. Recall the Tytler cycle. Nations move from bondage to spiritual faith and then to courage and to liberty. Contrary to media control and disinformation, this virus has further destabilized China as well. It is estimated that deaths in China are fifty times what they report. Communist China has been unable to eradicate religions, and although it has doubled down on persecuting them, they continue to expand their influence. There are a hundred million Christians in China, compared with ninety million in the Chinese Communist Party. There are many Muslims and various other sects. The Falun Gong began in 1992, teaching truthfulness, compassion, and forbearance and emphasizing morality and virtue. It already claims seventy million courageous members in spite of vicious persecution. This Falun Gong movement showcases the essential Christian virtue in the natural law, in our human nature.

Eventually, liberty will come to China. We must never confuse the official China with the Chinese people, nor can we ignore the psychopathic character of official Communist China. What I can predict is that there will be international blowback for the crime it unleashed with the Wuhan virus.

Trump has stood up to Communist China, and many countries respect his leadership. Moreover, Trump has always stressed the need to have a self-sufficient

America. With the virus, trusting in this hostile nation for our medications caught everyone's attention and should prioritize this effort to take vital businesses back.

Again, fear and anger are simply responses to threat. As China feels threatened, it is predictably going to compensate by becoming more belligerent. But communism's callous devaluation of life should alert the world, outshine communist disinformation, and alter the world's complacency. Fortunately, Trump salvaged our military, and China would now be foolish to wage that level of war. This outrage will have consequences, and we cannot allow this opportunity—this wake-up call—to go to waste.

As I write, the outcome of the November election is uncertain. Without Trump, all bets are off. Multiple scandals are proliferating about having a rigged election, with reckless broadcasting of unsolicited ballots and ballot harvesting (collecting thousands of blank ballots from unsuspecting seniors and forging them). The election will have come and gone before this book goes to print. Whatever the outcome, we can no longer be complacent in America. We surely cannot be complacent about China as well. But to end on an optimistic note, it is worth remembering that the Chinese character word for crisis is the combination both of danger *and opportunity*.

CONCLUSION

Thank you for reading this book. You know the saying, "If everybody thinks the same way, somebody isn't thinking." But we have trekked along together. I'm confident you have learned things and been startled by things and have most likely questioned some things as well. I'm sure, were we to get to know each other, that you could also teach me things.

Thinking back to the Tytler cycle, our Sitz im Leben would appear to be the counterpoint to the Chinese—from complacency to apathy and then to dependency on the way to bondage. Well, if I wasn't optimistic, I could not have written this book. I am *not* apathetic. You signed on to read this book. *You* are not apathetic. Those two million Tea Party marchers in 2009 were not apathetic, and the Americans who painted the map red and elected Donald Trump in 2016 are not apathetic.

And especially Donald Trump is not apathetic. He's convinced that we're not stuck with this Sitz im Leben. He and his supporters are committed to "make America great again." The rallies he had before the Wuhan virus were impressive, for example in New Jersey, a Democratic state. Many camped out a day ahead of the rally, in the winter, so they could get in the arena. A hundred thousand were left outside. Twenty-six percent of them were Democrats. Ten percent of those who pledged to vote in November had never voted before. This ratio appears to have carried for all his rallies. *Those* people are not apathetic.

Of all the things I have said in this book, this is the most important: what to do with this information. Put the book on the bookshelf with all the books you've read? Make a decision to do something one of these days? Yesterday's news goes under the birdcage. Instead, before you close this book and put it away, I am making a big request. Decide to do something—one tiny thing—now. Choose a specific small action at a specific time and do it. Perhaps call or even text a friend. Maybe talk a bit about what you've read and find a time to sit down together and get your friend's opinion about what should be done. The slogan that network marketers use is, "Book a meeting from a meeting," so agree to touch base again "on Friday evening"—a specific time—and note that on your calendar. Taking that first courageous step can lead to a journey. It takes that small, awkward first step. If you have children, remember your child's first stumbling steps and your child's glee when it worked. That joyous relief is ours when we actually take that step.

Too many Americans are part of the problem nowadays. Thank you for being part of the solution.

APPENDIX

THE NERVOUS SYSTEM AND OUR BRAIN

The goal of this appendix is to clarify three basic neurological facts while avoiding as much neurological jargon as possible; some jargon is necessary. The nervous system is made up of neurons and, stemming from that neuronal body, are relatively long axons, which you could imagine to be biological connecting wires reaching very close to the next dendrite of another neuron. We call these junctures synapses. Dendrites pick up the impulse, and that neuron may then repeat the signal.

Now when the electric charge gets to the end of the axon, it releases a neurotransmitter substance, and there are various kinds of these neurotransmitter substances in the body. They jump that minute gap, and with sufficient strength, the next neuron sends the charge along its axon. Think of this typically as a massed signal, coming more from the Mormon Tabernacle Choir than the lead soprano. However, one neuron could set off ten thousand others. This may seem inefficient, but should you put your index finger on a hot stove, it all works reflexively before you can blink your eye and call yourself an idiot.

Dr. Daniel Siegel[1] informs us that the skull-based portion of the nervous system consists of over one hundred *billion* of these neurons, which, collectively, are more than two million miles long. To circle the earth at the equator, you need to travel 24,902 miles. Thus, stretching out these neurons would get you around the equator more than eighty times! Even more incredible, each neuron, on average, has ten thousand connections with other neurons. Got a calculator? It is up to one million billion connections, "the most complex structure, natural or artificial, on earth"! So long as we are alive, at any moment, the number of these firings in the brain is incalculable, in continual response to our ongoing experience, and it remains a very interactive, organized system.

So what's the point of this? The reason for sharing this is to point out that, so long as we are alive, our *unique* individual experiences are constantly rearranging these myriad synaptic connections in our brain. Far from humans being equivalent to Karl Marx's herd of cows and flock of chickens, every individual human being, while sharing the same essence, the same human nature, is exquisitely individual. Even identical twins, growing up together, are unique human beings in immeasurable ways. I have forever said, "The frog in your backyard and the frog in a pond in Africa are more alike than any two human beings." One expert even ventured that the difference between the brain of a chimpanzee and a human is greater than the difference between a chimpanzee and a tulip. Don't know where he got his research, but you get the idea. "Can you not buy two sparrows for a penny? You are worth more than hundreds of sparrows." (Or a flock of chickens.)

OUR HUMAN EXECUTIVE FUNCTION

Let's focus now on particular brain structures instead of the brain as a whole. Given brain complexity, this is the mother of all oversimplifications in order to convey a basic idea. We think of emotion and reason as separate concepts, but all information processing is emotional. Emotion links various brain systems together and is the central, driving force of cognition. Emotion coordinates perceptions with memory and behavior. We do what we desire to do. Emotions give our lives meaning.

We speak of an old brain and a new brain. By "old brain," we mean those brain structures that have a lot in common with those of other animals. Animals are impulsive, emotion driven: pleasure-pain, fight-flight, stimulus-response. This emotion-driven linkage we call the limbic system—the "paleomammalian cortex" (how's that for a mouthful!). I am going to skip over the various subsystems in the brain that are involved in the limbic system since I merely want to make a point. In brief, the limbic system assists in various processes relating to cognition, including spatial memory, learning, motivation, emotional processing, and social processing. It is the motivation and emotional processing that are the issue here.

I mentioned neurotransmitters. The particular neurotransmitter involved here is called dopamine. Dopamine is the neurotransmitter that signals pleasure, and it is the motivational neurotransmitter, so it is the relevant neurotransmitter here. The limbic system extends into the "new brain," the specifically human brain, particularly the prefrontal cortex, the front part of our brain. This connection is basically called the ventromedial prefrontal cortex (VMPFC), although associated structures are involved. So the VMPFC is the emotional component, and it is activated by dopamine. (This is where Karl Marx stops.)

Human brains have an additional system. It is expressed basically in the dorsolateral prefrontal cortex (DLPFC). We call it the executive function. Think of the CEO in a company. That person doesn't put the nuts on the bolts and might be all thumbs. This is not their pay grade. They are the company's overseers whose decisions determine if the company will thrive or go bankrupt. That's the job description of the DLPFC.

So we can imagine the VMPFC getting all excited about something it desires. It tells the DLPFC about it, and the DLPFC says, "Well, we'll take a look at that." It might conclude, for example, "Well, that's valuable, and the risk is slight. Let's go for it." But it might say, "If you look beyond Stage 1, that looks like a disaster. Very high risk. We're not going to do it." It is this executive function, including working memory, in a word, figuring-things-out memory, which makes human beings entirely distinct from mammals, "created in the image and likeness of God." This is an obvious refutation of Karl Marx.

What can disrupt this partnership? Anything that juices up dopamine sufficiently that it overrides the DLPFC and shuts it down. I assume that is why alcoholics and substance abusers like what they do, no inhibitions. That is what happens in a bipolar flare. These events dehumanize human beings.

THE ROLE OF THE UNCONSCIOUS

With all that brain activity constantly going on, how can anyone keep on top of it? The answer is, nobody can. You know, there have been a lot of jokes about Sigmund Freud and his preoccupation with the unconscious mind, but modern neurological research bears him out. Our unconscious brain has to manage 99 percent of all brain activity for us. Our executive can't also be running the assembly line.

As I said, emotion directs action. We say that emotions are changes in the state of integration in the brain—everything working in harmony. Integration is emotional health. Emotion channels brain energy and complex incoming, sensory, and outgoing, motor responses that direct behavior to protect and sustain life. With emotional disturbance, though, the brain slips toward chaos or rigidity. What I didn't say is that these processes are unconscious processes. For example, if there is a sign of danger, the brain is, at first, unconsciously alerted.

This is one example of the way it works. If the brain is alerted to danger, it would register, in this case, fear in the orbitofrontal cortex. This fear then loops back to the senses that picked it up. In some interesting research, subjects were asked to contort their faces in specific ways. They were unaware that these contortions mimicked specific emotional states. While keeping up these grimaces, they then listened to a neutral story. The subjects unwittingly explained the story in line with their facial grimaces, looping back to the orbitofrontal cortex.

The important point is that this occurred *unconsciously* since they didn't make the connection consciously. By way of mirror neurons, our experiences reflect back on themselves. The mind appraises appraisals, cataloging our ongoing experiences and setting up expectations. This is a shortcut mechanism, but haste can make waste. This process locks in certain thought patterns and emotional states, like depression and anxiety. Accumulated experiences create habitual prototypes, we might say templates in the brain, causing it to prejudge what is going on and leap before we look. While this is efficient, we unconsciously are sizing things up in prefabricated ways. There is a saying: "If the only tool in your box is a hammer, everything looks like a nail." This is how persons can get trapped, for example, by a self-defeating attitude without realizing it. The *unconscious* brain then interprets everything that is happening as further evidence of failures and thinks of the future as hopeless, and people would view themselves as losers more and more. Thus, a chronic disabling state is created, still unconscious, getting more entrenched with each repetition.

For example, I will never watch a horror movie. I don't want my unconscious brain to get cluttered with those templates that could, behind my back, mess up the way I see things.

So take the example of Karl Marx. As you saw, his utterly dysfunctional, self-centered life, living like the world owed him a living, devoid of any social empathy or responsibility, established templates in his unconscious brain that programmed him to create an equally dysfunctional, antisocial vision, ignorant of his bias.

Memories of emotional experiences can *feel* as real and direct as the original physical responses and reestablish these experiences—for example, a cascade of terrifying associations so that the person experiences being traumatized again and again. This is the explanation for posttraumatic stress disorder. This primarily unconscious information can then pass to higher order memory, *conscious* thinking, almost as it were coincidental.

Moreover, fitting in by being socially appropriate, which children can feign by their facial expressions already at two years of age to mask their true emotional state, develops a chronic, unconscious false self, misaligned with their true nature. As has been seen with PTSD, these unconscious states are very difficult to transcend.

Finally, our ever increasing dependence on technological management in place of individual responsibility, previously a do-it-yourself American attribute, establishes passive-dependent paradigms in the people's unconscious brains, progressively replacing our former self-determination with the unconscious reliance on and expectation of external regulation at the cost of our self-directed liberty. Thus, it should come as no surprise that the younger generations are abandoning Christian values and are, instead, oriented unconsciously to be dependent and financially supported by government, replacing individualism with communalism.

A look at the 2016 electoral map finds the socialist Democrats concentrated in the areas of the densest population, relatively eclipsed from direct experience in nature and even more dependent on technology. Thomas Jefferson had observed, "I think our governments will remain virtuous for many centuries; as long as they are chiefly agricultural; and this will be as long as there shall be vacant lands in any part of America. When they get piled upon one another in large cities, as in Europe, they will become corrupt as in Europe."

WHAT IS BEHAVIORISM?

I am briefly going to mention behaviorism, a popular theory in psychology. Many volumes have been written about behaviorism. It posits that all learning comes from the training of responses to stimuli. Ivan Pavlov measured the saliva in dogs. They would salivate when given meat powder. He rang a bell whenever he gave them meat powder. He trained them to salivate when he rang the bell without any meat powder. This is Classical Conditioning.

Burrhus Frederic (B. F.) Skinner introduced another type of conditioning called Operant Conditioning. He would put a rat in a box, and somewhere in the box would be a lever. The rat ran around the box and, sooner or later, accidentally bumped the lever. *Ka-chink,* a food pellet appeared in the food dish. The rat soon figured out the connection and was getting fat. Skinner upped the ante. Now the rat had to push the lever, say five times, to get its pellet. Then it got even trickier. The rat never knew how many lever pushes it would need. It would end up starving, burning up more calories working the lever than it was getting in the dish.

Behaviorism replaced Sigmund Freud and his emphasis on the unconscious mind. I was never a behaviorist. These are valuable and useful theories but not enough. Behaviorism works well training flatworms. With progress in neurological research, Sigmund and I have been exonerated.

Moving from dogs and rats to monkeys, we have experiments with what were termed executive monkeys. Two monkeys are hooked up for training, and they get identical shocks. When a bell rings, one of the monkeys, the executive monkey, if it responds quickly enough and hits a button, avoids the shock to both monkeys. The other monkey can't do anything about it. The executive monkeys die of bleeding ulcers, but the passive monkeys are just fine.

This is one final observation. Addiction is an example of classical conditioning, but my point is that the human brain is immeasurably more complex than that of monkeys, and we function exponentially beyond simple stimulus-response. For one thing, we have the DLPFC.

NOTES

INTRODUCTION

1 https://www.pewforum.org/2019/10/17/in-u-s-decline-of-christia
2 William J. Federer, *Change to Chains: The 6000 Year Quest for Control,* vol. 1, *Rise of the Republic* (St. Louis, MO:Amerisearch Inc., 2011).
3 W. Cleon Skousen, *The Five Thousand Year Leap* (Franklin, TN: American Pub LLC, 2009).

SECTION I: MISUNDERSTANDINGS

Chapter 1: What Is Sitz im Leben About?

1 www.biographyonline.net/scientists/galileo.html.
2 https://en.wikipedia.org/wiki/Aristarchus_of_Samos.
3 *Kerygma und Mythos* (Johnson, 1991) 39, https://epdf.pub/kerygma-and-myth.html.
4 https://www.azquotes.com/author/42018-Rudolf_Bultmann.
5 https://en.wikipedia.org/wiki/Rudolf_Bultmann.
6 https://www.faith-theology.com/2006/01/bultmann-on-resurrection_21.html.
7 Conrad Hyers, *The Meaning of Creation: Genesis and Modern Science* (Westminster: John Knox Press, 1984).
8 Wilhelm Dilthey and H. P. Rickman, *Pattern & Meaning in History Thoughts on History & Society* (Clementon, NJ: Harper, 1962).
9 https://en.wikipedia.org/wiki/Being_and_Time.
10 https://www.britannica.com/biography/David-Friedrich-Strauss.
11 John Horvat II, *Return to Order* (York, PA: York Press, 2013).
12 Christopher Caldwell, *The Age of Entitlement* (New York: Simon & Schuster, 2020), 7.

Chapter 2: What About Primitive Africa?

13 J. A. Hunter and Daniel P. Mannix, *Tales of the African Frontier* (Long Beach, CA: Safari Press Inc., 1954).
14 Ibid., 62.
15 Ibid., 103.

16   Ibid., 65.

17   Ibid., 65–66.

18   Ibid., 71.

19   Ibid., 67.

20   Ibid., 75.

21   Ibid., 81.

22   Ibid., 78.

23   Ibid., 80.

24   Ibid., 72.

25   Ibid., 73.

26   Ibid., 79.

27   Ibid., 71.

28   Ibid., 106.

29   Ibid., 141.

30   Ibid., 74.

31   Ibid., 177.

32   J. A. Hunter, *Hunter* (New York: Harper & Brothers Pub., 1852), 73.

Chapter 4: What to Think of Thomas Jefferson?

33   https://www.virginia.edu/visit/grounds.

34   https://thefederalist.com/tag/university-of-virginia. See also Daniel Payne, "Leftists at UVA Are Proving President Trump Right About Thomas Jefferson Statues," September 13, 2017.

35   Gilbert Chinard, *Thomas Jefferson: The Apostle of Americanism*, 2nd ed., rev. (Ann Arbor, MI: University of Michigan Press, 1975), 86–7.

36   https://archive.org/stream/anessaytowardsf00jeffgoog.

37   G. Edward Griffin, *The Creature from Jekyll Island*, 5th ed. (Westlake Village, CA: American Media, 2010), 375.

38   www.americanyawp.com/reader/the-sectional-crisis/1860-republican-party-platform.

39   Thomas Jefferson, *Autobiography*, January 6–July 29, 1821, in *Thomas Jefferson Papers*, Library of Congress. Transcription available at Founders Online.

40   https://www.freedomunited.org/partner/walk-free.

41   https://www.npr.org/templates/story/story.php?storyId=6670689.

42   Caldwell, *The Age of Entitlement*, 6.

43   Ibid., 34.

44   Ibid., 35.

45 www.blackenterprise.com/black-billionaires-rich-forbes.

46 Andrew Sciascia, "City Announces 3% Tax for Reparations, Regardless of Slave Ancestry," *Western Journal News*, December 4, 2019.

47 Phillip C. McGraw, *Life Strategies* (New York: Hyperion, 1999).

48 woodsoncenter.org.

Chapter 5: What About Organized Religion?

49 https://www.biblestudytools.com/lexicons/hebrew/nas/anav.html.

50 https://biblehub.com/hebrew/6035.htm.

51 "List of religious leaders convicted of crimes," Wikipedia.

52 https://christiansfortruth.com/how-communists.

53 Theundergroundchurch.net/blog/2018/06/17/communist

54 www.cpusa.org/party_voices/on-religion.

55 www.cpusa.org/article/the-role-of-the-black-church. See also theunder-groundchurch.net/blog/2018/06/17/communist.

56 Douglas Valentine, *The CIA as Organized Crime* (Atlanta, GA: Clarity Press Inc., 2017).

57 Joseph Ratzinger, *Introduction to Christianity* (San Francisco: Ignatius Press, 1968).

58 Joseph Ratzinger, *In the Beginning: A Catholic Understanding of the Story of Creation and the Fall* (Michigan: Wm. B. Erdmans Publishing Co. 1995), 5. See also https://en.wikipedia.org/wiki/Theology_of_Pope_Benedict_XVI.

59 John F. Thornton and Susan B. Varenne, *The Essential Pope Benedict XVI* (New York: HarperCollins, 2005), 228.

60 https://remnantnewspaper.com/.../articles/item/4506-the-political-pope-by-george-neumayr.

61 https://www.washingtonpost.com/world/europe/with-call-for-pope-to-resign-divisions.

62 https://www.latimes.com/world/la-fg-pope-francis-catholic-schism-20180828-story.html.

63 https://en.wikipedia.org/wiki/Theodore_Edgar_McCarrick.

64 *Democracy Dies in Darkness*

65 https://www.catholicnewsagency.com/news/bishop.

66 https://www.cnn.com/2018/08/14/us/pennsylvania-catholic-church-grand-jury.

67   http://huffingtonpost.com/2012/07/18/vatican-bank-needs-more-trans-parency-regulators-say; https://www.washingtonpost.com/national/on-faith.

68   Eustace Mullins, "The CIA," chap. 5 in *The World Order: A Study in the Hegemony of Parasitism* (New York: Modern History Publishers, 1984).

69   https://en.wikipedia.org/wiki/Operation_Gladio.

70   https://en.wikipedia.org/wiki/Bologna_massacre.

71   https://www.Amazon.com/Vatican-Exposed-Money-Murder-Mafia/dp/1591020654.

72   www.pythiapress.com/wartales/colby.htm.

73   Pinop Arlacchi, *Mafia Business: The Mafia Ethic and the Spirit of Capital-ism* (New York: Oxford University Press, 1988), 40.

74   en.wikipedia.org/wiki/Hitchens_challenge.

75   Christopher Hitchens, *god Is Not Great: How Religion Poisons Everything* (New York: Hachette Book Group, 2009).

76   https://www.bbc.co.uk/news/world-us-canada-11843586.

77   David Horowitz (West Palm Beach, FL: Humanix Books, 2018), 17.

78   Hitchens, *god Is Not Great*, 102.

79   Ibid., 7.

80   Ibid., 23.

81   Ibid., 56.

82   Ibid., 52.

83   Ibid., 10.

84   Ibid., 8.

85   Jeff Jacoby, "The Extraordinary Generosity of Ordinary Americans," *Globe Columnist*, January 28, 2016.

86   Ibid, 16–17.

87   Ibid., 30.

88   Ibid., 34.

89   Ibid., 6.

90   Ibid., 153.

91   Ibid., 27.

SECTION II: ERADICATING CHRISTIAN CIVILIZATION

Chapter 7: What Is Communism About?

1   W. Cleon Skousen, *The Naked Communist* (Salt Lake City, UT: Ensign Pub. Co., 1962), 20.

2   Ibid., 22.

3   Ibid., 28.

4   Ibid., 1.

5   Ibid., 38.

6   www.shareyouressays.com/knowledge/3-important-laws-of-metaphysics-by-karl-marx/113090.

7   Skousen, *The Naked Communist*, 39.

8   marxistphilosophy.org/Aizenberg.pdf.

9   www.shareyouressays.com/knowledge/3-important-laws-of-metaphysics-by-karl-marx/113090.

10   en.wikipedia.org/wiki/Marxist_philosophy_of_nature.

11   www.people.howstuffworks.com/communism1.htm.

12   Skousen, *The Naked Communist*, 2–3.

13   Jamie Glazov, *United in Hate: The Left's Romance with Tyranny and Terror* (Los Angeles, CA: WND Books, 2009), 11.

14   Ibid., 14.

15   Ibid., 9.

16   Ibid., 10.

17   Ibid., 19.

18   Ibid., 17.

19   Ibid., 8–9.

20   commonsensegovernment.com/the-tytler-cycle-revisited.

21   https://www.lorencollins.net/tytler1.html.

22   Jamie Glazov, *United in Hate: The Left's Romance with Tyranny and Terror* (Los Angeles, CA: WND Books, 2009), xxx, 11.

23   G. Edward Griffin, *The Creature from Jekyll Island*, 5th ed. (Westlake Village, CA: American Media, 2010).

24   Ibid., 233.

25   Ibid., 503.

26   https://www.washingtontimes.com/news/2011/dec//7/labor-unions-and-communism.

27   https://www.redstate.com/diary/kcjw33/2011/03/11. See also www.unions-the-history-of-their-socialistagenda.

28 https://www.commieblaster.com/communists/index.html.

29 https://www.washingtontimes.com/news/2011/
dec/7labor-unions-and-communism.

30 Ibid.

31 www.freedomworks.org/content/
commerce-clause-not-grant-unlimited-congressional-power.

32 https://www.heritage.org/the-constitution/report/...

33 https://sites.gsu.edu/us-constipedia/wickard-v-filburn-1942.

34 https://www.breitbart.com/the-media/2019/10/14/
project-veritas-cnn-contractor-says...

35 Mark Steyn, *After America: Get Ready for Armageddon* (Washington, DC:
Regnery Publishing Inc., 2011), 82.

36 www.tn.gov/environment/program-areas/wr-water-resources/
watershed-stewardship/wetlands/what-is-...

37 https://thehill.com/opinion/op-ed/234685-epa-water...

38 https://en.wikipedia.org/wiki/
State-owned_enterprises_of_the_United_States.

39 https://tipsforsurvivalists.com/states-with-laws...

40 Ibid.

41 https://www.cbsnews.com/news/eminent-domain-being-abused. See also
www.martenlaw.com/newsletter/20070321-property-rights-after-kelo.

42 batr.org/forbidden/062315.html.

43 Ibid.

44 https://www.amazon.com/All-but-people-Franklin-Roosevelt/dp/
B0006BYJJQ,
https://conservativefiringline.com/the-commie-connection-fdr-and-sta-
lin. See also George Wolfskill and John A. Hudson, *All but the People:
Franklin D. Roosevelt and His Critics, 1933–39* (Kings Cross London, UK:
Macmillan, 1969).

45 https://www.thenewamerican.com/culture/history/
item/17147-the-communist-agent-who-caused-pearl-...

46 https://en.wikipedia.org/wiki/Harry_Hopkins.

47 https://www.breitbart.com/national-security/2013/08/05/
did-the-roosevelt...

48 https://therainmanperspective.blogspot.com/2012/05/united-na-
tions-is-communist.html.

49 https://www.bibliotecapleyades.net/sociopolitica/un_exposed04.htm.

50 https://www.unwatch.com/un_communist.html.

51   https://www.bibliotecapleyades.net/sociopolitica/un_exposed04.htm.

52   Ibid.

53   https://unsdg.un.org.

54   https://americanpolicy.org/agenda21.

55   Tom DeWeese, *Erase* (The DeWeese Company Inc., 2016).

56   https://www.proliberty.com/observer/20091223.htm; en.wikipedia.org/
     wiki/Earth_First!.

57   www.environmentandsociety.org/mml/
     un-world-commission-environment-and-development-ed-r...

58   www.sustainable-environment.org.uk/Action/Earth_Summit.php.

59   byebyebluesky.com/
     who-is-maurice-strong-ipcc-the-brainchild-of-maurice-strong.

60   https://clintonwhitehouse2.archives.gov/PCSD/Publications.

61   Reed F. Noss, "The Wildlands Project," *Wild Earth*, special issue (1992):
     13–15.

62   https://climate.news/2019-08-26-bill-gates...

63   https://www.congress.gov/bill/116th-congress/house-bill/1111.

64   Skousen, *The Naked Communist*, 38.

65   en.wikipedia.org/wiki/Tom_Cryer.

66   https://www.zerothposition.com/2015/10/21/
     eight-observations-on-the-death-of-irwin-schiff.

67   https://www.History.com/topics/early-us/alien-and-sedition-acts.

68   Thomas E. Woods Jr., Nullification (Washington, DC: Regnery Publish-
     ing Inc., 2010).

69   Porter Stansbury, *The American Jubilee: A National Nightmare Is Closer
     than You Think* (Stansbury Research Pub., 2017).

70   Ibid., ii.

71   Ibid., 11.

72   www.cnbc.com/2017/07/19/survey-shows-majority-of-business-o...

73   myemail.constantcontact.com/A-Newsletter-from...

74   Leonard C. Lewin, *Report from Iron Mountain on the Possibility and Desir-
     ability of Peace* (Liberty, MO: Dial Press, 1966).

75   Ibid., xxix.

76   Ibid., 29.

77   Ibid., 68.

78   Ibid., 46.

79   http://www.c3headlines.com/global-warming-quotes-climate-change-
     quotes.html.

80 http://en.wikipedia.org/wiki/The_Limits_to_Growth.

81 en.wikipedia.org/wiki/2052:_A_Global_Forecast_for_the_Next_Forty_Years.

82 https://www.huffpost.com/entry/jim-inhofe-climate-snow_n_6763868.

83 John L. Casey, *Dark Winter How the Sun Is Causing a 30-Year Cold Spell* (West Palm Beach, FL: Humanix Books, 2014).

84 Marc Morano, *The Politically Incorrect Guide to Climate Change* (Washington, DC: Regnery Publishing, 2018).

85 https://www.pewresearch.org/fact-tank/2017/08/09/m.

86 Brigitte Gabriel, *They Must Be Stopped: Why We Must Defeat Radical Islam and How We Can Do It* (New York: St. Martin's Press, 2008).

87 https://www.csmonitor.com/World/Security-Watch/terrorism-security/2015/0113/How-many...

88 http://www.majorrreligions.com/Muhammad.php.

89 https://www.thereligionofpeace.com/pages/quran/taqiyya.aspx.

90 muslimfact.com/.../islam-permits-lying-to-deceive-unbelievers-and-bri-shtm.

91 https://www.snopes.com/fact-check/churchill-on-islam.

92 https://www.gatestoneinstitute.org/12693/sweden-radicalization-muslims.

93 humansarefree.com/2019/10/sweden-one-in-four-women-are-afraid-to-leave-their-homes-in-fea...

94 Skousen, *The Five Thousand Year Leap*, 59–60.

95 Adrienne Ed Koch, *The American Enlightenment* (New York: George Braziller Pub., 1965), 239.

96 Clyde Cleveland and Edward F. Noyes, *Restoring the Heart of America* (New York: Barnes & Noble, 2002), 59.

97 *Business Weekly*, August 2007, 27.

98 Frederick T. Gates, *The Country School of Tomorrow* (London, UK: Forgotten Books, 2016), https://archive.org/details/countryschooloft00gates. See also https://www.thrivemovement.com/followmoney-education.

99 B. K. Eakman, *Educating for the New World Order* (Portland, OR: Halcyon House), 127–8.

100 http://www.thrivemovement.com/follow-money-education.

101 Connor Boyack, *Passion-Driven Education* (Salt Lake City: Libertas Press, 2016), 33. See also http://www.crossroad.to/text/articles/tnmfobe1196.html.

102   Edward J. Wheeler, ed. *Current Opinion*, vol. 62, (New York: Current Literature Pub. Co., 1917), 195.

103   ampp.mega.nu/ampp/samuelson.html.

104   Ibid.

105   B. K. Eakman, *Educating for the New World Order*, 132.

106   https://www.washingtontimes.com/news/2016/oct/6/...

107   https://www.redstate.com/brandon_morse/2018/07/02/course-millennials-want-socialism...

108   Howard Zinn, *A People's History of the United States*, rev. ed. (New York: HarperCollins Publishing Inc., 1995).

109   https://newrepublic.com/.../112574/howard-zinns-influential-mutilations-american-history.

110   https://www.zinnedproject.org.

111   https://www.barnesandnoble.com/w/debunking-howard-zinn-mary-grabar/1131770453.

112   https://www.wsj.com>Opinion>Commentary The '1619 Project' Gets schooled-WSJ

113   B. K. Eakman, *Educating for the New World Order*.

114   Joel Turtel, *Public Schools, Public Menace: How Public Schools Lie to Parents and Betray Our Children* (Staten Island, NY: Liberty Books, 2005), 1.

115   John Taylor Gatto, *Dumbing Us Down* (Gabriola Island, BC: New Society Pub., 2005), xxxiii.

116   John Stormer, *None Dare Call It Education* (Florissant, MO: Liberty Bell Press, 1998).

117   Conner Boyack, *Passion-Driven Education* (Salt Lake City, UT: Libertas Press, 2016), 31.

118   Samuel Blumenfeld and Alex Newman, *Crimes of the Educators* (Washington, DC: WND Books, 2014).

119   Charlotte Thompson Iserbyt, *A Chronological Paper Trail, The Deliberate Dumbing Down of America*, abr. ed. (Parkman, OH: Conscience Press, 2011).

120   https://en.Wikipedia.org/wiki/Charlotte_Thomson_Iserbyt.

121   Mary Grabar, *Debunking Howard Zinn: Exposing the Fake History That Turned a Generation Against America* (Washington, DC: Regnery Pub, 2019).

SECTION III: RESTORING CHRISTIAN CIVILIZATION

Chapter 12: What Will It Take?

1   Alana Semuels, "The Town That Decided to Send All Its Kids to College," *The Atlantic*, August 18, 2015, https://www.theatlantic.com/business/archive/2015/...

2   Alexis de Toqueville, *Democracy in America*, vol. 2 (Cambridge: Sever & Francis, 1862), 129.

3   Christopher Caldwell, *The Age of Entitlement* (New York: Simon & Schuster, 2020), 6.

Chapter 13: What to Do About Public Education?

4   John Taylor Gatto, *Dumbing Us Down* (Gabriola Island, BC: New Society Publishers, 2005), 1–10.

5   Boyack, *Passion-Driven Education*.

6   https://blog.nomorefakenews.com/2018/03/05/suppose-you-write-to-your-child-and-then...

7   https://www.rt.com/usa/nyc-graduates-unable-to-read-011.

8   "Wendy Lecker: Leaving math standards to politicians doesn't add up," *Stamford Advocate*, November 28, 2015, https://www.stamfordadvocate.com/news/article/...

9   https://www.infowars.com/fbi-instructs-high... March 11, 2016.

10   Boyack, *Passion-Driven Education*, 54–5.

11   Ibid.

12   www.thoughtco.com/high-school-course-requirements-college-admissions-788858.

13   https://www.ronpaulcurriculum.com/Online/Homeschool.

14   https://www2.ed.gov/news/staff/bios/devos.html.

15   Skousen, *The Five Thousand Year Leap*, 59–60.

16   Peter Schweizer, *Profiles in Courage* (Nashville, TN: HarperCollins Publishers, 2020).

17   Ibid., 100.

18   Ibid., 88.

19   Ibid., 86.

20   Thomas Sowell, *Applied Economics: Thinking Beyond Stage One*, rev. ed. (New York: Basic Books, 2009), 6.

Chapter 14: How Will All Truth Seekers Unite?

21 https://www.amazon.com/Learned-Optimism-Change...

22 Edwin Vieira Jr., *Constitutional Homeland Security*, vol. 1, rev. ed. (Ashland, OH: BookMasters Inc., 2007).

23 Ibid., 75.

24 en.wikipedia.org/wiki/Milgram_experiment.

APPENDIX

1 Daniel J. Siegel, *The Developing Mind*. 2nd ed. New York/London: The Guilford Press, 2012. See also:

Doidge, N. *The Brain that Changes Itself: Stories of Personal Triumph from the Frontiers of Brain Science*. New York: Penguin, 2007.

T., S. Green, F. Neinemann, and J. F. Gusella. "Molecular Neurobiology and Genetics: Investigation of Neural Function and Dysfunction." *Neuron* 20.

E. R. Kandel, J. H. Swartz, and T. M. Jessell. *Principles of Neural Science*. 4th ed. New York: McGraw-Hill, 2000.